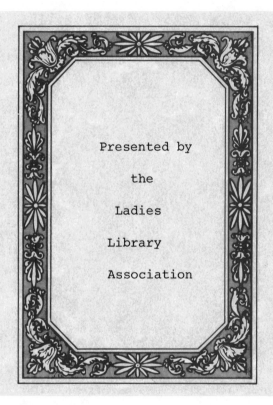

THE FAMILY
IN AMERICA
OPPOSING
VIEWPOINTS®

Other Books of Related Interest in the Opposing Viewpoints Series:

THE FAMILY IN AMERICA
OPPOSING VIEWPOINTS®

David L. Bender & Bruno Leone, *Series Editors*

Viqi Wagner, *Book Editor*
Karin L. Swisher, *Assistant Editor*

OPPOSING VIEWPOINTS SERIES ®

Greenhaven Press, Inc.   PO Box 289009   San Diego, CA 92198-9009

Library of Congress Cataloging-in-Publication Data

The Family in America : opposing viewpoints / Viqi Wagner, book editor; Karin L. Swisher, assistant editor.
    p.   cm. — (Opposing viewpoints series)
    Includes bibliographical references and index.
    Summary: Presents differing views on such family-related topics as reproduction, divorce, working mothers, and government assistance. Includes critical thinking activities.
    ISBN 0-89908-194-0 (lib. : alk. paper). — ISBN 0-89908-169-X (pbk. : alk. paper)
    1. Family—United States. 2. Family policy—United States. [1. Family. 2. Family policy.]   I. Wagner, Viqi, 1953-   . II. Swisher, Karin L., 1966- . III. Series: Opposing viewpoints series (Unnumbered)
HQ536.F368   1992
306.85'0973—dc20   92-8150
                                           CIP
                                           AC

"We would like to note that several articles contained within this anthology are from a newsletter called *The Family in America*, published by the Rockford Institute, and wish to point out that the Rockford Institute has no affiliation with Greenhaven Press and the similarities in our titles are purely coincidental."

"Congress shall make no law . . .
abridging the freedom of speech,
or of the press."

First Amendment to the U.S. Constitution

The basic foundation of our democracy is the first amendment guarantee of freedom of expression. The Opposing Viewpoints Series is dedicated to the concept of this basic freedom and the idea that it is more important to practice it than to enshrine it.

97362

Contents

Page

Why Consider Opposing Viewpoints? — 9

Introduction — 13

Chapter 1: What Is the Status of the Family?

Chapter Preface — 16
1. The Family Is in Decline — 17
   David Popenoe
2. The Family Is in Transition — 25
   Dennis K. Orthner
3. The Traditional Family Is Obsolete — 33
   Diane Fassel
4. The Definition of Family Is Expanding — 40
   Teresa Marciano & Marvin B. Sussman
5. The Definition of Family Should Remain Limited — 47
   Bryce J. Christensen
6. Homosexual Partners Are Changing the Family — 55
   Brent Hartinger
7. Homosexual Partners Are Undermining the Family — 63
   Bradley P. Hayton
8. Reproductive Technology Is Changing the Family — 71
   Ruth Macklin
9. Reproductive Technology Is Undermining the Family — 79
   Donald DeMarco
A Critical Thinking Activity:
   Understanding Words in Context — 87
Periodical Bibliography — 89

Chapter 2: How Does Divorce Affect the Family?

Chapter Preface — 91
1. Divorce Is Normal — 92
   Constance R. Ahrons & Roy H. Rodgers
2. Divorce Is Abnormal — 100
   Fred Moody
3. Divorce Harms Children — 108
   Judith S. Wallerstein & Sandra Blakeslee
4. Divorce May Not Harm Children — 115
   Diane Fassel

5. Divorce Laws Harm Women Economically 120
   Lenore J. Weitzman

6. Divorce Is Not the Cause of Women's Economic
   Hardships 129
   Susan Faludi

A Critical Thinking Activity:
   Distinguishing Between Fact and Opinion 136
Periodical Bibliography 138

Chapter 3: How Are Two-Career Parents Affecting the Family?

Chapter Preface 140
1. Working Mothers Benefit the Family 141
   Robin Parker

2. Working Mothers Harm the Family 147
   Juli Loesch Wiley

3. Businesses Are Meeting the Needs of Two-Career
   Parents 152
   Sylvia Ann Hewlett

4. Businesses Are Not Meeting the Needs of
   Two-Career Parents 159
   Jan Fletcher

5. More Day Care Is Needed to Support Two-Career
   Couples 167
   Kenneth Labich

6. More Day Care Will Not Solve the Problems of
   Two-Career Couples 175
   Mothers at Home

7. Two-Career Parents Spend Too Little Time with
   the Family 183
   William R. Mattox Jr.

8. Two-Career Parents Have Enough Time to Spend
   with the Family 191
   Gary Burtless & Robert J. Samuelson

A Critical Thinking Activity:
   Evaluating Sources of Information 198
Periodical Bibliography 200

Chapter 4: What Government Policies Would Help the Family?

Chapter Preface   202

1. The Government Should Support Traditional
   Families   203
   William R. Mattox Jr.

2. Government Support for the Traditional Family
   Is Unnecessary   211
   Stephanie Coontz

3. The Government Should Mandate Family Leave   219
   T. Berry Brazelton & Patricia Schroeder

4. The Government Should Not Mandate Family Leave   227
   Bryce J. Christensen

5. Funding Social Programs Would Benefit Families   234
   Ruth Sidel

6. Tax Cuts Would Benefit Families   242
   Robert Rector & Stuart M. Butler

A Critical Thinking Activity:
   Recognizing Statements That Are Provable   250

Periodical Bibliography   252

Organizations to Contact   253
Bibliography of Books   257
Index   259

Why Consider Opposing Viewpoints?

"It is better to debate a question without settling it than to settle a question without debating it."

Joseph Joubert (1754-1824)

The Importance of Examining Opposing Viewpoints

The purpose of the Opposing Viewpoints Series, and this book in particular, is to present balanced, and often difficult to find, opposing points of view on complex and sensitive issues.

Probably the best way to become informed is to analyze the positions of those who are regarded as experts and well studied on issues. It is important to consider every variety of opinion in an attempt to determine the truth. Opinions from the mainstream of society should be examined. But also important are opinions that are considered radical, reactionary, or minority as well as those stigmatized by some other uncomplimentary label. An important lesson of history is the eventual acceptance of many unpopular and even despised opinions. The ideas of Socrates, Jesus, and Galileo are good examples of this.

Readers will approach this book with their own opinions on the issues debated within it. However, to have a good grasp of one's own viewpoint, it is necessary to understand the arguments of those with whom one disagrees. It can be said that those who do not completely understand their adversary's point of view do not fully understand their own.

A persuasive case for considering opposing viewpoints has been presented by John Stuart Mill in his work *On Liberty*. When examining controversial issues it may be helpful to reflect on this suggestion:

9

The only way in which a human being can make some approach to knowing the whole of a subject, is by hearing what can be said about it by persons of every variety of opinion, and studying all modes in which it can be looked at by every character of mind. No wise man ever acquired his wisdom in any mode but this.

Analyzing Sources of Information

The Opposing Viewpoints Series includes diverse materials taken from magazines, journals, books, and newspapers, as well as statements and position papers from a wide range of individuals, organizations, and governments. This broad spectrum of sources helps to develop patterns of thinking which are open to the consideration of a variety of opinions.

Pitfalls to Avoid

A pitfall to avoid in considering opposing points of view is that of regarding one's own opinion as being common sense and the most rational stance, and the point of view of others as being only opinion and naturally wrong. It may be that another's opinion is correct and one's own is in error.

Another pitfall to avoid is that of closing one's mind to the opinions of those with whom one disagrees. The best way to approach a dialogue is to make one's primary purpose that of understanding the mind and arguments of the other person and not that of enlightening him or her with one's own solutions. More can be learned by listening than speaking.

It is my hope that after reading this book the reader will have a deeper understanding of the issues debated and will appreciate the complexity of even seemingly simple issues on which good and honest people disagree. This awareness is particularly important in a democratic society such as ours where people enter into public debate to determine the common good. Those with whom one disagrees should not necessarily be regarded as enemies, but perhaps simply as people who suggest different paths to a common goal.

Developing Basic Reading and Thinking Skills

In this book, carefully edited opposing viewpoints are purposely placed back to back to create a running debate; each viewpoint is preceded by a short quotation that best expresses the author's main argument. This format instantly plunges the reader into the midst of a controversial issue and greatly aids that reader in mastering the basic skill of recognizing an author's point of view.

A number of basic skills for critical thinking are practiced in the activities that appear throughout the books in the series. Some of the skills are:

Evaluating Sources of Information. The ability to choose from among alternative sources the most reliable and accurate source in relation to a given subject.

Separating Fact from Opinion. The ability to make the basic distinction between factual statements (those that can be demonstrated or verified empirically) and statements of opinion (those that are beliefs or attitudes that cannot be proved).

Identifying Stereotypes. The ability to identify oversimplified, exaggerated descriptions (favorable or unfavorable) about people and insulting statements about racial, religious, or national groups, based upon misinformation or lack of information.

Recognizing Ethnocentrism. The ability to recognize attitudes or opinions that express the view that one's own race, culture, or group is inherently superior, or those attitudes that judge another culture or group in terms of one's own.

It is important to consider opposing viewpoints and equally important to be able to critically analyze those viewpoints. The activities in this book are designed to help the reader master these thinking skills. Statements are taken from the book's viewpoints and the reader is asked to analyze them. This technique aids the reader in developing skills that not only can be applied to the viewpoints in this book, but also to situations where opinionated spokespersons comment on controversial issues. Although the activities are helpful to the solitary reader, they are most useful when the reader can benefit from the interaction of group discussion.

Using this book and others in the series should help readers develop basic reading and thinking skills. These skills should improve the reader's ability to understand what is read. Readers should be better able to separate fact from opinion, substance from rhetoric, and become better consumers of information in our media-centered culture.

This volume of the Opposing Viewpoints Series does not advocate a particular point of view. Quite the contrary! The very nature of the book leaves it to the reader to formulate the opinions he or she finds most suitable. My purpose as publisher is to see that this is made possible by offering a wide range of viewpoints that are fairly presented.

David L. Bender
Publisher

Introduction

"Whoever said that death and taxes are the only inevitable things in life was overlooking an obvious third one: family."

William J. Doherty,
Psychology Today, May/June 1992.

The traditional family of the twentieth century consists of a working father, a mother that stays home, and their children. Many people romanticize this family structure, hearkening back to television shows of the 1950s and 1960s like "Leave It to Beaver" and "Ozzie and Harriet." In these shows the mother was always nurturing and available, the father always gave good advice, and the children were always well-behaved. These shows made traditional families look especially loving, supportive, and successful. Many parents of today compare their turbulent, hectic lives with those of a fictionalized past and find their own situations wanting. Deborah Edler Brown and Michele Donley, writing in *Newsweek's* fall 1990 special issue on families, support this theory: "Much of the turmoil felt by parents in the '90s derives from the fact that so many are children of the '50s. Their image of an ideal family comes from TV shows like 'Father Knows Best.'"

This idealized version of the traditional family, however, has never really existed. While a greater number of traditional families may have existed in the 1950s, most families were not the romantic versions that appeared on television. Between 1940 and 1960, for example, the number of working wives doubled from 15 to 30 percent. In addition, the divorce rate of the 1950s was higher than any previous time, except for a brief upsurge after World War II. Many families in the 1950s may have felt the same sense of upheaval that prompts parents now to long for an idealized image of the traditional family.

Today, 70 percent of America's families are nontraditional. The most common family type is composed of either a two-career married couple and their children or a single parent and his or her children. These two groups each comprise 29 percent of all families, making them almost as common as the traditional family. Stepfamilies are also increasingly common. In addition to these types, a minority of Americans—homosexual couples with children, grandparents raising grandchildren, communal families—have broadened the definition of "family" still further.

Thus, while many people may believe the traditional family is best—63 percent of Americans polled claimed it as ideal—they have found it to be unfulfilling or unattainable. According to William J. Doherty, a professor of family and social science, one explanation may be that "traditional family structures are no longer appropriate for the modern age" because such structures no longer meet some families' emotional and economic needs. Another explanation may be that many Americans, especially single mothers, may not have a choice in their family structure. Many single mothers were either abandoned by their husbands, forced to leave abusive situations, or never married the father of their children. Many may still believe in the importance of the traditional family, but circumstances have not allowed them to live in one.

As the American family changes, the roles traditional and nontraditional families will play in the future remain uncertain. *The Family in America: Opposing Viewpoints* debates the following topics surrounding the changing American family: What Is the Status of the Family? How Does Divorce Affect the Family? How Are Two-Career Parents Affecting the Family? What Government Policies Would Help the Family? As more Americans find themselves living in new types of families, these issues will gain in importance.

What Is the Status of the Family?

Chapter Preface

In November 1991 the National Commission on Children issued its final report based on two surveys conducted over a two-and-a-half year period. Called *Beyond Rhetoric: A New American Agenda for Children and Families,* it revealed that a majority of American adults were discouraged about the status of America's families. More than half of the adults surveyed believed that parents were not doing as good a job as the previous generation and 88 percent believed that parenting was more difficult now than in the past.

In the same report, however, most of the parents surveyed described their own families as successful. Ninety-seven percent of the parents said their relationship with their children was either good or excellent. In addition, 70 percent of families said they ate dinner together regularly, a factor many experts believe is an indication of a strong family.

The contradictions apparent in this report indicate a disparity between people's perception of their own families and the perception of families outside their own. What these findings reveal about the strength of the family is debated in the following chapter.

"During the past 25 years, the institution of the family has weakened substantially."

The Family Is in Decline

David Popenoe

In the following viewpoint, David Popenoe argues that declining birth rates, sexual liberation, working mothers, and increased divorce rates have led to the decline of the traditional family. He describes gains in women's status and material standards of living as positive results of this decline, but believes the welfare of children has been sacrificed. While Popenoe rejects a return to rigid traditional family forms, he believes Americans should recommit themselves to children and strong families. Popenoe is professor of sociology and associate dean for the social sciences at Rutgers University in New Brunswick, New Jersey.

As you read, consider the following questions:

1. What are the characteristics of the traditional nuclear family, as Popenoe defines it?
2. What is the crucial difference between social change affecting the family in the last twenty-five years and previous family change, according to the author?
3. According to Popenoe, what is the main drawback to government programs that support the family?

Adapted from "Family Decline in America" by David Popenoe, in *Rebuilding the Nest: A New Commitment to the American Family*, David Blankenhorn, Steven Bayme, and Jean Bethke Elshtain, eds. Milwaukee: Family Service America, Inc., 1990. Reprinted with permission.

The recent social transformation of the family has been so momentous that, in my opinion, we are witnessing the end of an epoch. Today's societal trends are bringing to a close the cultural dominance of what historians call the modern (I will use the term "traditional") nuclear family, a family situated apart from both the larger kin group and the workplace; focused on the procreation of children; and consisting of a legal, lifelong, sexually exclusive, heterosexual, monogamous marriage, based on affection and companionship, in which there is a sharp division of labor, with the female as full-time housewife and the male as primary provider and ultimate authority. Lasting for only a little more than a century, this family form emphasized the male as "good provider," the female as "good wife and mother," and the paramount importance of the family for child rearing. (Of course, not all families were able to live up to these cultural ideals.) During its cultural heyday, the terms "family," "home," and "mother" ranked extraordinarily high in the hierarchy of cultural values.

In certain respects, this family form reached its apogee in the middle of the 20th century. By the 1950s—fueled in part by falling maternal and child mortality rates, greater longevity, and a high marriage rate—it is probably the case that a higher percentage of children than ever before were growing up in stable, two-parent families. Similarly, this period witnessed the highest ever proportion of women who married, bore children, and lived jointly with their husbands until at least age 50.

Flight from the Nuclear Family

In the 1960s, however, four major social trends emerged to signal a widespread "flight" from both the ideal and the reality of the traditional nuclear family: rapid fertility decline, the sexual revolution, the movement of mothers into the labor force, and the divorce revolution. None of these changes was new to the 1960s; each represented a tendency that was already evident in earlier years. However, a striking acceleration of these trends occurred in the 1960s, which was made more dramatic by the fact that during the 1950s these trends had leveled off and in some cases even reversed their direction.

• The Decline in Fertility. First (taking up these four trends without reference to their relative importance or causal priority), fertility declined in the United States by almost 50% between 1960 and 1989, from an average of 3.7 children per woman to only 1.9. Although fertility has been gradually diminishing for several centuries (the main exception being the two decades following World War II), the level of fertility during the past decade was the lowest in U.S. history and below that necessary for the replacement of the population. As a percentage of the total population, children over the past 25 years have dropped from more than a third to about one-fourth.

Growing dissatisfaction with parenthood is now evident among adults in our culture, along with a dramatic decrease in the stigma associated with childlessness. Some demographers now predict that between 20% and 25% of today's young women will remain completely childless, and nearly 50% will be either childless or have only one child.

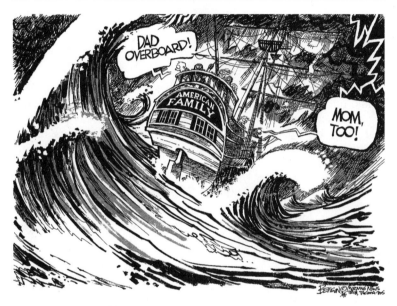

Steve Benson. Reprinted by permission: Tribune Media Services.

• The Sexual Revolution. Second, what is often called the sexual revolution has shattered the association of sex and reproduction. The erotic has become a necessary ingredient of personal well-being and fulfillment, both in and outside marriage, as well as a highly marketable commodity. The greatest change has been in the area of premarital sex: from 1971 to 1982, the proportion of unmarried girls in the United States aged 15-19 who engaged in premarital sexual intercourse jumped from 28% to 44%. This behavior reflects a widespread change in values: in 1967, 85% of Americans "condemned premarital sex as morally wrong," compared with only 37% in 1979. . . .

• Working Married Mothers. Third, although unmarried women have long been in the labor force, the past quarter century has witnessed a striking movement into the paid work force of married women with children. In 1960, only 19% of married women with children younger than 6 were in the labor force (39% with children between 6 and 17); by 1986, this figure had climbed to 54% (68% of those with older children).

• Increased Divorce Rate. Fourth, the divorce rate in the United States over the past 25 years (as measured by the number of divorced persons per 1,000 married persons) has nearly quadrupled, increasing from 35 to 130. This increase has led many to refer to a divorce revolution. A landmark of sorts was passed in 1974, when for the first time in American history more marriages ended in divorce than in death. The probability that a marriage contracted today will end in divorce ranges from 44% to 66%, depending upon the method of calculation.

Reshaped Family Experience

These four trends signal a widespread retreat from the traditional nuclear family in its terms of a lifelong, sexually exclusive unit, focused on children, with a separate-sphere division of labor between husband and wife. Unlike most previous family change, which reduced family functions and diminished the importance of the kin group, the family change of the past 25 years has tended to break up the "nucleus" of the family unit—the bond between husband and wife. Nuclear units, therefore, are losing ground to single-parent families, serial and stepfamilies, and unmarried and homosexual couples.

The number of single-parent families, for example, has risen sharply as a result not only of marital breakup, but also of marriage decline (fewer persons who bear children are getting married) and widespread abandonment by males. In 1960, only 9% of children in the United States younger than 18 were living with one parent; by 1986, this figure had climbed to nearly one-fourth of all children. (The comparable figures for blacks are 22% and 53%, respectively.) Of children born between 1950 and 1954, only 19% of whites (48% of blacks) had lived in a single-parent family by the time they reached age 17. But for children born in 1980, the figure is projected to be 70% (94% for blacks).

During the past quarter century there has also been a retreat from family living in general. For instance, the percentage of "nonfamily" households (households other than those containing two or more persons living together and related by blood, marriage, or adoption) has nearly doubled, from 15% to 28% of all households. Approximately 85% of these new households consists of a person living alone. . . .

Despite the dramatic nature of the recent social transformation of the family, many family experts are still reluctant to refer to the transformation as "family decline." This is unfortunate, because the concept of the family as a declining or weakening institution provides a "best fit" for many of the changes that have taken place. The concept also alerts us to examine the consequences of a rapidly changing institution.

During the past 25 years, the institution of the family has weakened substantially in a number of ways. Individual family members have become more autonomous and less bound by the family group, and the group has become less cohesive. Fewer of its traditional social functions are now carried out by the family; these have shifted to other institutions. The family has lost more power and authority to other institutions, especially to the state and its agencies. The family has grown smaller, less stable, and has a shorter life span; people are therefore family members for a smaller percentage of their life. The outcome of these trends is that people have become less willing to invest time, money, and energy in family life. It is the individual him- or herself, not the family unit, in whom the main investments are increasingly made. . . .

Social Consequences

How are we to evaluate the social consequences of recent family decline? At the outset, it must be stressed that the issue is extremely complex. Society has been ill-served by the simplistic, either/or terms used by both the political right and left in the national debate.

Certainly, one should not jump immediately to the conclusion that family decline is necessarily bad for our society. A great many positive aspects of the recent family changes stand out as noteworthy. During this same quarter century of family decline, women (and many minorities) have clearly improved their status and probably the overall quality of their lives. Much of women's gain in status has come through their release from family duties and increased participation in the labor force. In addition, given the great emphasis on psychological criteria for choosing and keeping marriage partners, it can be argued persuasively that those marriages today that endure are more likely than ever before to be emotionally rewarding companionships.

This period has also seen improved health care and longevity as well as widespread economic affluence, all of which have produced, for most people, a material standard of living that is historically unprecedented. . . .

Negative Consequences

Despite these positive aspects, the negative consequences of family decline are real and profound. The greatest negative effect, in the opinion of nearly everyone, is on children. Because children represent the future of a society, any negative consequences for them are especially significant. Substantial, if not conclusive, evidence indicates that, partly due to family changes, the quality of life for children in the past 25 years has worsened. Much of the problem is of a psychological nature and thus is difficult to measure quantitatively.

The Fifties Were Better

We did value families in the fifties, especially families with children. We knew it was difficult and sometimes expensive to raise them, but we thought they were worth the sacrifices we had to make. Their welfare was more important than ours. To blame the plight of children today on lack of government-sponsored social services or cutbacks in Medicaid funding or a retreat from the commitment to the welfare state is naive and self-serving. The welfare state was much smaller in 1954, and Medicaid didn't exist. Most children were still far better off than most children are today. The plight of today's children can be blamed on one thing and one thing alone: we no longer care what happens to them.

Orania Papazoglou, *First Things*, January 1992.

Perhaps the most serious problem is a weakening in many families of the fundamental assumption that children are to be loved and valued at the highest level of priority. The general disinvestment in family life that has occurred has commonly meant a disinvestment in children's welfare. Some refer to this as a national "parent deficit." Yet the deficit goes well beyond parents to encompass an increasingly less child-friendly society. The parent deficit is all too easily blamed on newly working women. But it is men who have left the parenting scene in large numbers, a phenomenon one scholar has called "a disappearing act by fathers." More than ever before, fathers are denying paternity, avoiding their parental obligations, and are absent from home (at the same time there has been a slow but not offsetting growth of the "housefather" role). Indeed, a persuasive case can be made that men began to abandon the "good provider" role at about the same time that many women started to relinquish the role of the full-time homemaker. Thus, men and women may have been equally involved in triggering the recent flight from the traditional nuclear family.

The Breakup of the Nuclear Family

The breakup of the nuclear unit has been the focus of much concern. Virtually every child desires two biological parents for life, and substantial evidence exists that child rearing is most successful when it involves two parents, both of whom are strongly motivated for the task. This is not to say that other family forms can not be successful, only that as a group they are not

22

as likely to be successful. This is also not to say that the two strongly motivated parents must be organized in the patriarchal and separate-sphere terms of the traditional nuclear family.

Regardless of family form, a significant change has occurred over the past quarter century in what can be called the social ecology of childhood. Advanced societies are moving ever farther from what many hold to be a highly desirable child-rearing environment consisting of the following characteristics: a relatively large family that does a lot of things together, has many routines and traditions, and provides a great deal of quality contact time between adults and children; regular contact with relatives, active friendships in a supportive neighborhood, and contact with the adult world of work; little concern on the part of children that their parents will break up; and the coming together of all these ingredients in the development of a rich family subculture that has lasting meaning and strongly promulgates family values such as cooperation and sharing. . . .

What should be done to counteract or remedy the negative effects of family decline? This is the most controversial question of all, and the most difficult to answer. . . .

Among the broad proposals for change that have been put forth, two extremes stand out prominently in the national debate: (1) a return to the structure of the traditional nuclear family characteristic of the 1950s and (2) the development of extensive governmental family policies.

Aside from the fact that it is probably impossible to return to a situation of an earlier time, the first alternative has major drawbacks. Such a shift would require many women to leave the work force and to some extent become "de-liberated," an unlikely occurrence indeed. Economic conditions necessitate that even more women take jobs, and cultural conditions stress ever greater equality between the sexes.

The Traditional Family May Be Flawed

In addition to such considerations, the traditional nuclear family form, in today's world, may be fundamentally flawed. As an indication of this, one should realize that the young people who led the transformation of the family during the 1960s and 1970s were brought up in 1950s families. If the 1950s families were so wondferful, why didn't their children seek to emulate them? In hindsight, the 1950s families seem to have been beset with problems that went well beyond patriarchy and separate spheres. . . .

Despite such difficulties, the traditional nuclear family is still the family of choice for millions of Americans. They are comfortable with it, and for them it seems to work. It is reasonable, therefore, at least not to place roadblocks in the way of couples

23

with children who wish to conduct their lives according to the traditional family's dictates. Women who freely desire to spend much of their lives as mothers and housewives, outside the labor force, should not be economically penalized by public policy for making that choice. Nor should they be denigrated by our culture as second-class citizens.

Government Programs Have Drawbacks

The second major proposal for change that has been stressed in national debate is the development of extensive governmental programs offering monetary support and social services for families, especially for the new "nonnuclear" families. In some cases these programs assist with functions that families are unable to perform adequately; in other cases, the functions are taken over, transforming them from family to public responsibilities.

This is the path followed by the European welfare states, but it has been less accepted by the United States than by any other industrialized nation. The European welfare states have been far more successful than the United States in minimizing the negative economic impact of family decline on family members, especially children. In addition, many European nations have established policies making it much easier for women (and increasingly men) to combine work with child rearing. With these successes in mind, it seems inevitable that the United States will (and I believe should) move gradually in the direction of European countries with respect to family policies, just as we are now moving gradually in that direction with respect to medical care.

There are clear drawbacks, however, in moving too far down this road. If children are to be best served, we should seek to make the family stronger, not to replace it. At the same time that welfare states are minimizing some of the consequences of family decline, they may also be causing further decline of the family unit. . . .

Although each of the above alternatives has some merit, I suggest a third alternative, which is premised on the fact that we cannot return to the 1950s family, nor can we depend on the welfare state for a solution. Instead, we should strike at the heart of the cultural shift that has occurred, point up its negative aspects, and seek to reinvigorate the cultural ideals of "family," "parents," and "children" within the changed circumstances of our time. We should stress that the individualistic ethos has gone too far, that children are being woefully shortchanged, and that, in the long run, strong families represent the best path toward self-fulfillment and personal happiness. We should bring again to the cultural forefront the old ideal of parents living together and sharing responsibility for their children and for each other.

"Everyone agrees that the American family is changing."

The Family Is in Transition

Dennis K. Orthner

Dennis K. Orthner maintains in the following viewpoint that analysts are too quick to chart family decline. He believes the family is more accurately in transition. Orthner argues that fundamental values, such as caring for children and the importance of kinship, have not changed. What is changing and has yet to be sorted out are the ways people choose to live with each other. He believes this upheaval will settle if government, corporate, and community support networks are strengthened. Orthner is professor of sociology and director of the Human Services Research Laboratory at the University of North Carolina at Chapel Hill.

As you read, consider the following questions:

1. How does Orthner interpret contradictory marital statistics?
2. What is the difference between the terms *values* and *norms*, according to the author?
3. What is the fourth wave of institutional change, according to Orthner?

Adapted from "The Family in Transition" by Dennis K. Orthner, in *Rebuilding the Nest: A New Commitment to the American Family*, David Blankenhorn, Steven Bayme, and Jean Bethke Elshtain, eds. Milwaukee: Family Service America, Inc., 1990. Reprinted with permission.

Everyone agrees that the American family is changing. Divorce rates are rising, women are entering the labor force in record numbers, children are more likely to be left unattended or in group day-care arrangements, nonmarital cohabitation is increasingly common, and the number of single persons in the population is rising. All of these trends are quite familiar to the public.

But there has been less agreement on the meaning of these changes. Is the family system in America falling apart or reorganizing? Are we seeing institutional decline or change? Are families losing their ability to foster healthy individuals or are they gaining the freedom to customize their patterns? Are family values no longer important or have new beliefs and values begun to replace outdated ones? If it is possible to do so, we must find policies that will: (1) mitigate the negative impacts of change and (2) foster emerging family patterns and values that help the family adapt to contemporary cultural drifts.

The fundamental question is not how to stop family changes from occurring, but rather how to shape family change in a direction that minimizes the disruptions of these changes on potentially vulnerable groups, such as children and the poor, and maximizes the effectiveness of other organizations in society, such as businesses and community services.

The Family Reflects Widespread Social Change

I believe that the family changes now occurring are connected to, and perhaps rooted in, fundamental shifts in norms and values in American society. Much of the current discussion of the family focuses on changes in family structures and functions. However, these are but behavioral manifestations of what is occurring in the soul of our society. The beliefs that used to form the basis for relational stability are being reexamined. . . .

Norms of family behaviors—and the values that underlie those behaviors—are in transition. The result: unstable and widely varying interpretations of appropriate and inappropriate behavior. During major transitions such as these, any organization (e.g., family, corporation, or government) will find it difficult to establish firm rules for organizational formation, maintenance, and dissolution. The family system is not alone in this struggle: we can see similar organizational stresses and redefinitions being deliberated in businesses, in schools, in governments, and in communities. Nearly all social systems are currently renegotiating their fundamental bases for order. The oft-noted "crisis" of reorganization is much broader than the family, but it is within the family that we can see both the seeds for new organizational patterns and the high costs of failing to achieve a new level of stability. . . .

Those who speculate that the family system is declining claim that marriage as an ideal is less important today. They suggest that positive values associated with voluntary singleness have become more common, making marriage more of a choice than a necessity among those who traditionally have been in the marriage market. If this is true, marriage as a valued institution is indeed in trouble and other forms of nonmarital living arrangements may replace marriage in the future.

Evidence to support this thesis comes from several sources, including the increased proportion of unmarried persons in the population and the rising number of nonmarital cohabitants. Clearly, the decision not to marry is no longer considered a disgrace, and delaying marriage is less likely to foster predictions of spinsterhood. More adults in America today (33%) are ambivalent about whether it is better to be married than single for life, and a minority (16%) even disagree with that assumption. Likewise, the acceptance of nonmarital cohabitation is growing, with 33% of adults considering these relationships "O.K." in 1989 compared with 22% in 1986.

But this concern can be overblown. A consistent 96% of the American public during the past 30 years has expressed a personal desire for marriage. Only 8% of adult women consider remaining single an ideal; this has not changed in the past two decades. More than 80% of the high school classes of 1972 and 1980 said it was "very important" to marry and have a happy family life, and these beliefs increased after graduation. Surveys of college freshmen have also remained consistent: 70% of those surveyed in 1970 and 1985 expressed a strong desire to rear a family. . . .

If anything, the value of marriage as a preferable living arrangement appears to be holding its own during this time of institutional transition.

Individualism vs. Collectivism

A second concern is that individualism has become so strong in America that interest in the collectivities of family and community has declined. Robert Bellah and his colleagues note that "individualism lies at the very core of American culture. . . . We believe in the dignity, indeed the sacredness, of the individual. . . . Our highest and noblest aspirations, not only for ourselves, but for those we care about, for our society and for the world, are closely linked to our individualism." David Popenoe worries, however, that "cultural trends associated with the growing importance placed on 'self-fulfillment' . . . could be regarded as another important contributor to the high family-dissolution rate.". . .

Studies conducted during the 1950s found a strong sense of obligation among family members to help other family members. This finding surprised some researchers, because they too had come to believe that familism had declined in favor of individualism. These researchers discovered frequent visitations between families, financial help being given to younger and older families, help with child care and other household tasks, and frequent exchanges of advice. In fact, though most people admitted that they preferred to prove their independence by not always seeking help, few were reluctant to accept help when it was offered.

The situation today is not that different. Visits among relatives, especially with parents, have not declined significantly since the 1950s. More than half (53%) of adults with living parents see them at least once a month, and a similar percentage (51%) agree that aging parents should live with their adult children. Among the sample of families participating in the 1988 National Survey of Families and Households, the majority (55%) believe that they can call on their relatives in the middle of the night if they have an emergency, and two out of three (66%) say they can borrow $200 from a relative in an emergency.

Do Not Confuse Change with Decay

I agree . . . that family life is changing; I don't agree that the family is in decline. Whenever social institutions shift their functions and structure, the usual perception is of decay. We shouldn't exaggerate the pleasures associated with an earlier world. The family life of the 1950s was neither as monolithic as is often portrayed, nor was it as happy. There are major differences between current family problems and those of earlier generations, but little is gained by viewing the current situation as unprecedented.

Sanford M. Dornbusch, *Family Affairs*, Summer/Fall 1989.

This is not a gloomy picture of rampant individualism. Rather, it suggests that collective interests remain strong in American families, even within the context of a culture that promotes individual interests. There is little evidence that Americans are giving up on familism. . . .

Commitment vs. Autonomy

The inability of many couples to sustain lifelong commitments is often taken as evidence that family commitments are not as strong today as they once were. Furthermore, a large proportion of youth and adults worry that this trend will continue. In a [1989] survey, only 39% of those polled believed that people who get married today expect the marriage to last forever. Nevertheless, it is difficult to sort out this general sense of pessimism from a personal sense of optimism about their own relationships. The vast majority of adults (71%) believe that "marriage is a lifelong commitment that should not be ended except under extreme circumstances." Even more Americans (85%) say they would remarry their spouses if they had to do it all over again. Even the divorced and separated hold positive ambitions: most people who can do so will remarry and 81% still believe that marriage is a commitment for life.

These statistics do not indicate that Americans are running away from marriage and commitment. Instead, they indicate an underlying search for meaningful commitments and a healthy fear of the negative consequences if these do not last. Perhaps social scientists have been all too successful in pronouncing the decline in commitments: the fear of marital failure has continued to rise through the 1980s even though divorce rates have stabilized, even declined, in the past decade and a half. . . .

Changing Family Norms

Although basic family *values* have not changed dramatically, the *norms* of family behavior have, in fact, undergone dramatic transformations. Family norms, as I define them here, refer to the behavioral expectations associated with the statuses and roles of family members. Whereas values are attached to beliefs, norms are attached to and directly guide behavior. (Also, behavioral changes can change norms.) Thus, norms guide our actions; they serve as cues to appropriate and inappropriate behavior.

Many contemporary family problems are not tied to value transitions at all. Instead, they represent norm transitions. To a large extent, family processes today are confused by conflicting, incongruent, and absent family norms. The rules of family behavior have changed so dramatically in some areas that many men, women, and children do not know how to respond to one another's expectations. With so many alternative cues to guide behavior, confusion is more the rule than the exception in intimate relationships.

Joan Aldous refers to this confusion as a period in which *role making* is dominating the process of *role taking*. During an earlier era, family roles were firmly defined. Expectations for the socialization of children were clear, as were the qualities one looked for in a mate. Most women and men simply adopted the roles of their parents and got the cues for their behavior from relatively well-defined norms. This is not the case today. Although traditional roles remain the norm in some subsets of society, most men and women are unsure of others' expectations of them and of their own expectations of themselves. . . .

Another normative change is the shift away from ascribed

family roles toward achieved family roles. Family roles—mother, father, son, daughter—are no longer defined by larger societal norms. Instead, each role is customized; it is defined within the context of the particular family system. My role as a father, for example, is defined more by the expectations my wife and children have of me than by society's notion of what a father should do for his family. Although this gives me more freedom to develop a father role that is rewarding and personally enjoyable, it also increases the level of anxiety associated with the role because my success as a father is contingent upon ongoing and ever-changing reinforcements. . . .

Normative Issues Define Public Debate

We are now confronted by a veritable revolution in family norms. While the dominant values undergirding the family have been slowly shifting, norms of family behavior have moved more quickly to take advantage of the freedoms permitted by greater independence and autonomy. The family system that had once been called "the haven" and "respite" from the changes occurring in other organizations, notably business and government, is now even more vulnerable to the status and role confusion in the larger society.

These normative issues have become the new battleground in public debate. What is considered "pro-family" can be interpreted as ultraliberal, ultraconservative, or somewhere in between. Though some family advocates argue about family "values," the real debate generally focuses on norms and expectations of family members, most often parents. Answers to James A. Levine's plaintive question *Who Will Raise the Children?* are not framed in terms of whether children should be taken care of. We all agree that they should. What we disagree about is whether this responsibility, which fairly recently was solely the responsibility of mothers, should now be shared more by fathers and other caregivers. I do not believe that the value associated with children has been diminished that much. What has changed are the expectations regarding the responsibilities for their nurturance. . . .

We are in the early stages of a new "wave" of institutional change, perhaps as significant as the major social reorganizations that have occurred in the past. Three major family system waves have sequentially dominated human history.

The *first wave* was represented by wandering family and communal units in the preagricultural period. In this system, community interests overshadowed family interests because little to no property was controlled by individual families.

The *second family wave* occurred after the domestication of agriculture. Extended families dominated this period because property lines had to be much more clearly differentiated.

The *third wave* emerged after industrialization, and again, a major reorganization of the family took place. Property was no longer as important to family survival, so norms and values were built around independent family units with new, differentiated member roles and responsibilities. This transition into the industrial family, as reviewed by Edward Shorter, Philippe Ariès, and Robert Bellah and colleagues, resulted in significant family disorganization and in concern about the survivability of the family as an institution.

Family Changes

For most Americans the model of a father at work and a mother at home has been relegated to history. Economic reality, if nothing else, is rapidly making it an antique, rather than an icon that must be defended. . . .

"People grew up with one set of norms and values and now they are living another," said Arlene Skolnick, a research psychologist at the University of California, Berkeley. "As a result we have a tremendous amount of ambivalence. People believe in the family quite firmly, but they do not want to, or they are not able, to go back to the old patterns of family life."

Robert Suro, *The New York Times*, December 29, 1991.

The *fourth wave* of institutional change is now upon us. The lack of defined family norms and adequate support systems to help us meet some of our basic needs are evidence of this significant transformation. This fourth wave, when it stabilizes, will represent a significant departure from the way in which families are currently viewed or have been viewed in the recent past. I suspect that this new wave will encourage more relationship testing in early adulthood and more coalescence around children in the lives of parents. Divorce rates will probably go down somewhat, in part because formal marriages may not take place until later, but also because the norms and guidelines for forming and maintaining these relationships will be clearer than they are today.

Defining the New Family

This suggestion that we are at the beginning of a major cultural transformation in relationships is not an isolated one. Many behavioral and social scientists who have attempted to describe marriage and family relationships in nonfunctionalist terms have had to struggle with redefining the concept of family in terms that are not proscribed by static and equilibrium-oriented assumptions. Two decades ago, for example, John Edwards tried to express a process-theory-oriented view of the family in his critique of Charles Hobart's functionalist view of family norms and values. Edwards has continued to refine his thinking and stated:

> We desperately need an alternative model of normal development, a model devoid of the present nuclear family bias. . . . It would focus, instead, on the processual nature of youthful development. Crucially, it would delineate the components of well-being and the patterns of "healthy" families, regardless of their structural configurations.

John Scanzoni and his colleagues recently attempted to define the nature of this emerging institution. They replace the functionalist, equilibrium-oriented view of institutions, which is very resistant to change, with a nonfunctionalist process definition of institutions such as the one proposed by Anthony Giddens: "by institutions I mean structured social practices that have a broad spatial and temporal extension . . . and which are followed or acknowledged by the majority of the members of a society."

This new paradigm suggests that institutions represent the accumulations of norms, rules, and roles that reflect contemporary thinking and that they are changed, therefore, by current social processes. This is in contrast with the traditional, equilibrium-oriented paradigm in which institutions are considered outside the perimeter of the contemporary environment and apart from—even resistant to—normative changes that are occurring in the larger society.

If, following this line of thinking, the family is indeed in the midst of a major institutional transformation, then the current level of family instability is temporary. As the attitude surveys earlier reviewed suggest, the hope for a new level of stability lies with the young. The older generations are very concerned about family changes, because they have witnessed significant disruptions in their traditional family roots. Although concerned, the current parent generation is not nearly as anxious about these changes. The young are more hopeful. They see these changes as largely positive, but they worry that the rules and support they need are not there to guide their relationships.

> *"The first step in supporting family in all its forms is to let go of the myth of the intact family."*

The Traditional Family Is Obsolete

Diane Fassel

In the following viewpoint, Diane Fassel challenges those who idealize the traditional nuclear family. Traditional families may have worked well a century ago, she argues, but not in modern society where people live much longer, are more mobile, and can end bad marriages more easily. In addition, she finds, an intact family is no insurance against such problems as family violence and drug abuse. She believes the traditional family is no more valuable than many other family forms. Fassel is a family counselor in Colorado specializing in divorce and child custody cases.

As you read, consider the following questions:

1. How does Fassel support her view that short-term relationships have become the accepted norm in modern society?
2. In what ways is the traditional intact family *not* a haven for its members, according to the author?
3. According to the author, what happens when society wrongly insists that intact families are the norm and divorce is the exception?

From *Growing Up Divorced: A Road to Healing for Adult Children of Divorce* by Diane Fassel. Copyright © 1991 by Diane Fassel. Reprinted by permission of Pocket Books, a division of Simon and Schuster, Inc.

The refusal to admit that the intact family is not a panacea for society's ill, and that, in fact, it is less and less common, prevents us from recognizing and exploring other alternatives to the intact family.

How does society perpetuate the myth of the intact family? In large part, it does so through a series of assumptions that, I believe, have until now gone largely unexamined.

• *The first societal assumption states that staying together in long-term relationships is good; short-term relationships are bad.* This assumption underlies a double standard that is actively supported by the major religious groups and the civil society itself. It is reflected in vows in which couples promise "till death do us part." The standard is the commitment to the long-term relationship. The reality is that fewer and fewer people remain in such relationships. The major social and religious institutions choose to look the other way rather than face the reality that long-term relationships may no longer be as viable as they once were.

Because of the spread of AIDS, we are told that there is a rise in monogamy and a second baby boom. Yet even with a return to traditional values, the divorce rate remains constant at one out of two marriages. We keep trying the nuclear family, but we are not becoming more successful at it.

Long-Term Is Not Better than Short-Term

All around us we see a world that is changing, and it is changing with a rapidity unknown to previous generations. Our beliefs about longevity seem to lag behind our experience. In the United States, many people will change occupations seven times in their lifetime, and a majority of the population changes residence or geographic location every five years. In a research study I did of urban communes in Boston in the early 1970s, I found that 80 percent of the urban commune dwellers considered two years a "long time" to have the same group in a house. Their usual experience was a turnover of housemates every six months.

The belief that long-term relationships are good, short-term bad, sets longevity as an external standard against which to measure ourselves. Neither long-term nor short-term is good nor bad. When, as a society, we value one over the other, we are not open to possibilities for other forms for relationships. We persist in our determination that the family of old is possible. Moreover, we establish the traditional family as the ideal and measure every other relational form against it. This assumption prevents us from looking at our reality and working within it.

Inevitably, if we abandoned our assumptions about relationships there would continue to be those who entered into long-term relationships and stayed in them over the years. Others would move in and out as they needed. In a society that valued the process of relating rather than a static standard of the "right" relationship, all forms of relating would receive appropriate support. In addition, the guilt and shame that many [adult children of divorce] now carry because they cannot meet the societal expectation would be greatly reduced. . . .

Longer Life Spans

• *A second societal assumption states that a society in which people will live to age seventy-five can operate with the same relationship commitments as a society in which people live to age forty-five.* Surely, the kinds of marriages and the relationship expectations a culture has for those who will spend only twenty years together are different for those who can conceivably live almost twice as long. Our societal expectations for marriage seem to be based on life in the 1850s, rather than the 1990s.

Ozzie and Harriet Were No Role Models

The bemoaning of the loss of the "traditional" family has reached epic proportions. In general, the loss is blamed for the deterioration of American society; specifically it is said to cause divorce, drug and alcohol abuse, child neglect and abuse, delinquency, and thoughtless violence. Proponents of the traditional family claim these problems didn't exist when the TV family of Ozzie and Harriet were the role model for all families. The proponents say that if we could only get back to those ideals, all would again be right with the world, life would again be full of bliss, all people would be happy, and abuse and violence would vanish.

Rubbish. This ideal produced narrowly defined acceptable behaviors for men and women that also produced the long list of ills. The children of these traditional families are both the victims and the cause of the myriad of problems our society now faces. How could a standard that was so wonderful have produced children who are so disenchanted with the structure in which they grew up? If this structure was so ideal and produced satisfied children, then what is the source of the problems of our times?

J. Donovan, *Full-Time Dads*, August/September 1991.

Like present societies, earlier societies experienced war, chaos, and political upheavals. Yet, in those earlier periods, the family, extended families, and communities appeared to be a bulwark against the outside world. We like to believe the family was a place of safety, into which one could retreat from the hazards of society. However, historical studies of the family are raising questions about just how ideal the family of old really was. There is evidence that women and children did not fare well and that physical abuse was as common in the pre-twentieth-century family as it is today.

Perhaps all we can conclude is that prior to the late 1950s, there was tremendous societal and community pressure on husbands and wives to stay together. [Sociologist] Judith Wallerstein, quoting a conversation with Margaret Mead, says that our society is radically different because "we have created in the last twenty years *a world in which marriage is freely terminable at any time for the first time in history.*" Moreover, with the relative loss of societal pressure to stay together, the nature of our stress differs from our predecessors'. They seemed to bond in the face of cultural upheaval; we seem to fragment. Rather than becoming a haven, the intact family is a victim of cultural distress.

We expect to adjust to change in every sphere of science, technology, and the environment. The most dramatic change is in the complexity of the human psyche. How can we expect that the choices we make at twenty-one are still appropriate at fifty or at eighty, not to mention all the decades in between?

Everything around us has changed since the turn of the century, yet the culturally bound expectation of long-term relationships seems blind to the fact that the human person is not the same in needs, expectations, and skills. A great deal of the emotional investment in the myth of the intact family comes from a rigid adherence to modes of thought based on an earlier time and a shorter life span. This adherence keeps us in denial about our experience, which does not coincide with earlier cultural experience, nor with the myths about marriage and divorce that we inherited from that time.

Social Value Is Overrated

• *The third societal assumption is that the family is the basic social unit and it should be strengthened.* Underlying this assumption is the understanding that "family" usually refers to a mother, father, and children.

I believe we must question the assumption that the family is the basic social unit. . . . There is no question that the way many are experiencing family today is detrimental to the family members. Should the family as a primary social unit be strengthened? And if it were, would it make a difference?

I think we need to examine such issues as the isolation of the family, our mobile society, and the corporate world. All of these militate against the integrity of the traditional family unit. Families are without the support of older generations and relatives. Mobility keeps people from establishing roots in neighborhoods and from developing the support groups that could enhance family life. The corporate world of business is driven by a basic concern for profit, which results in workaholic standards for those who choose a career there. The family is a casualty of those trends. Although political leaders claim to be profamily, little real support in the form of legislation has been enacted that would actually have strengthened this floundering family unit. Again, the rhetoric of "family" is for the purpose of supporting the myth of the intact family. Yet what is going on in these intact families?

Intact Families Are Increasingly Troubled

Everywhere I go I hear that the family is in trouble. Educators complain they are now performing tasks of physical care and emotional nurturing that rightfully belong to parents, but are not being done at home. Violence is reported in 38 percent of families, and there is increasing awareness of incest. Multiple addictions are found in almost every family. In just twenty years, we have witnessed "broken families," single-parent families, and lately parentless families as crack-cocaine-addicted parents have neither the inclination nor the ability to parent their offspring.

Traditional Families Are Extinct

Some people think we're still living in an "Ozzie and Harriet" world where most fathers work, comfortably supporting a stay-at-home wife and two children. But that family idea is so close to extinction, it has a display case waiting for it in the Smithsonian, alongside the dodo bird.

Bonnie Erbe, *St. Paul Pioneer Press*, October 21, 1990.

I believe our adherence to the myth of the intact family prevents us from acknowledging the existence and the viability of the many alternatives as legitimate family forms. If the society were to respond to the fact that a great variety of family forms exist—single parents by divorce, single parents by choice, unmarried couples with children, gay and lesbian parents, grandparents, aunts and uncles raising children—perhaps there would be some help for the family. However, little is done to develop or foster other social units. This is unfortunate because to admit the reality of such forms would benefit parents, children, and ultimately the society itself.

We can hardly ignore the fact that "Mom, Pop, and the kids" is rapidly becoming a minority family form, while other arrangements are on the rise. I believe that the traditional family has been declining as the basic social unit for at least twenty years.

• *A fourth societal assumption is that divorce results in disturbed children and dysfunctional adults.* This is an assumption that needs to be challenged, both from the popular view and the research perspective. . . .

We need to question the level of denial in the society when we believe that divorce results in dysfunctional adults and children, while giving less weight to the numbers of intact families where affairs are common, marriages feel dead, and abuse is an everyday occurrence. We also need to question our persistence in believing that the intact family is the norm and divorce is the problematic exception. Twenty years of statistics on divorce now show that divorce is very common. It is the choice of 50 percent of all people who marry. The function of denying the prevalence of divorce is to prevent us from taking steps to claim divorce as a very real aspect of relational life among people. It is a normal response and a viable choice. To deny this keeps the society focused on one marriage form and one type of family unit that may not be the best solution. It is to prop up one option of relating, while ignoring the possibilities inherent in the other, divorce. We abhor divorce at the cost of maintaining our myth about the supremacy of the intact family. Regrettably, the dysfunction of intact families is not clearly seen, so troubled families do not receive help, just as children and adults of divorce do not get the support they need to move on to healthier situations. . . .

Letting Go of the Myth

I am persuaded that the intact family is greatly idealized. I do not dispute that millions of people are married. I question how functional that form is. I question its viability in our rapidly changing culture, and I wonder at the intensity with which so many hold on to it. I am astounded at the longing I find in many [adult children of divorce] to achieve a "normal" family when such an entity rarely exists. . . .

The concomitant development of multiple family forms, which are growing everywhere, promises alternatives to the traditional family. Some have observed that the nuclear family cannot survive without something around it. The nuclear family exists in a vacuum. It needs to be held in place by a support structure outside itself. The myth of the intact family has precipitated this distress for the nuclear family by isolating it into a form unto itself. . . .

The intact family will become a reality when it takes its place on an equal footing with other family forms. Hopefully, we will drop such confusing terms as "intact" and "broken," and we will be "family," whatever that means in our individual situations. As the world shrinks, we will extend our notion of family to include the global community. This awareness itself may move us to redefine the size and function of the family unit. It seems to me that throughout society we witness the demise of our illusions about family. This is a process. Although it is painful, it is necessary. We make the process more painful when we resist it. The first step in supporting family in all its forms is to let go of the myth of the intact family. It is essential to do this for the sake of ourselves, our families, and our society.

"The wider family has become more visible, is evolving rapidly and is being more enthusiastically embraced."

The Definition of Family Is Expanding

Teresa Marciano and Marvin B. Sussman

Traditional definitions of family are too narrow for today, argue sociologists Teresa Marciano and Marvin B. Sussman. In the following viewpoint, Marciano and Sussman identify the characteristics and functions of what they term "the wider family." They believe wider families can provide flexibility and benefits that cannot be found in traditional families. Marciano is professor of sociology at Fairleigh Dickinson University in Teaneck, New Jersey. Sussman is professor emeritus of human behavior at the College of Human Resources, University of Delaware in Newark.

As you read, consider the following questions:

1. What is the place of marriage and children in the wider family, according to the authors?
2. What three subcategories of wider families will evolve over time, according to Marciano and Sussman?
3. How might the legal system have to change in response to an expanded definition of the family, according to the authors?

From "Wider Families: An Overview" by Teresa Marciano and Marvin B. Sussman, from *Wider Families: New Traditional Family Forms*, Teresa Marciano and Marvin B. Sussman, eds., © 1991 by Haworth Press. Reprinted with permission of Haworth Press, 10 Alice St., Binghamton, NY 13904.

No adequate definition of "the family" exists, though anthropologists have spent decades elaborating family types. Any text or monograph will offer its own definition of family, or borrow a definition from someone else according to the author's preferences or topical concerns. At best the student of families describes the characteristics that families share with one another. These descriptions tend to be judgment free and are not unlike the following definition that a family consists of husband and wife living with their issue in neolocal residence, engaged in intimate interaction and ruled by its oldest members.

Characteristics include most or all of the following: the idea that children must or were or will be present, thus fulfilling the procreative function; legal marriage will have occurred resulting in rules for responsibility and orderly descent; kinship bonds will be the foundation of family; that bonding and inheritance transfers will effect intergenerational continuity: implied lifetime commitment provides time and sanctuary for expressions of intimacy, nurturance, caring, and love; and nuclear units in the family will share a lifestyle based on the parental or ancestral socioeconomic status. Whatever lifestyle is lived will have its genesis in the family.

Defining the Wider Family

The notion of wider families does not ignore some of these family realities, but maintains that families exist as social constructions, coexisting with the traditionally-defined families and frequently overlapping with them in expressing family-like behaviors. Wider families characteristics include:

• Wider families form without being limited to age distributions found in traditionally defined families. Relationships between generational cohorts are unnecessary. The actual mixture by age is a result of the reason the family got formed. Children in the wider family precede rather than define the wider families' existence.

• Legal marriage need not ever bind any of the members of a wider family to each other. It is a voluntary association. Individuals can leave and are under no legal obligation to remain. If contracts exist such as those regarding property ownership, settlements are made according to contract law.

• Wider families may exist which include kin-bonded people, but kinship bonds are incidental to the wider family.

• Permanence varies, and is not objectively normative for families, i.e., there are no legal, contractual bases for the continuation of wider families; there is no necessary degree of intergenerational permanence, though it may occur. Wider families have varying degrees of permanence and fluidity, and may disappear altogether or fragment and reconstitute in different forms, with sub-groups of the original wider family and with new members.

- Wider family emerges from lifestyle; it is a bonding of the type felt as "family," and deserves to be called that in wider settings. Perhaps we should adopt the wisdom of Swahili, wherein the word for family is "jamaa," and the word for nationhood is "ujamaa." The nation is the wider conceptualization of family.
- Wider families arise spontaneously in or apart from planned activities. They are logically or emotionally the "next step" for people connected by needs, activities, and interests.
- Wider families are autonomous, free, uncoerced types of families. If anything, coercion cancels the wider family notion, which springs from free choices made to enhance rather than limit one's life.
- Wider families can become primary groups for many members. The intensive interaction found in many of them results in in-group formation where members create a "we" or "in" group and view all others as outsiders.

Some part of the continuum between nuclear families and nation contains wider families. They may temporally coexist with kin- and marriage-based families. They may support and enhance kin/marriage families, or may be sources of conflict with them. Wider families are not necessarily "big, happy families." They may be filled with nasties, or with uncomfortable mixtures who may find a modus vivendi, fragment, or disappear.

What Families Do

Wider families come into existence for economic and emotional concerns. Services, exchanges, help, caring, advice, and emotional support can be found in wider families when traditional family resources are unavailable or inimical to the person's lifestyle. . . . Education, health, job, children, become major ingredients requiring services and supports. Longevity extends those needs, which often create burdens for traditional families. The wider family is the frequent and possible—though by no means inevitable—outcome, not only here and today but also in other times and places in the world.

The communards whose numbers grew so visibly and significantly in the Sixties and Seventies were forming wider families out of wider arrays of economic and social options. . . . The enlargement of possibilities, the assertion of rights of oppressed or stigmatized groups, found their dynamic in collective action, the civil rights and liberation movements for people of color, women, gay people. These assertions of freedom to live nonviolently in one's own pursuit of happiness, have had outcomes such as . . . lesbian mothers forming supportive communities. Redefinitions of "family," when those new definitions are lived, become powerful forces for changing contemporary ideas of acceptable and legal precepts and institutions.

The wider family has become more visible, is evolving rapidly and is being more enthusiastically embraced. The consequence is more frequent challenges to the traditional family system as a social and legal construct. . . . John Scanzoni and William Marsiglio extend the idea of marriage itself to encompass a variety of forms, placing marriage within a category of similar relationships rather than seeing marriage sui generis, as a category unto itself. If what was a unique and solely valid type becomes one of many valid types, the cultural and symbolic bases for accepting a wider form has been established. . . .

The Changing American Household

Household Composition: 1970 to 1988
(Percent of total households)

	1970	1980	1988
Married couples with children*	40.3	30.9	27
Married couples without children*	30.3	29.9	29.9
Other families with children*	5	7.5	8
Other families without children*	5.6	5.4	6.6
Men living alone	5.6	8.6	9.7
Women living alone	11.5	14	14.4
Other nonfamily household	1.7	3.6	4.4

*Own children under 18

Source: U.S. Department of Commerce, Bureau of the Census. *Population Profile of the United States 1989.* Series P-23, 159:25, April 1989.

Hospitality is endemic to the activity patterns of wider families. Kris Jeter establishes the vital role of hospitality in creating wider families. Her analysis of this phenomenon from the beginnings of recorded history, with focus upon mythological origins of Jewish and Muslim customs of hospitality is a powerful testament to the essence of hospitality in creating and maintaining wider families. Hospitality provides a sanctuary for the seeker, a release from the exigencies of everyday life, a suspension of time and space. What more important function can a wider family provide?

The social dynamic of wider families, whether or not recognized as families by the legal or larger social systems, draws much power from the bonds of affection, remembrance, nurturance, support and "there-ness" of members for one another. When major changes have occurred, whether divorce, marriage, or on a more far-reaching scale when successive generations of a biological family live different lifestyles in different class and cultural arenas, the wider family may be the only group which meets deep personal needs. . . .

Continuing Change

The concept of the wider family is a sensitizing rather than a definitive concept. It points to the path of inquiry rather than telling us what will or must be found. Sensitizing concepts are more open to dramatic or subtle empirical changes. They enable quicker naming, and therefore understanding of the processes we create and which influence us.

This is ever more important as we look to what becomes of aging adults who may never have married, or who have had no children, or who live without contact with biological kin. Those who respond to dependent members of wider families, providing needed care, nurturance and emotional support, are substituting for traditional family members and emerge into the patterns of serial reciprocity. Thus, families are "made" out of other affectionate and service-providing groupings—wider families—where generational transfers of equity, status transfers, whole new lines of monetary and class inheritance, become possible. Children and grandchildren who are that because they act like that, friends' children who are "shared" children, who inherit from nonbiological "aunts" and "uncles," are such examples.

Certainly there is more freedom to be creative in wider families, since they are not constrained by the structures, normative patterns, and legal obligations of traditional families. There is the possibility of concentrating on fewer goals, or concentrating on goals obscured or blocked by the very memories and involvements that form so many of the bonds of biological families. Time is also available to do things in wider families that traditional family requirements may prevent. Holidays, birthdays, days of mourning and days of rejoicing, can be remade in voluntaristic ways, free of traditions and their sanctions. Wider families are arenas of creation, so that levels of expectation emerge, rather than being pre-existent to action and character development.

Still, habitual action does become patterned, and long-lived wider families may give rise to new kinds of traditions. These remain to be studied, as well as the question of whether over time, the spontaneous, transformed into the expected, may cause the perpetuation or the breakup of wider families. Wider families may be temporary, complementary, or latent groups. Temporary in the sense that through spontaneous formation they meet a current need or desire or solve a vexing problem. Then they cease to exist. Complementarity is functioning in tandem with traditional groups such as biological families, enhancing and supporting the life ways of its members. Latent wider families maintain their informal networks, experience times of quiescence and become active when issues stimulate members to activity.

Wider families are rescues both from isolation and independence; in all cases, the freedom to enter and the freedom to leave the wider family may be matters of optimal time and mass, of the right circumstances and the right people, at the right time.

New Areas of Research

How contact is maintained is also a matter of study and exploration: do wider families necessarily exist physically proximate? Are fax and bitnet families wider families? [Fax and bitnet families are groups of unrelated people who "meet," "talk," and form strong friendships by fax machine correspondence or through computer networks. They may never physically meet each other.] The technologically based wider family may be a future network whose significance we already perceive from the modem-based groups that form interlocking grids across the country.

A Definition of the Wider Family

A family consists of two or more people, whether living together or apart, related by blood, marriage, adoption or commitment to care for one another.

Board of Directors of Family Service America, Inc., *1992-1993 Family Agenda.*

Is wider family the key to the success of organized crime? By adding emotional and relational components to any contractual structure, that structure's demands become far more binding. The cynical and shadow-negative realm of such wider families have their equivalent in positive ways, e.g., in administrative structures in industry and other corporate entitites, where team groupings may expand beyond the corporate realm into other parts of workers' lives.

There is also the question of whether the wider family will rescue the kin/marital family from overloads that build through the multiplication of roles, demands, and options. If wider families become safety valves for need expression, emotional support and services, resource transfers and voluntary inheritance lines may expand the traditional lines of what is known as "family" along many, complex dimensions. Such takeovers may result in new forms of family based on the institutionalization of the properties of wider families. Formalization is inevitable in the transition from informal and voluntary groupings to establishment forms with endemic dominance and power. . . .

Define It, and Knowledge Follows

Today, we hear so much about the minimal impact sociology seems to have on larger social understandings. Sociological, and psychological, and economic, and scientific terminology do get into everyday discourse, but the disparity between what has been learned from studies and the public awareness of it, signifies insufficient contribution on sociology's part to enriching that discourse. People want to make sense out of their lives. Religion traditionally has helped to do so, but it is not the only place that the quest for understanding can be served. In fact, to make sense out of the world we must be able to recognize what is happening, to name the phenomena of which we are part and which we create; things that have names are far less frightening than those which are nameless.

The notion of "wider family" emerges from observation, elaborating a grounded theoretical formulation. If it is observed, if it can be explored and explained, it should be done in order to serve the needs of those who seek sense and definitions in their lives. For example, narrow social definitions may enable narrow legal definitions to persist; both cause much pain and deprivation. This is experienced by same-sex couples who say they are married, act lovingly and caringly, but must fight in court for access to each other if illness claims one and separates the couple, and for survivors' rights on the death of one. "Domestic partnership" laws which protect such survivors still encounter questions of duration or permanence, and conditions of dissolution. Perhaps just legitimating, through more empirical research, the existence of families that do not, or only partly, meet legal definitions of family, laws will be less calcified than they currently are in comparison to the dynamic flow of relationships in our society.

46

"Family *refers to that social unit composed of a married father and mother and their children.*"

The Definition of Family Should Remain Limited

Bryce J. Christensen

In the following viewpoint, Bryce J. Christensen argues that the word *family* should not be redefined to include nontraditional groups of people. He believes politicians, sociologists, and feminists use the word *family* because its favorable connotations help advance their causes—expansion of the welfare state and abandonment of traditional male/female roles. Christensen is director of the Rockford Institute Center on the Family in America, a conservative organization focusing on family issues.

As you read, consider the following questions:

1. According to the author, how does Socrates' defense of a limited, strict definition of words apply to broadening the meaning of family?
2. How does expanding the definition of family sabotage meaningful debate on family issues, according to Christensen?
3. What government programs undertaken in the broadened name of family are harmful, according to Christensen?

From *Utopia Against the Family* by Bryce J. Christensen. San Francisco: Ignatius Press, 1990. Copyright 1990 by Ignatius Press. Reprinted with permission.

Not long ago, utopians of various political stripes were willing to attack the family openly. Feminists like Germaine Greer and Kate Millett rejected the family as "the prison of domesticity" and "patriarchy's chief institution." New Left thinkers like R.D. Laing and Peter Irons denounced the family for its "repressive functions" in enforcing monogamy, sexual restraint, and the capitalist work ethic. Now, however, many leading feminists proclaim themselves "profamily," while the political heirs of the New Left declaim passionately on the need for a "national family policy."

What's going on here? In a few instances, the feminists and radicals of the 1960s and 1970s have outgrown their utopian passions and have accepted the post-Edenic responsibilities of marriage and child rearing. However, a careful examination of the new family-policy forces reveals that most of their leaders still carry deep grudges against the traditional family but find it politically useful to cloak their utopian agenda in profamily rhetoric. . . . In adopting the family label as their own, many feminists and politicians hope to play a semantic shell game with the American people, capturing the widespread popular sentiments that attach to the word *family* while quietly slipping the word's historical, moral, and paternal content into the "memory hole." In this ideological redefinition of family, we are witnessing what C.S. Lewis aptly describes as "verbicide, the murder of a word."

Appropriation of the Word *Family*

For most people, *family* refers to that social unit composed of a married father and mother and their children. In extension, the term is often applied to grandparents, aunts, uncles, cousins, and other relatives. Modern redefiners of family propose a quite different set of meanings. In a typical redefinition, the American Home Economics Association (AHEA) cheerfully disposes of centuries of semantic and moral tradition.

> AHEA defines the family unit as two or more persons who share resources, share responsibility for decisions, share values and goals, and have commitment to one another over time. The family is that climate that one "comes home to" and it is this network of sharing and commitments that most accurately describes the family unit, regardless of blood, legal ties, adoption, or marriage.

Only slightly less radical than the AHEA redefinition of family is the functional definition of the term provided by [sociologist] Ira Reiss . . . "The family institution is a small kinship-structured group with the key function of nurturant socialization of the newborn." The virtue of this definition, in Reiss' view, is that it can apply to "any type of family structure" that provides

48

care for an infant: "The structure of a kinship group, like the family, can vary tremendously. The biological mother can be alone with her child or she may not be present at all. . . . Whoever performs the major share of the nurturant function for the newborn comprises the heart of the family unit." In Reiss' definition of *family*, references to "father" or "marriage" are about as important as references to "sunroof" or "bucket seats" in the definition of *automobile*.

Practical Considerations Aside

Practical considerations require us to pin down what the family is all about. Tax bills, welfare and insurance payments, adoption rights and other real-life events can turn on what constitutes a family. Our expectations of what a family ought to be will also shape the kinds of social policies we want. Webster's offers 22 definitions. The Census Bureau has settled on "two or more persons related by birth, marriage or adoption who reside in the same household." New York state's highest court stretched the definition: [in 1989] . . . the court set four standards for a family: (1) the "exclusivity and longevity of a relationship"; (2) the "level of emotional and financial commitment"; (3) how the couple "conducted their everyday lives and held themselves out to society"; (4) the "reliance placed upon one another for daily services." That approach incenses social critic Midge Decter. "You can call homosexual households 'families,' and you can define 'family' any way you want to, but you can't fool Mother Nature," says Decter. "A family is a mommy and a daddy and their children."

Jerrold K. Footlick, *Newsweek*, Special Issue, Winter/Spring 1990.

Some utopians are quite candid about their motives for redefining family. In a critique of "the definition of family," David Allen, professor of women's studies at the University of Wisconsin, argues that "an overly rigid definition of the family and its responsibilities can contribute to limiting women's participation in the work force, perpetuating constrictive gender identities, and sustaining a sense of entrapment." To advance "emancipatory interests," Allen argues that he and his colleagues must go about "opening up a plurality of definitions" for the term. Not happy about this kind of scholarship, Professors Larry and Janet Hunt of the University of Maryland acknowledge that many sociologists are "obscuring [social] trends with infinitely flexible conceptions of family."

Trying to create such semantic plurality, feminist writer Letty Cottin Pogrebin attacks the applications of family to any "particular living unit" or to any social grouping that is "concrete, secure, and orderly." Pogrebin complains that when family is "used prescriptively" the word serves to "coerce people into roles" and "to create a national ethos out of a myth of domestic bliss." Better in her view to acknowledge the confusion in "current varieties of usage" of the word. "*What* is family is a contradictory mess," she declares in a sentence laden with more passion than grace. Family, Pogrebin informs her readers, carries "different meanings and produces different results in different contexts." Consequently, Pogrebin argues that it is time to discard terms like "broken family" and "single-parent family." Broadcasting on the same feminist wavelength, Joan Walsh has urged feminist leaders to curry political advantage by declaring themselves "profamily" while they "generously define the family to include women and the people they care for."

Redefinition Demeans Marriage

Joining in the ideological redefinition of family, Bob Frishman of People for the American Way rejects any attempts to define family normatively, maintaining that "the family in America always has had a changing and changeable form." "At any time in our history," Frishman writes, "one could find many kinds of people living in many kinds of households." In defending a pluralistic vision of "families of many types," Frishman takes particular pains to erase the significance of marriage: "Unmarried and married couples are alike in most respects. There are the same ups and downs, the same strong emotions, and an equal emphasis on monogamy." Within the context of this radical redefinition of family, Frishman contends that "nobody deserves to be called 'antifamily' for rejecting the simplistic, unrealistic, and incomplete assessment and solutions of the 'pro-family' movement."

Even more daring is Karen Lindsey of Emerson College, who argues that unless it is "recognized that the family, historically, *was* a prison," then "the family becomes . . . a creation of false naming." In challenging "the oppressive definitions of family," Lindsey proposes that "for people who have shared history, who have loved each other and lived through major parts of each other's lives together, the concept of 'family' should apply." The time has come, she announces, for people to "reclaim for themselves the power of naming" by declaring their circle of friends to be a "consciously chosen family" or an "intentional family." Such intentional "families" may be made up of those who share professional interests, economic needs, political views, or sexual preference. "We can all translate our ideas of deeper, freer family structures into reality. We can name, and we can create."

Popular journalists naturally are carried along by such utopian tides. *Ladies' Home Journal* has suggested that "we are witnessing a renaissance of the family," while informing readers that "the family of the mid-eighties is very different from the one most Americans were reared in. In fact *family* in the singular is somewhat of a misnomer. Better: the plural *families.* . . . The family is flourishing in a multiplicity of forms—single parent family, stepfamily, extended family." "At bottom, the basic American concept of family is being transformed," concluded a trendy article in *Women's World*. Redefiners of family are scoring points in the public schools as well. In a 1986 survey of the social studies texts most commonly used in grade schools, psychologist Paul Vitz found "no explicit, objective definition of family." Instead, he found such "vague and inaccurate" notions as "a family is a group of people" or "a family is defined as 'the people you live with.'". . .

Socrates vs. Humpty Dumpty

Stripped of every self-justifying rationale, the motive of those now redefining family is well illustrated in a famous episode in Lewis Carroll's *Through the Looking Glass* in which Alice expresses confusion at the strange way Humpty Dumpty uses the word *glory:*

"I don't know what you mean by 'glory'," Alice said.

Humpty Dumpty smiled contemptuously. "Of course you don't—till I tell you. I meant 'there's a nice knock-down argument for you!'"

"But 'glory' doesn't mean 'a nice knock-down argument'," Alice objected.

"When I use a word," Humpty Dumpty said, in rather a scornful tone, "it means just what I choose it to mean—neither more nor less."

"The question is," said Alice, "whether you *can* make words mean so many different things."

"The question is," said Humpty Dumpty, "which is to be master—that's all."

Indeed, when [advocates] unitedly defend the use of family in innovative ways because of the political advantages so gained, they implicitly declare themselves disciples of Humpty Dumpty semantics. For them, the semantic question is neither more nor less than a question of political mastery. Acknowledging no abiding norm or ideal to be re-presented as family, they see merely a cluster of popular emotions waiting to be captured at the hustings. This way lies verbal deception and rhetorical confusion.

Humpty Dumpty's word tricks may have baffled Alice, but the ancient Greek philosopher Socrates would have understood very well the significance of willful redefinitions of words. In a profound discussion of language in Plato's *Cratylus*, Socrates disputes the Protagorean view that "all is convention" and "relative to individuals" in the use of names. Socrates declares that "things have a permanent essence of their own" and that proper names must therefore be given "according to a natural process . . . and not at our pleasure." Names show themselves "false," he explains, if they do not help us "distinguish natures, as the shuttle . . . distinguish[es] threads of the web." In his search for their "original meaning," Socrates reasons that it is "the ancient form" of words that "shows the intention of the giver of the name" and that bears most clearly the imprint of "the minds of gods, or of men, or of both."

"Family" Must Be Restricted

The "family" is now so loosely defined that it can mean any combination of individuals in almost any situation, including a fishing boat crew or a coffee klatch. Family defenders often say "traditional family" to describe what "family" used to mean. Few would contest that "traditional families" are embattled. But current terminology is due less to social changes than the sexual radicals' campaign to deny the importance of the two-parent, heterosexual family. Under the new definition, that "type" of family ceases to be the foundational unit of civilization and becomes just one among many "choices."

Robert Knight, *The Washington Times*, January 17, 1992.

Evidently, Socrates is no inspiration for those now redefining family, for they want to use the word not for "distinguishing natures" but for confounding the traditional distinctions between family and nonfamily, between family and state. In their hands, the word *family* serves not as a shuttle for separating the threads of the web, but instead as a crude spindle for spinning together many kinds of diverse social and political threads into one statist fabric. Nor do the redefiners of family follow Socrates' teachings on the primacy of the ancient meaning of words: The Indo-European roots of *family* are decidedly marital and patriarchal.

Modern Arguments for Strict Definition

Dead now for two millennia, Socrates could not persuade all of his contemporaries to accept his views on language and may convince fewer living now. But the redefining of family appears troubling even when analyzed within modern theoretical frameworks far removed from the philosophical premises of the *Cratylus*. For instance, in his 1964 book *Language in Thought and Action*, semantics scholar S.I. Hayakawa observed that fruitful political discourse about democracy can occur only when citizens share "reasonable agreement as to the extensional meaning of 'democracy'." Without such agreement, he cautioned, political arguments will "go on indefinitely," splitting society into "bitterly opposed groups" unable to understand one another. The same may be said about current political debates over family policy if family is redefined to apply to every sort of domestic arrangement but none in particular.

In his *Theory of Semiotics* (1976), the Italian scholar Umberto Eco offers an analysis of code-switching that helps to explain the sudden popularity of *family* among people who have never much cared for the word before. As Eco describes it, code-switching occurs whenever advertisers, propagandists, politicians, and others engaged in "rhetorical discourse" choose to "*switch* from one code to another without making the process evident." In this switching, words with a favorable "emotional connotation" are invoked to camouflage denotative "incompatibilities." Eco notes, for example, how advertisers change their catch phrases every time the public mood changes. In the code-switching now being performed by many advocates of a national family policy, the favorable connotations of family are being used to dispel concerns about growing government paternalism and to quell fears about declining personal morality. . . . Eco observes, however, that code-switching may fail in the long run because denotative incompatibilities eventually poke through, causing the "explosion" of the contrived system of meaning.

Utopian Programs

In the short run, the advocates of a national family policy may succeed in winning political support for their utopian programs. But in the long run, these code-switchers will probably trigger the kind of cultural "explosion" described by Eco, for far from reinforcing the moral, emotional, and spiritual commitments that make family life possible, the utopian appropriation of family can only weaken those bonds. Legal theorist Christopher Stone notes correctly that "the way we employ morally significant words embeds cues to right conduct." Semantic "cues" that point to marriage, fidelity, and parental responsibility all vanish when family is redefined to include cohabiting couples, unwed mothers, and every other social grouping. (It is also worth noting in passing that while Johnson's *Dictionary* defined *marriage* as "the act of uniting a man and woman for life," current dictionary makers hazard no guess as to how long wedlock may last.) [Government] initiatives—subsidized day care, generous welfare benefits for unwed mothers, guaranteed maternal leave—can make the decline of the family less visible and (temporarily) less painful. But people will eventually notice that nothing government does in the name of family aptly compensates for the disappearance of intact marriages and parental care for children. None of the deep and reassuring feelings found in the traditional family will easily transfer to the day-care administrator, the social worker, or the child-support officer.

Changing Vocabulary

Looking specifically at changes in the vocabulary of the family and of sex roles, Professor L.B. Cebik of the University of Tennessee makes a telling observation in the *Journal of Home Economics*: "From Aristotle onward, we took language to be a fixed entity whose nature we sought as one seeks the analysis of a rock. Then . . . we reversed our field and definitions became arbitrary. . . . By stipulation we could make a concept mean whatever we wanted it to mean. The result has been chaos." Cebik believes that in home economics, as in other academic disciplines, "when we attempt to alter concepts, the situation becomes frightful, for we usually do so without investigating the consequences of either the old or the new meanings. . . . This sort of short-sightedness can spell . . . a well-intentioned disaster.". . .

When a word has become so elastic as to be applicable to everything, soon no one cares if the word simply disappears from use. Despite all the changes in modern life, the intact family continues to prove Socrates' assertion that "things have a permanent essence of their own." The indiscriminate application of the word *family* can only signal a betrayal of that essence. . . .

"Tongues, like governments, have a natural tendency to degeneration," observed Samuel Johnson, who yet challenged his fellow English speakers to "make some struggles for our language." The time is now to fight for the word *family*, to prevent it from losing its historical, moral, and descriptive content, for the loss of this particular piece of our linguistic heritage will not be without serious cultural and political consequences. Inaccurate words are dangerous, Orwell warned, because "the slovenliness of our language makes it easier for us to have foolish thoughts." Foolish thoughts quickly translate into ruinous policies. A normative definition of family must be vigorously affirmed. . . . Christians and Jews have a particular stake in avoiding a change in language which would make Scripture appear irrelevant. The word *family* can retain the meaning preserved through centuries of moral effort only if those in our cultural centers insist that it not be applied indiscriminately to cohabiting couples, unwed mothers, or the federal government.

"Gay marriage wouldn't weaken the family; it would strengthen *it."*

Homosexual Partners Are Changing the Family

Brent Hartinger

In the following viewpoint, Brent Hartinger makes the case for legalizing homosexual marriage and recognizing homosexual families as a legitimate family form. Hartinger argues that gay marriage would strengthen the concept of family for all Americans. Hartinger is a free-lance writer based in Seattle, Washington.

As you read, consider the following questions:

1. According to the author, what percentage of homosexual men and women are in long-term, committed relationships?
2. Why does Hartinger conclude that allowing same-sex marriage is essentially a conservative, not liberal, act?
3. How does the author counter the argument that sanctioned marriage must be linked to childbearing?

Brent Hartinger, "A Case for Gay Marriage," *Commonweal*, November 22, 1991. Reprinted with permission. This article was one of three debating the issue of gay marriage and does not represent the views of *Commonweal* on this issue.

In San Francisco in 1991, homosexuals won't just be registering for the draft and to vote. In November 1990, voters approved legislation which allows unmarried live-in partners—heterosexual or homosexual—to register themselves as "domestic partners," publicly agreeing to be jointly responsible for basic living expenses. Like a few other cities, including New York and Seattle, San Francisco had already allowed bereavement leave to the domestic partners of municipal employees. But San Francisco lesbians and gays had been trying for eight years to have some form of partnership registration—for symbolic reasons at least—ever since 1982 when then-mayor Diane Feinstein vetoed a similar ordinance. A smattering of other cities provide health benefits to the domestic partners of city employees. In 1989, a New York court ruled that a gay couple is a "family" in that state, at least in regard to their rent-controlled housing (the decision was reaffirmed late in 1990). And in October of 1989, Denmark became the first industrialized country to permit same-sex unions (since then, one-fifth of all marriages performed there have been homosexual ones).

However sporadic, these represent major victories for gay men and lesbians for whom legal marriage is not an option. Other challenges are coming fast and furious. Two women, Sandra Rovira and Majorie Forlini, lived together in a marriage-like relationship for twelve years—and now after her partner's death, Rovira is suing AT&T, Forlini's employer, for refusing to pay the death benefits the company usually provides surviving spouses. Craig Dean and Patrick Gill, a Washington, D.C., couple, have filed a $1 million discrimination suit against that city for denying them a marriage license and allegedly violating its human rights acts which outlaw discrimination on the basis of sexual orientation; the city's marriage laws explicitly prohibit polygamous and incestuous marriages, but not same-sex ones.

Benefits of Legal Marriage

Legally and financially, much is at stake. Most employee benefit plans—which include health insurance, parental leave, and bereavement leave—extend only to legal spouses. Marriage also allows partners to file joint income taxes, usually saving them money. Social Security can give extra payment to qualified spouses. And assets left from one legal spouse to the other after death are not subject to estate taxes. If a couple splits up, there is the issue of visitation rights for adopted children or offspring conceived by artificial insemination. And then there are issues of jurisprudence (a legal spouse cannot be compelled to testify against his or her partner) and inheritance, tenancy, and conservatorship: pressing concerns for many gays as a result of AIDS.

In terms of numbers alone, a need exists. An estimated 10

percent of the population—about 25 million Americans—is exclusively or predominantly homosexual in sexual orientation, and upwards of 50 percent of the men and about 70 percent of the women are in long-term, committed relationships. A 1990 survey of 1,266 lesbian and gay couples found that 82 percent of the male couples and 75 percent of the female ones share all or part of their incomes.

Domestic Partnership Status Is Inadequate

As a result, many lesbians and gays have fought for "domestic partnership" legislation to extend some marital and family benefits to unmarried couples—cohabitating partners either unwilling or, in the case of homosexuals, unable to marry. In New York City, for example, unmarried municipal workers who have lived with their partners at least a year may register their relationships with the personnel department, attesting to a "close and committed" relationship "involving shared responsibilities," and are then entitled to bereavement leave.

Numbers of Gay Parents Are Growing

According to Roberta Achtenberg, executive director of the National Center for Lesbian Rights, there are more than 2 million gay mothers and fathers. Most of their children are from earlier, heterosexual relationships, but she estimates that some 5,000 to 10,000 lesbians have borne children after "coming out," and hundreds of gay and lesbian couples have adopted.

Jean Seligmann, *Newsweek*, Special Issue, Winter/Spring 1990.

But such a prescription is inadequate; the protections and benefits are only a fraction of those resulting from marriage—and are available to only a small percentage of gays in a handful of cities (in the above-mentioned survey, considerably less than 10 percent of lesbian and gay couples were eligible for any form of shared job benefits). Even the concept of "domestic partnership" is seriously flawed. What constitutes a "domestic partner"? Could roommates qualify? A woman and her live-in maid? It could take an array of judicial decision making to find out.

Further, because the benefits of "domestic partnership" are allotted to couples without much legal responsibility—and because the advantages of domestic partnership are necessarily allowed for unmarried heterosexual partners as well as homosexual ones—domestic partnership has the unwanted consequence of weakening traditional marriage. Society has a vested interest in stable, committed relationships—especially, as in the case of most heterosexual couples, when children are concerned. But by eliminating the financial and legal advantages to marriage, domestic partnership dilutes that institution.

Society already has a measure of relational union—it's called marriage, and it's not at all difficult to ascertain: you're either married or you're not.

Gay Parenting Does Not Harm Children

Yet for unmarried heterosexual couples, marriage is at least an option. Gay couples have no such choice—and society also has an interest in committed, long-lasting relationships even between homosexuals. An estimated 3 to 5 million homosexuals have parented children within heterosexual relationships, and at least 1,000 children were born to lesbian or gay couples in the San Francisco area alone since 1986. None of the recent thirty-five studies on homosexual parents has shown that parental sexual orientation has any adverse effect on children (and the children of gays are no more likely to be gay themselves). Surely increased stability in the relationships of lesbians and gay men could only help the gays themselves and their many millions of children.

Some suggest that legal mechanisms already exist by which lesbian and gay couples could create some of the desired protections for their relationships: power-of-attorney agreements, proxies, wills, insurance policies, and joint tenancy arrangements. But even these can provide only a fraction of the benefits of marriage. And such an unwieldy checklist guarantees that many lesbian and gay couples will not employ even those available.

There is a simpler solution. Allow gay civil marriage. And throw the weight of our religious institutions behind such unions.

Same-Sex and Interracial Marriage Compared

In 1959, Mildred Jeter and Richard Loving, a mixed-race Virginia couple married in Washington, D.C., pleaded guilty to violating Virginia's ban on interracial marriages. Jeter and Loving were given a suspended jail sentence on the condition that they leave the state. In passing the sentence, the judge said, "Almighty God created the races white, black, yellow, Malay, and red, and he placed them on separate continents. And but for the interference with his arrangements, there would be no cause for such marriages. The fact that he separated the races shows that he did not intend for the races to mix." A motion to overturn the decision was denied by two higher Virginia courts until the state's ban on interracial marriage was declared unconstitutional by the United States Supreme Court in 1967. At the time, fifteen other states also had such marital prohibition.

Clearly, one's sexual orientation is different from one's race. While psychological consensus (and compelling identical and fraternal twin studies) force us to concede that the homosexual *orientation* is not a choice (nor is it subject to change), homosexual behavior definitely is a choice, very unlike race. Critics maintain that gays can marry—just not to members of their same sex.

But with regard to marriage, whether homosexual behavior is a choice or not is irrelevant, since one's marriage partner is *necessarily* a choice. In 1959, Richard Loving, a white man, could have chosen a different partner to marry other than Mildred Jeter, a black woman; the point is that he did not. The question is whether, in the absence of a compelling state interest, the state should be allowed to supersede the individual's choice.

No Break with Convention

Some maintain that there are compelling state interests to prohibiting same-sex marriages: that tolerance for gay marriages would open the door for any number of unconventional marital arrangements—group marriage, for example. In fact, most lesbian and gay relationships are probably far more conventional than most people think. In the vast majority of respects, gay relationships closely resemble heterosexual ones—or even actually improve upon them (gay relationships tend to be more egalitarian than heterosexual ones). And in a society where most cities have at least one openly gay bar and sizable gay communities—where lesbians and gays appear regularly on television and in the movies—a committed relationship between two people of the same sex is not nearly the break from convention that a polygamous one is. More important, easing the ban on same-sex marriage would make lesbians and gays, the vast majority of whom have not chosen celibacy, even more likely to live within long-term, committed partnerships. The result would be more people living more conventional life-styles, not more people living less conventional ones. It's actually a conservative move, not a liberal one.

Reducing Stigma

Similarly, there is little danger that giving legitimacy to gay marriages would undermine the legitimacy of heterosexual ones—cause "the breakdown of the family." Since heterosexuality appears to be at least as immutable as homosexuality (and since there's no evidence that the prevalence of homosexuality increases following the decriminalization of it), there's no chance heterosexuals would opt for the "homosexual alternative." Heterosexual marriage would still be the ultimate social union for heterosexuals. Gay marriage would simply recognize a consistent crosscultural, transhistorical minority and allow that significant minority to also participate in an important social institution. And since marriage licenses are not rationed out, homosexual partnerships wouldn't deny anyone else the privilege.

Indeed, the compelling state interest lies in *permitting* gay unions. In the wake of AIDS, encouraging gay monogamy is simply rational public health policy. Just as important, gay marriage would reduce the number of closeted gays who marry heterosexual partners, as an estimated 20 percent of all gays do, in an effort to conform to social pressure—but at enormous cost to themselves, their children, and their opposite-sex spouses. It would reduce the atmosphere of ridicule and abuse in which the children of homosexual parents grow up. And it would reduce the number of shameful parents who disown their children or banish their gay teenagers to lives of crimes, prostitution, and drug abuse, or to suicide (psychologists estimate that gay youth comprise up to 30 percent of all teen suicides, and one Seattle study found that a whopping 40 percent of that city's street kids may be lesbian or gay, most having run away or been expelled from intolerant homes). Gay marriage wouldn't weaken the family; it would *strengthen* it.

Families of Affinity

Is a lesbian couple a family? Yes, a Minnesota appeals court ruled in December 1991 in a case that has been a focus of gay-rights activism since 1984. Ordering that Karen Thompson, a physical-education professor, be granted guardianship of her brain-damaged lover Sharon Kowalski, the three-judge panel said, "Thompson and Sharon are a family of affinity, which ought to be accorded respect.". . .

Thompson's cause won widespread support from gay-rights groups, which want homosexual partners to enjoy legal rights comparable to those of married couples. The decision, says Paula Ettelbrick, attorney with the Lambda Legal Defense and Education Fund in New York City, a gay-rights group, "begins the process of recognizing that lesbian and gay couples share the kind of commitment that married couples do."

Time, December 30, 1991.

The unprecedented social legitimacy given gay partnerships—and homosexuality in general—would have other societal benefits as well: it would dramatically reduce the widespread housing and job discrimination, and verbal and physical violence experienced by most lesbians and gays, clear moral and social evils.

Of course, legal and religious gay marriage wouldn't, as some writers claim, "celebrate" or be "an endorsement" of homosexual sexual behavior—any more than heterosexual marriage celebrates heterosexual sex or endorses it; gay marriage would celebrate the loving, committed relationship between two individuals, a relationship in which sexual behavior is one small part. Still, the legalization of gay marriage, while not making homosexual sexual behavior any more prevalent, would remove much of the stigma concerning such behavior, at least that which takes place within the confines of "marriage." And if the church sanctions such unions, a further, moral legitimacy will be granted. In short, regardless of the potential societal gains, should society and the church reserve a centuries-old moral stand that condemns homosexual sexual behavior?

Acknowledge Biological Imperatives

We have no choice; the premises upon which the moral stand are based have changed. Science now acknowledges the existence of a homosexual sexual *orientation*, like heterosexuality, a fundamental affectional predisposition. Unlike specific behaviors of, say, rape or incest, a homosexual's sexual behavior is the logical expression of his or her most basic, unchangeable sexual make-up. And unlike rape and incest, necessarily manifestations of destruction and abuse, sexual behavior resulting from one's sexual orientation can be an expression of love and unity (it is the complete denial of this love—indeed, an unsettling preoccupation with genital activity—that makes the inflammatory comparisons of homosexual sex to rape, incest, and alcoholism so frustrating for lesbians and gays).

Moral condemnation of homosexual sexual behavior is often founded on the belief that sex and marriage are—and should be—inexorably linked with child-rearing; because lesbians and gay men are physiologically incapable of creating children alone, all such sexual behavior is deemed immoral—and gays are considered unsuitable to the institution of marriage. But since moral sanction is not withheld from infertile couples or those who intend to remain childless, this standard is clearly being inconsistently—and unfairly—applied.

Reinforce Monogamy

Some cite the promiscuity of some male gays as if this is an indication that all homosexuals are incapable or undeserving of marriage. But this standard is also inconsistently applied; it has never been seriously suggested that the existence of promiscuous heterosexuals invalidates all heterosexuals from the privilege of marriage. And if homosexuals are more likely than heterosexuals to be promiscuous—and if continual, harsh condemnation hasn't altered that fact—the sensible solution would seem to be to try to lure gays back to the monogamous fold by providing efforts in that direction with some measure of respect and social support: something gay marriage would definitely provide.

Human beings are sexual creatures. It is simply not logical to say, as the church does, that while one's basic sexual outlook is neither chosen nor sinful, any activity taken as a result of that orientation is. One must then ask exactly where does the sin of "activity" begin anyway? Hugging a person of the same sex? Kissing? Same-sex sexual fantasy? Even apart from the practical impossibilities, what about the ramifications of such an attempt? How does the homosexual adolescent formulate self-esteem while being told that *any* expression of his or her sexuality *ever* is unacceptable—or downright evil? The priest chooses celibacy (asexuality isn't required), but this *is* a choice—one made well after adolescence.

Cultural condemnations and biblical prohibitions of (usually male) homosexual behavior were founded upon an incomplete understanding of human sexuality. To grant the existence of a homosexual orientation requires that there be some acceptable expression of it. Of course, there's no reason why lesbians and gays should be granted moral leniency over heterosexuals—which is why perhaps the most acceptable expression of same-sex sexuality should be within the context of a government sanctioned, religiously blessed marriage. But before we can talk about the proper way to get two brides or two grooms down a single church aisle, we have to first show there's an aisle wide enough to accommodate them.

"When compared to the traditional heterosexual marriage form of the family, homosexual partnerships greatly lack social benefit."

Homosexual Partners Are Undermining the Family

Bradley P. Hayton

Because homosexual relationships are unstable and abnormal, they harm the stability of the traditional heterosexual family, Bradley P. Hayton argues in the following viewpoint. He believes same-sex couples do not form lasting relationships and are not good role models for children. Rather than legalizing homosexual marriage, society should enact laws that support the traditional family form, Hayton concludes. Hayton, a family counselor in private practice in Newport Beach, California, is a former research analyst with Focus on the Family, a conservative social policy organization in Colorado Springs.

As you read, consider the following questions:

1. What are the necessary functions of a family, according to the author?
2. According to Hayton, why does society have a right to keep homosexual relationships illegal?
3. Why does Hayton believe the effects of homosexual parenting on children are similar to those of divorce?

Bradley P. Hayton, "To Marry or Not: The Legalization of Marriage and Adoption of Homosexual Couples." Reprinted with permission. A footnoted version of this paper is available from the author, 3416 Via Oporto, Suite 203, Newport Beach, CA 92663.

Should homosexuals be allowed to marry? And should homosexuals be given the legal privilege of adopting children as their own? As the "traditional" family continues to break down in America, these questions are increasingly answered in the affirmative. In fact, an affirmative answer to these questions is considered "progressive" by many who believe that past family forms were indicative of a lower form of evolution.

Rather than citing increasing divorce rates, premarital and extramarital sexual behavior, single parenthood, cohabitation, and homosexuality as symptoms of family breakdown, they believe that these are merely indications of a higher form of social adaptation to modern times. Rather than stable relationships, our society actually needs highly unstable, fleeting relationships, based upon the meeting of individual needs. The family isn't breaking apart; rather we must merely redefine its ever-changing form.

Arguments on behalf of homosexual marriages and homosexual child-adoption are a part of this movement. . . . But before we redefine the family, redefine sexuality, redefine moral behavior, redefine sexual differences and roles, and even redefine human nature itself, it would be good for us to examine some of the rational arguments on behalf of the traditional family, defined as a group of individuals related to one another by marriage, birth, or adoption.

Arguments That Support Traditional Families

First, heterosexual couples reproduce children, something necessary for the continuation of both the human race and a particular society and culture. Without children, a population and a culture soon die. . . . Second, heterosexual couples raise children, providing for their physical, emotional, spiritual, and educational needs. Parents are the best providers of all the needs of children. An impersonal state is never a better substitute. Medical doctors, psychologists, and educators all agree that physical, mental, emotional, spiritual, social, and educational health all begin in the home. No other institution is more powerful in shaping the future of a child.

Third, heterosexual couples teach and model sound morals to children that will be useful to civilization. These morals include truthfulness, respect of others, commitment, perseverance, kindness, committed long-term sexuality, self-control, and others. Without these virtues, the fabric of the social community soon disintegrates. These virtues are the foundation for economic, political, and social wealth in every society.

Fourth, the heterosexual marital bond anchors sexuality, which is more male- than female-related. In every culture, males have always been more sexual than females. This is likewise true in the American homosexual community. While 28 percent of male homosexuals in San Francisco reported having more than a thousand partners and 75 percent had more than a hundred partners, 50 percent of the lesbians reported only having one partner. . . . The heterosexual marital bond ties sexually active men to one woman. When a society endorses divorce or alternative family forms, then the woman always loses. . . .

Social Stability

Fifth, the stable family is the foundation to a stable social order. Broken marriages are at the root of many of America's present social problems. Literally hundreds of studies have correlated broken families with decreased mental health and increased crime, child abuse, unemployment, poverty, substance abuse, and reliance upon welfare.

Individual rights are rooted in the responsibilities of a family. Male incomes are highly correlated with the number of children that the man must support. Families provide the environment to care for the physicial, emotional, spiritual, moral, and educational needs of future citizens. Families cater to specific needs of individuals, rather than to masses. They are the training grounds for community living.

Once we have examined the rational benefits of the "traditional" family, the problems with alternative forms of the family, like homosexual marriages, become easily evident.

Inability to Bear and Raise Children

First, homosexual couples do not reproduce their own children. Any society which accepts homosexual behavior as normal and encourages homosexuality by officially recognizing its validity is on the road to destruction simply by the fact that it will soon be extinct. Homosexuals do not reproduce their lifestyle by having children, but by converting heterosexuals and youth to become homosexual. Lesbian couples can give birth to a child, but the biological father is thus separated from the child as father.

Second, homosexuals cannot meet the psychological, emotional, spiritual, social, and educational needs of children. Homosexuals have very unstable relationships. Studies during the later 1970s and early 1980s, researched mostly by homosexuals, indicated that the average homosexual has between 20 to 106 different partners per year. About one-quarter report having over a thousand partners thus far in their lives. Even after the AIDS crisis, it appears that homosexuals average about 50 different partners per year. Twenty-eight percent of homosexuals have had sodomy with 1000 or more partners, 70 percent with 50 or more partners, and only 2 percent have had what could be described as monogamous or semi-monogamous relationships.

Male homosexual couples continue to be highly promiscuous during their "commitment." And the average couple only stays together only 9 to 60 months. This promiscuity indicates a lack of stability in same-sex relationships. Though psychologists might differ over the cause of homosexual promiscuity, these unstable relationships are not conducive to the stable emotional and social development of children. By nature homosexual behavior is physically and emotionally abnormal, and thus trains children in behavior and virtues that are destructive to the social fabric.

Modeling Immoral Behavior

Third, homosexual promiscuity models and trains children in immoral behavior, behavior that every culture around the world throughout all of history has punished either civilly or socially. Though homosexual advocates are labelling cultures that prohibit homosexual behavior as barbarian or archaic, there is no scientific proof that homosexual sexual behavior is beneficial to society or culture. It is highly probable that prohibitions of homosexual behavior for thousands of years have some cultural and social wisdom. Even a sociobiologist would acknowledge that such social prohibitions have genetic wisdom for human survival.

Deprived Children

A child receives incalculable benefits in the maturing process by the joint instruction, consolation, oversight and love of a father and mother—benefits that are unavailable in homosexual households. The child enjoys the opportunity to understand and respect both sexes in a uniquely intimate climate. The likelihood of gender prejudice is thus reduced, an exceptionally worthy social objective.

Bruce Fein, *ABA Journal*, January 1990.

Many advocates of the legitimization of homosexual behavior argue that civil law should not legislate morality, or that one's sexual morality is relative. There are two primary arguments against such beliefs. First, all law legislates morality. When a state taxes for welfare, education, national defense, or even scientific research, the state makes moral statements about the virtues of these endeavors. When a state outlaws murder, child abuse, prostitution, theft, and other acts, it does so on the basis that these acts are immoral and not beneficial to society.

Groups that want to legitimize homosexual behavior and marriage are indeed making many moral statements: that homosexual marriages *are* moral, that homosexuality is a *right*, and that the state must endorse such behavior. It is interesting that the modern American concept of human "rights" is derived from Jefferson's American Declaration of Independence. Yet in this document "rights" are endowed by our Creator. The vast majority of biblical scholars have always believed that God in the Scriptures prohibited homosexual behavior. And Jefferson himself believed homosexual behavior was worse than bestiality, and prescribed civil punishment for acts of sodomy. Homosexual acts as a "right" were far from Jefferson's mind.

Second, few rarely believe that all sexual morality is relative. Few would seriously endorse wife abuse, incest, pedophilia, bestiality, polygamy, or even adultery. Though some of these acts are made illegal and punishable by the state while others are not, these very "private" acts have grave consequences to society. When a state legitimizes by formally recognizing sexual acts, it endorses these acts as both moral and socially beneficial. Homosexual behavior is neither.

To argue that homosexuals keep their sexual preference private, and that heterosexual youth don't necessarily become homosexual misses the point. Thousands of studies have demonstrated that children imitate the values of the significant adults in their lives. And one's life speaks volumes more than mere words. At the very least, homosexuals teach their children to become more tolerant of homosexual behavior.

Encouraging Promiscuity

Fourth, it is doubtful that homosexual promiscuity will ever change, even with the legitimization of marriage. It has thousands of years of history. Sometimes it was accepted and sometimes not, and in both cases sexual promiscuity was high.

There are several lines of evidence in support of this contention. Homosexual sexuality, especially among males, tends to be highly impersonal. Kinsey and his associates reported that about one half of homosexuals reported that 60 percent or more of their sexual partners were persons with whom they had sex only one time. Between a quarter and a third reported having been robbed by a sexual partner. Two-fifths reported that their longest sexual relationship lasted less than a year, and about 25 percent reported that kissing occurred in one-third or less of their sexual encounters. Thirty percent reported never having had sex in their own homes.

Even homosexual couples aren't very stable. Before moving in together, 64 percent knew each other less than a year. Indeed, their relationships are fast lived, and quickly burn out. Only 26 percent believe that commitment was most important in a marriage relationship. Only a minority share major expenses and purchases as couples. Though the relationships of lesbians last considerably longer than gays, about half are already in their third relationship. Based on their own definition of a "marriage," almost half have been "married" two or more times at the time of their interview. Finding no difference between lesbians and gays, the average length of a relationship is two to three years. . . .

Adoption by Homosexuals

Although the subject is related, whether or not a homosexual should be allowed to adopt a child is a separate issue. Usually every adoption agency investigates the "suitability" of the future parent before the adoption is made. Thus, we must investigate the suitability of the homosexual parent for the best interests of the child.

It must be noted that adoption is also a separate issue than child custody. Sometimes heterosexual couples split, and the courts must decide custody questions regarding the child's natural parents. It must investigate the suitability of each natural parent in the best interests of the child. Sometimes a homosexual parent might actually be better than the heterosexual parent. This viewpoint will center on adoption by non-biological parents.

Effects of Unstable Relationships

Courts must examine the detrimental effects that homosexual adoption would have on the child. First, the unstable nature of homosexual relationships do not make them conducive to child-rearing. . . .

Though there is little direct research on the effects of this instability upon children, there is much research on the effects of divorce upon children. Even after ten years, the effects can still be devastating. Judith Wallerstein and Sandra Blakeslee found that 41 percent were still doing poorly, entering adulthood as worried, underachieving, angry, and with a diminished capacity to parent. They say that only victims of natural disaster could be more seriously harmed than the victims of divorce. At the same time, there is no predicting the long-term effects of divorce upon children from how they initially react.

If one divorce has major effects upon children, we might suspect that multiple "divorces" from multiple relationships, as well as hundreds if not thousands of sexual partners, would even do greater damage. Like watching violent television, a child would simply become emotionally blunted.

Effects of Same-Sex Parenting

Second, hundreds of studies have demonstrated the effects upon children of not having either a mother or a father. Since single parenting is primarily a recent phenomenon in Western culture due to the breakdown of the family, these studies are mostly of recent origin. Summarizing the research on the effects of single parenthood upon children, [Cornell professor Urie] Bronfenbrenner writes:

> [The] results indicate that, controlling for associated factors such as low income, children growing up in such households are at greater risk for experiencing a variety of behavioral and educational problems, including extremes of hyperactivity or withdrawal, lack of attentiveness in the classroom, difficulty in deferring gratification, impaired academic achievement, school misbehavior, absenteeism, dropping out, involvement in socially alienated peer groups, and, especially, the so-called "teenage syndrome" of behaviors that tend to hang together—smoking, drinking, early and frequent sexual experience, a cynical attitude towards work, adolescent pregnancy, and in the more extreme cases, drugs, suicide, vandalism, violence, and criminal acts. Most of these effects are much more pronounced for boys than for girls. . . .

The empirical research on absent mothers also could apply to homosexual adoptions. Hundreds of studies have demonstrated the importance of a mother in child rearing and bonding. Fathers simply do not appear to have the capacity as a mother for child nurture.

Views of Marriage

Homosexuals model a poor view of marriage to children. They are taught by example and belief that marital relationships are transitory and mostly sexual in nature. Sexual relationships are primarily for pleasure rather than procreation. And they are taught that monogamy in a marriage is not only the norm, but should be discouraged if one wants a good "marital" relationship.

Bradley P. Hayton, "To Marry or Not: The Legalization and Adoption of Homosexual Couples," February 1992.

Numerous studies have linked the effects of lesbian parenting upon children to the same effects that single parenthood has upon children. In fact, many of these studies demonstrated that these children experience the same emotional and behavioral problems as children of divorce.

Sexual Identity Requires Opposite-Sex Models

The absence of either the mother or the father has long been the subject of study in psychoanalytically-oriented psychology. Healthy sexual identity only occurs when both a mother and a father are in the home where the child can work through Oedipal feelings of love, rage, and anxiety. Without both parents of the opposite sex, a healthy resolution of these feelings is rarely possible. Sexual identity and superego development are at risk in same-sex homes, as well as single parent homes.

Numerous studies have also demonstrated that children of homosexual parents experience a great deal of difficulty with the "stepparents," in other words, living with parents who have high rates of splitting and then rejoining with new family groups.

And last, though no studies have been done with children who have lived with two homosexual parents, some studies with children from marriages with one homosexual present have demonstrated noticeable results. Children fear being labelled homosexual themselves, fear ostracism from peers, experience much confusion and withdrawal from family and peers, boys feel left out, girls increasingly worry about their own sexual identity, and many children simply reject their parents' lifestyle. The rotating partners of homosexuals cause many children to compete for the affection of their mothers and feel left out of their own families. . . .

Though the effects of homosexual adoption have not been studied empirically, we have every reason to believe that they are not as healthy as intact heterosexual relationships. Clearly, however, the effects of homosexual parenting should be studied directly. . . .

Society Should Not Sanction Homosexual Families

In sum, it must be concluded that when compared to the traditional heterosexual marriage form of the family, homosexual partnerships greatly lack social benefit. Homosexuals highly sexualize human relationships which are usually very temporary. They cannot reproduce children, except through extraordinary technology, and influence children in unhealthy ways, not unlike other forms of single parenthood or stepfamily relationships. Homosexual parents also model what society has traditionally called immoral sexual behavior. Today, in face of an epidemic of STDs [sexually transmitted diseases], AIDS, and teenage pregnancy, we must not teach our children that sexual promiscuity is merely an alternative lifestyle. Rather, children should be encouraged to live in mutual monogamy with one sexual partner in marriage. This is not the behavior that is either desired nor lived by the homosexual community.

"We need a richer concept than that of biological relatedness to flesh out our understanding of the family."

Reproductive Technology Is Changing the Family

Ruth Macklin

Ruth Macklin is professor of bioethics at Albert Einstein College of Medicine, Bronx, New York. In the following viewpoint, Macklin supports the view that reproductive technologies such as artificial insemination, in vitro fertilization, and surrogacy redefine the family but do not undermine it. She argues that societies traditionally define the family by law, by established custom, or by personal choice, and believes these methods can define families formed by the new technologies as well.

As you read, consider the following questions:

1. According to the author, what are the limitations of a strict biological definition of family?
2. How might laws governing adoption be applied to surrogacy cases, according to the author?
3. Which issues in reproductive technology are public domain and which are private family matters, according to Macklin?

Adapted from "Artificial Means of Reproduction and Our Understanding of the Family" by Ruth Macklin, *Hastings Center Report*, January/February 1991. Reprinted with permission.

It is an obvious truth that scientific and technologic innovations produce changes in our traditional way of perceiving the world around us. We have only to think of the telescope, the microscope, and space travel to recall that heretofore unimagined perceptions of the macrocosm and the microcosm have become commonplace. Yet it is not only perceptions, but also conceptions of the familiar that become altered by advances in science and technology. . . .

Now questions are being raised about how a variety of modes of artificial means of reproduction might alter our conception of the family. George Annas has observed:

> Dependable birth control made sex without reproduction possible. . . . Now medicine is closing the circle . . . by offering methods of reproduction without sex; including artificial insemination by donor (AID), in vitro fertilization (IVF), and surrogate embryo transfer (SET). As with birth control, artificial reproduction is defended as life-affirming and loving by its proponents, and denounced as unnatural by its detractors.

Opponents of artificial reproduction have expressed concerns about its effects on the family. This concern has centered largely but not entirely on surrogacy arrangements. Among the objections to surrogacy made by the Roman Catholic Church is the charge that "the practice of surrogate motherhood is a threat to the stability of the family." But before the consequences for the family of surrogacy arrangements or other new reproductive practices can be assessed, we need to inquire into our understanding of the family. Is there a single, incontrovertible conception of the family? And who are the "we" presupposed in the phrase, "our understanding"? To begin, I offer three brief anecdotes.

Subjective Perceptions of Family

The first is a remark made by a long-married, middle-aged man at a wedding. The wedding couple were both about forty. The bride had been married and divorced once, the groom twice. During a light-hearted discussion about marriage and divorce, the middle-aged man remarked: "I could never divorce my wife. She's family!"

The second is a remark made by a four-year-old boy. I had just moved to the neighborhood and was getting to know the children. The four-year-old, named Mikey, was being tormented by a five-year-old named Timmy. I asked Mikey, "Is Timmy your brother?" Mikey replied: "Not any more. Not the way he acts!"

The third story appears in a case study presented as part of a bioethics project on everyday dilemmas in nursing home life. A resident, Mrs. Finch, is a constant complainer who seeks more choices and independence than the nursing home allows. A social worker at the home talked to Mrs. Finch about her adaptation, suggesting that she think of the residents and staff group as a large family where "we all make allowances for each other" and "we all pull our weight." Mrs. Finch responded that she is in the nursing home because she needs health care. She already has a family and does not want another one.

In my commentary on the case of Mrs. Finch, I gave an analysis that suggests some of the complexities in understanding the concept of the family. I wrote:

> Mrs. Finch is quite right to reject the social worker's suggestion that the nursing home be viewed as "a large family." A family is a well-defined social and cultural institution. People may choose to "adopt" unrelated persons into their own family, and biologically related family members may choose to "disown" one of their members (which doesn't sever the kinship ties, though it may sever relations). But an organization or institution does not become a "family" because members or residents are exhorted to treat each other in the way family members should. The social worker's well-intended chat with Mrs. Finch is an exhortation to virtue rather than a proper reminder about the resident's obligations to her new "family."

It is possible, of course, to settle these conceptual matters simply and objectively by adopting a biological criterion for determining what counts as a family. According to this criterion, people who are genetically related to one another would constitute a family, with the type and degree of relatedness described in the manner of a family tree. This sense of *family* is important and interesting for many purposes, but it does not and cannot encompass everything that is actually meant by *family*, nor does it reflect the broader cultural customs and kinship systems that also define family ties.

Family Anecdotes

What makes the first anecdote amusing is the speaker's deliberate use of the biological sense of *family* in a nonbiological context, that is, the context of being related by marriage. In saying that he could never divorce his wife because "she's family," he was conjuring up the associations normally connected with biologically related family and transferring those associations to a person related by the convention of marriage. In a society in which the divorce rate hovers around 50 percent, being a family member related by marriage is often a temporary state of affairs.

What makes the second anecdote amusing is Mikey's denial, based solely on Timmy's behavior, that his biologically related sibling was his brother. When two people are biologically related, they cannot wave away that kinship relation on grounds of their dislike of the other's character or conduct. They can sever their relationship, but not their genetic relatedness. Whether family members ought to remain loyal to one another, regardless of how they act, is an ethical question, not a conceptual one.

The third story also relies on the biological notion of family. Mrs. Finch construed the concept literally when she insisted that she already had a family and "didn't need another one." When I observed in my commentary that a family is a well-defined social and cultural institution, I meant to rebut the social worker's implication that anything one wants to call a family can thereby become a family. Yet considered from a moral perspective, our conception of the family does draw on notions of what members owe to one another in a functional understanding of the family:

> Families should be broadly defined to include, besides the traditional biological relationships, those committed relationships between individuals which fulfill the functions of family.

It seems clear that we need a richer concept than that of biological relatedness to flesh out our understanding of the family. Although the biological concept is accurate in its delineation of one set of factors that determine what is a family, it fails to capture other significant determinants.

Essential Bonds Are Social, Not Genetic

Caring for, nurturing, and nourishing a child in the context of an ongoing social, emotional, and loving relationship is more important than physically begetting a child, however ineradicable and significant the physical/biological connection that is created thereby. . . .

It is the social relationship to a child that makes the parent, and while genetic connection may foster relational bonds, it is the bonds that are crucial, not the genetic ties.

Paul Lauritzen, *Second Opinion*, July 1991.

Newly developed artificial means of reproduction have rendered the term *biological* inadequate for making some critical conceptual distinctions, along with consequent moral decisions. The capability of separating the process of producing eggs from the act of gestation renders obsolete the use of the word *biological* to modify the word *mother*. The techniques of egg retrieval, in vitro fertilization (IVF), and gamete intrafallopian transfer (GIFT) now make it possible for two different women to make a biological contribution to the creation of a new life. It would be a prescriptive rather than a descriptive definition to maintain that the egg donor should properly be called the biological mother. The woman who contributes her womb during gestation—whether she is acting as a surrogate or is the intended rearing mother—is also a biological mother. We have only to reflect on the many ways that the intrauterine environment and maternal behavior during pregnancy can influence fetal and later child development to acknowledge that a gestating woman is also a biological mother. I will return to this issue later in considering how much genetic contributions should count in disputed surrogacy arrangements.

In addition to the biological meaning, there appear to be three chief determinants of what is meant by *family*. These are law, custom, and what I shall call subjective intentions. All three contribute to our understanding of the family. The effect of artificial means of reproduction on our understanding of the family will vary, depending on which of these three determinants is chosen to have priority. There is no way to assign a priori precedence to any one of the three. Let me illustrate each briefly.

Law as a Determinant of Family

Legal scholars can elaborate with precision and detail the categories and provisions of family law. This area of law encompasses legal rules governing adoption, artificial insemination by donor, foster placement, custody arrangements, and removal of children from a home in which they have been abused or neglected. For present purposes, it will suffice to summarize the relevant areas in which legal definitions or decisions have determined what is to count as a family.

Laws governing adoption and donor insemination stipulate what counts as a family. In the case of adoption, a person or couple genetically unrelated to a child is deemed that child's legal parent or parents. By this legal rule, a new family is created. The biological parent or parents of the child never cease to be genetically related, of course. But by virtue of law, custom, and usually emotional ties, the adoptive parents become the child's family.

The Uniform Parentage Act holds that a husband who consents to artificial insemination by donor (AID) of his wife by a physician is the legal father of the child. Many states have enacted laws in conformity with this legal rule. I am not aware of any laws that have been enacted making an analogous stipulation in the case of egg donation, but it is reasonable to assume that there will be symmetry of reasoning and legislation.

Commenting on the bearing of family law on the practice of surrogacy, Alexander M. Capron and Margaret J. Radin contend that the "legal rules of greatest immediate relevance" to surrogacy are those on adoption. These authors identify a number of provisions of state laws on adoption that should apply in the case of surrogacy. The provisions include allowing time for a "change of heart" period after the agreement to release a child, and prohibition of agreements to relinquish parental rights prior to the child's birth. . . .

Consider first the case of the gestational surrogate who is genetically unrelated to the child. Does society's traditional respect for biological ties give her or the genetic mother the right to "reclaim" (or claim in the first place) the child? Society's traditional respect is more likely a concern for genetic inheritance than a recognition of the depth of the bond a woman may feel toward a child she has given birth to.

Parenthood Made Possible

Despite all the problems engendered by the new reproductive methods and their uses, they have the potential of helping many infertile couples to have children. It is hard to object to this. These children are badly wanted and greatly prized in a world where this is too often not the case.

Marcia Angell, M.D., *The New England Journal of Medicine*, November 25, 1990.

Secondly, consider the case of egg donation and embryo transfer to the wife of the man whose sperm was used in IVF. If the sperm donor and egg recipient were known to the egg donor, could the donor base her claim to the child on "society's traditional respect for biological ties"? As I surmised earlier, it seems reasonable to assume that any laws enacted for egg donation will be similar to those now in place for donor insemination. In the latter context, society's traditional respect for biological ties gave way to other considerations arising out of the desire of couples to have a child who is genetically related to at least one of the parents.

The most telling examples of custom as a determinant of family are drawn from cultural anthropology. Kinship systems and incest taboos dictated by folkways and mores differ so radically that few generalizations are possible.

Ruth Benedict writes: "No known people regard all women as possible mates. This is not in an effort, as is so often supposed, to prevent inbreeding in our sense, for over great parts of the world it is an own cousin, often the daughter of one's mother's brother, who is the predestined spouse." In contrast, Benedict notes, some incest taboos are

extended by a social fiction to include vast numbers of individuals who have no traceable ancestors in common. . . . This social fiction receives unequivocal expression in the terms of relationship which are used. Instead of distinguishing lineal from collateral kin as we do in the distinction between father and uncle, brother and cousin, one term means literally "man of my father's group (relationship, locality, etc.) or his generation.". . . Certain tribes of eastern Australia use an extreme form of this so-called classificatory kinship system. Those whom they call brothers and sisters are all those of their generation with whom they recognize any relationship.

One anthropologist notes that "the family in all societies is distinguished by a stability that arises out of the fact that it is based on marriage, that is to say, on socially sanctioned mating entered into with the assumption of permanency." If we extend the notion of socially sanctioned mating to embrace socially sanctioned procreation, it is evident that the new artificial means of reproduction call for careful thought about what should be socially sanctioned before policy decisions are made.

Subjective Intention as a Determinant of Family

This category is most heterogeneous and amorphous. It includes a variety of ways in which individuals—singly, in pairs, or as a group—consider themselves a family even if their arrangement is not recognized by law or custom. Without an accompanying analysis, I list here an array of examples, based on real people and their situations.

• A homosexual couple decides to solidify their relationship by taking matrimonial vows. Despite the fact that their marriage is not recognized by civil law, they find an ordained minister who is willing to perform the marriage ceremony. Later they apply to be foster parents of children with AIDS whose biological parents have died or abandoned them. The foster agency accepts the couple. Two children are placed in foster care with them. They are now a family.

• A variation on this case: A lesbian couple has a long-term monogamous relationship. They decide they want to rear a child. Using "turkey-baster" technology, one of the women is inseminated, conceives, and gives birth to a baby. The three are now a family, with one parent genetically related to the child.

• Pat Anthony, a forty-seven-year-old grandmother in South Africa, agreed to serve as gestational surrogate for her own daughter. The daughter had had her uterus removed, but could still produce eggs and wanted more children. The daughter's eggs were inseminated with her husband's sperm, and the resulting embryos implanted in her own mother. Mrs. Anthony gave birth to triplets when she was forty-eight. She was the gestational mother and the genetic grandmother of the triplets. . . .

My point in elucidating this category of heterogeneous examples is to suggest that there may be entirely subjective yet valid elements that contribute to our understanding of the family, family membership, or family relationships. I believe it would be arbitrary and narrow to rule out all such examples by fiat.

The open texture of our language leaves room for conceptions of family not recognized by law or preexisting custom. . . .

Balancing Public and Private Needs

What can we conclude from all this about the effects of artificial means of reproduction on the family and on our conception of the family? Several conclusions emerge, although each requires a more extended elaboration and defense than will be given here.

A broad definition of *family* is preferable to a narrow one. A good candidate is the working definition proposed by Carol Levine: "Family members are individuals who by birth, adoption, marriage, or declared commitment share deep personal connections and are mutually entitled to receive and obligated to provide support of various kinds to the extent possible, especially in times of need."

Some of the effects of the new reproductive technologies on the family call for the development of public policy, while others remain private, personal matters to be decided within a given family. An example of the former is the determination of where the presumptions should lie in disputed surrogacy arrangements, whose rights and interests are paramount, and what procedures should be followed to safeguard those rights and interests. An example of the latter is disclosure to a child of the facts surrounding genetic paternity or maternity in cases of donor insemination or egg donation, including the identity of the donor when that is known. These are profound moral decisions, about which many people have strong feelings, but they are not issues to be addressed by public policy. . . .

There is no simple answer to the question of how artificial means of reproduction affect our understanding of the family. We need to reflect on the variety of answers, paying special attention to what follows from answering the question one way rather than another. Since there is no single, univocal concept of the family, it is a matter for moral and social decision just which determinants of "family" should be given priority.

"The family should be safeguarded against the threats . . . of reproductive technology."

Reproductive Technology Is Undermining the Family

Donald DeMarco

Families are undermined when children are conceived through reproductive technology rather than by sexual intercourse between a married couple, Donald DeMarco argues in the following viewpoint. DeMarco believes reproductive technologies that replace the male or female partner, or involve fertilizing an egg outside the body, make the terms *mother, father, husband,* and *wife* too ambiguous; without clear definition, the family disintegrates. He also believes medical research should focus on curing infertility, not circumventing natural conception, and he advocates traditional adoption for infertile couples. DeMarco is professor of philosophy at the University of St. Jerome's College in Waterloo, Ontario, Canada.

As you read, consider the following questions:

1. What fundamental problem does reproductive technology cause in the family, according to DeMarco?
2. According to the author, why is adoption an acceptable solution to infertility while surrogacy is unacceptable?
3. Why does DeMarco believe that surrogacy threatens children?

Adapted from "The Brave New World of Reproductive Technology" by Donald DeMarco, *The Family in America* magazine, April 1990. Reprinted with permission.

The prevailing myth in our Age of Science is that technology gives us greater control of our lives. Like most myths, this one is true only up to a point. It begins to crumble precisely when moral questions arise. Henry Miller's remark that we live in an "air-conditioned nightmare" underscores the insufficiency of technology. It can provide us with practical comforts such as air-conditioning, but it cannot furnish our lives with moral meaning. Technology, therefore, can benefit the family, which is essentially a moral institution, only marginally. The essential strength of the family will always come from non-technological qualities such as love, fidelity, solidarity, and commitment.

Regulating Fertility

During the 1970s, educational and medical authorities vigorously promoted contraception, abortion, and sterilization. They argued that these technologies would strengthen the family by allowing married couples to regulate their fertility so that all their children would be wanted and would arrive when they wanted them. But these anti-fertility measures, rather than granting people more control over their own reproduction, helped foster the very opposite condition—a lack of reproductive control manifest in a pandemic of infertility.

Many family planners were surprised that an anti-fertility program resulted in widespread infertility, but this outcome has a logical explanation. The prefixes "anti" and "in" denote *opposition* and *deprivation*, respectfully. *Anti-fertility* practices logically lead to *infertility* consequences in the same way that any action that opposes something has a negative impact on the thing it opposes. Insults cause injury. In the same way, anti-intellectualism breeds unenlightenment, just as anticlericalism tends to diminish the supply of clerics.

Nonetheless, America's confidence in the myth that technologies grant people more control over the reproductive aspect of their lives remains unshaken. Consequently, many Americans look optimistically to a variety of new reproductive technologies with the hope that they will rectify current infertility problems. Unfortunately, reproductive technologies create more problems for the family than they solve. At the same time, pursuit of these technological remedies distracts attention away from the more important task of employing the moral and spiritual forces that are needed to strengthen the family.

Anonymous Fatherhood

The essential strength of the family does not lie in the spouses' fertility, but in the faithful love they have for each other. An infertile couple can build a strong, unified family with adopted children. What is critical is that nothing be done to compromise the unity between husband and wife. This unity is indispensable, the *sine qua non* for a good family.

The fundamental problem with reproductive technologies such as AID (artificial insemination by donor, required for the practice of surrogate motherhood) as well as IVF (*in vitro* fertilization), ET (embryo transfer), and extra-corporeal gestation, is that they compromise spousal unity. This compromise entails a loss of the moral significance of the way spouses naturally confer parenthood upon one another, as well as the very meanings of motherhood and fatherhood themselves. This is readily apparent in AID and the effect that sperm donation has on the donor's understanding of his relationship with his procreative partner as well as his understanding of his own parenthood.

Jimmy Margulies. Reprinted with permission.

A medical student, for example, provides semen for AID for the customary fee of $50. His relationship with the woman who might make him a father is, on a personal level, completely alienated. He never meets her, nor does he know who she is. Secondly, his understanding of his own possible fatherhood is purely hypothetical. As far as he is concerned, whether his sperm contribution has made him a father and how many times is a mere abstraction. Yet fatherhood with its attendant moral responsibilities is a concrete reality. This estranged attitude toward both one's procreative partner and one's own paternity greatly weakens cultural appreciation of the moral significance of marital procreation as well as the moral significance of fatherhood. This twofold weakening can only be injurious to society's understanding of the spousal integrity that is at the very heart of the family. . . .

A child conceived through artificial insemination may have no natural father, may not be begotten by a father, or may be begotten by a "father" who is a woman! When fatherhood is reduced to the plane of the biological, it edges perilously close to oblivion. At the same time, the other dimensions of fatherhood—psychological, moral, spiritual, and legal—are subjects for the Court's sometimes arbitrary ruling.

In Pipersville, Pennsylvania, a man sued his former wife, contending that she used his sperm without permission to conceive a child through the University of Pennsylvania's fertility program. The man gave sperm samples to his wife believing that she was using them to take his sperm count. He is asking that he be freed from supporting their daughter. In this case, the man who is allegedly the biological father acknowledges no moral grounds for his role as a provider. Unlike men whose wives have conceived through AID and want to be considered fathers, this man (who is probably the biological father) wants to disclaim any paternal relationship.

AID technology reduces fatherhood to mere paternity, so stripping fatherhood of its moral and personal significance. AID conveys the social message that marital unity and parental integrity are compromisable in the interest of having a child. This message is detrimental to healthy family life. And now that it is possible to freeze eggs, women have the opportunity to become gamete donors and experience the same estrangement from procreation and their own parenthood as do male sperm donors. Thus, the potential for weakening the family proceeds from both the female and male sides.

Exploiting Children

Children should come into being as a consequence of their parents' unselfish love. By removing procreation from the context of loving, marital intercourse, advocates of the new reproductive technologies make the exploitation of children more likely. When the Repository for Germinal Choice opened its vaults in Escondido, California, in 1979, it was proclaimed a sperm bank for geniuses. In April of 1982, a Phoenix woman named Joyce Kowalski gave birth to a healthy, 9-pound daughter—the first of the "Nobel Sperm Bank" babies. In an exclusive interview with the *National Enquirer*, her husband pledged, "We'll begin training Victoria on computers when she's 3, and we'll teach her words and numbers before she can walk."

As parents, however, the Kowalskis may be less than ideal. They had lost custody of Mrs. Kowalski's two children from a previous marriage because of child abuse. Mrs. Kowalski confessed to abusing these children in an attempt to "make them smart." Moreover, the two are convicted felons. They served a one-year sentence in a federal prison for a scam that used records of dead children to secure loans and credit cards. A spokesman for the sperm bank conceded that its screening of would-be-mothers was inadequate. "We have to rely on their honesty," he said.

Lesbian Couples Increase

The absence of adequate screening standards in sperm banks affords single women and lesbian couples the opportunity of having children of their own. In fact, there is at least one program in the United States that already uses sperm donated by homosexual men to impregnate lesbian women through AID. But the use of new technologies to form single-parent and homosexual family units is not only an affront to the traditional family, but such use conveys the philosophy that there should be no moral standards whatsoever in the establishing of a family. . . .

Reproductive Technologies Ignore Children's Needs

Time magazine (September 30, 1991) reported that fertility clinics ask parents to sign over the "excess embryos" created from their ova and sperm to other couples or to research. But is it moral to "harvest" children from anonymous ovaries? To give away our sons and daughters in a vial of sperm? Can it be moral deliberately to create an individual whose sole knowledge of her parents is that they "donated" her? Regardless of the care she may receive from psychological parents, will she not feel betrayed, created as their substitute child, to fill their needs without any thought of hers?

Sue Martin, *Second Opinion*, January 1992.

As male expendability increases, lesbian couples grow more numerous. According to a *New York Times* report, thousands of lesbians are inseminating themselves. Informal networks have been established to help them find sperm donors; support groups sponsor picnics, parties, and other social events to keep lesbians who have children from feeling isolated. A lawyer in Columbus, Ohio, says that she knows at least thirty lesbian mothers in and around Columbus. About 40 percent of the women inseminated at the Sperm Bank of Northern California identify themselves as lesbians—twice as many as in 1982 when the sperm bank opened. The director of the Gay and Lesbian Parents Coalition in Washington, D.C., states that one in twenty lesbians had babies through artificial insemination; three years ago, they estimated one in fifty or a hundred.

Dr. Richard Green, a professor of psychology at UCLA, is well aware of the growing phenomenon of husbandless marriages and fatherless families, although he is not particularly disturbed by it, because he believes "the issue of children raised without a man in the family has not been studied to be able to predict whether that could lead to other problems." Do we need studies to affirm the importance of a father to his children? What could these "other problems" be if being born and raised without a father is not a problem itself? And how could we recognize these other problems? Bioethicist John Fletcher remarks that "a physician can act ethically to help a lesbian couple with AID, if the partners show a prevailing pattern of responsibility." But would it be unethical to deny AID to such a couple? Is not Fletcher himself, as well as the AID physicians, also depreciating the male role in marriage and parenting?

The Perils of Surrogate Motherhood

AID has also created the possibility of surrogate motherhood. In its conventional mode, surrogacy offers an infertile wife the hope of raising a child that is genetically linked to her husband. In specific terms, a fertile woman (the "surrogate") is fertilized artificially by sperm from the infertile woman's husband. She then carries the pregnancy to term and surrenders the child to the infertile couple who commissioned the pregnancy. But the usual nomenclature of surrogacy is somewhat misleading. It is the adoptive mother who is truly the surrogate, since it is she who raises a child borne by another. The woman usually called a surrogate mother is really a "surrogate wife."

In the traditional family, marriage and parenthood go together. Husband and wife become parents to their children and assume the responsibility for them. Surrogacy severs the connection between marriage and parenthood. The woman ("surrogate") who provides the egg and who conceives and carries the child to term has no preconception relationship with the biological father and no postdelivery relationship with the child she bears. She is personally estranged from both her inseminator and her child.

Unlike adoption, however, surrogacy means a severance between marriage and parenthood that is fully intended even before conception. The child is conceived and carried with the clear purpose of placing it into another family. Adoption is traditionally understood as a response to some unforeseen disruption in the family structure—divorce or death, for example—or as a way of placing an illegitimate child with both a mother and a father. Prior to the practice of surrogacy, people did not plan to have children for the specific purpose of placing them in another family environment.

Surrogacy entails other disruptions, as well. The child, who is genetically related to the surrogate, is cut off from all its blood relatives on its mother's side. These relations are important to the child not only for identity, but for social and biological reasons as well. Surrogacy cuts the child off from half its genetic relations so that it can be attached to another family with whom it has no maternal ties.

Surrogacy also represents the threat of disruption for other children that the surrogate mother may have already borne. Surrogacy brokers prefer to use women who already have children of their own, so demonstrating the quality of their reproductive capacities. But when a mother keeps one child and gives away (or sells) another, the contradiction must have its impact on those she is raising. Angela Holder, president of the American Society of Law and Medicine, expresses her concern that granting a mother the freedom to give away some of her children could very well make those remaining at home feel insecure. "I think we have to consider," she says, "how those children feel when their mamas sell a little brother or sister, and they start wondering if they're going to be sold." On the other hand, a sibling might find the prospect of giving away a brother or sister much to his liking. According to one newspaper account, when a surrogate mother informed her nine-year-old daughter that she planned to give away her new baby, the girl replied: "Oh, good. If it's a girl, we can keep it and give Jeffrey [her two-year-old brother] away."

Alienation from the Family

Consideration must also be given to the alienation from the family that the surrogate's husband must feel. He knows that his wife is carrying another man's child. It is unlikely that this could be a neutral experience for him. Under normal circumstances, when a wife is carrying her husband's child, the pregnancy provides abundant opportunities for the couple to grow closer to each other as they anticipate the arrival of their child. The husband thrills at feeling his child kick in his wife's womb. Together, they pick out names for the child, select godparents, plan where the baby will sleep, and so on. As a result of these kinds of shared experiences, they deepen their awareness of parenthood as they prepare to assume its exacting responsibilities.

But how does a husband benefit from his wife's bearing a child for an infertile couple? What can his motivation be to want her to go through with the process? The pregnancy will surely place demands on their marriage and inconvenience the husband in a thousand ways. But these difficulties are borne outside of the typical context that would give them meaning. The discomforts and deprivations that a married couple endure during pregnancy have meaning in the anticipation of *their* child and *their* shared intimacy. Surrogacy inevitably brings about innumerable divisions and disruptions that are obviously antithetical to an integrated and happy family. Surrogacy assumes that a woman's carrying a child for another is simply a matter of fulfilling a contract. But such a pregnancy disrupts the family's organic structure. Perhaps the greatest strain is placed on the relationship between the surrogate mother and her husband. The breakdown of the Whitehead marriage during the Baby M legal imbroglio may be testimony to this. . . .

Future of the Family

New reproductive technologies offer the hope of strengthening the family by adding to it. At the same time, however, such technologies introduce so many risks, disruptions, and forms of alienation into the organic web of marriage and the family that they prove, on balance, to be more hazardous than helpful. Society's naive confidence that technology can cure all ills deserves closer examination. There are no technological substitutes for moral responsibilities.

The dilution of the meaning of motherhood and fatherhood, the weakening of the bond between husband and wife, the commodification of progeny, the alienation between family members, and opportunities for exploiting infertile couples by the medical profession and clever merchandisers are some of the more important perils that society should take into account. The moral health of the family deserves priority over the presumed right of married couples to have their own genetically linked offspring.

The indispensable foundation for the strength of the family is the faithful, uncompromisable love and fidelity that husband and wife have for one another. If reproductive technologies threaten this relationship, then they come at too high a price. Society must place greater emphasis on the importance of a loving marriage and on the recognition that children are gifts of love that proceed from the foundational love between the married partners.

Reproductive technologies do not restore normal fertility, they circumvent it. More research is needed into ways of restoring fertility. Complementing this effort, programs should be developed that aim at preventing the causes of infertility. Such measures would be fully in accord with traditional and time-honored norms of medical ethics. Finally, adoption should be encouraged more enthusiastically.

The family as a moral entity is the fundamental unit of civilization. Accordingly, the family should be safeguarded against the threats posed by those forms of reproductive technology that compromise its moral quality.

Understanding Words in Context

Readers occasionally come across words they do not recognize. And frequently, because they do not know a word or words, they will not fully understand the passage being read. Obviously, the reader can look up an unfamiliar word in a dictionary. By carefully examining the word in the context in which it is used, however, the word's meaning can often be determined. A careful reader may find clues to the meaning of the word in surrounding words, ideas, and attitudes.

Below are excerpts from the viewpoints in this chapter. In each excerpt, one of the words is printed in italics. Try to determine the meaning of each word by reading the excerpt. Under each excerpt you will find four definitions for the italicized word. Choose the one that is closest to your understanding of the word.

Finally, use a dictionary to see how well you have understood the words in context. It will be helpful to discuss with others the clues that helped you decide on each word's meaning.

1. Characteristics of a family include the idea that children must be or were or will be present, thus fulfilling the family's *PROCREATIVE* function.

   PROCREATIVE means:

   a) intellectual   c) reproductive
   b) humorous   d) social

2. Wider families are free, *UNCOERCED* types of families that spring from the free choices one makes to enhance one's life.

UNCOERCED means:

a) unforced   c) helpful
b) unconnected   d) bright

3. Even if new laws defining family do nothing more than recognize the existence of alternative families, they will be less *CALCIFIED* than current laws. The law must reflect the changing, dynamic flow of relationships of our modern society.

CALCIFIED means:

a) metallic   c) milky
b) inflexible   d) loose

4. The family is a small kinship-structured group with the key function of *NURTURANT* socialization of the newborn. This definition of the family applies to any type of family structure that provides care for an infant.

NURTURANT means:

a) outside   c) expensive
b) negative   d) caring

5. The family of the nineties is very different from the one most Americans were reared in. In fact, the word "family" in the singular is somewhat of a *MISNOMER*. Better: The plural "families" when applied to today's situation.

MISNOMER means:

a) silly joke   c) unjust verdict
b) wrong name   d) bad relation

6. Nothing the government does in the name of the family can aptly *COMPENSATE* for the disappearance of intact marriages and parental care for children.

COMPENSATE means:

a) make up for   c) search intensely
b) run into   d) unite with

7. The woman who contributes her womb during a pregnancy—whether she is a *SURROGATE* or the intended rearing mother—is also a biological mother.

SURROGATE means:

a) nurse   c) female
b) parent   d) substitute

Periodical Bibliography

The following articles have been selected to supplement the diverse views presented in this chapter.

Katrine Ames et al. "And Donor Makes Three," *Newsweek*, September 30, 1991.

Aimee Lee Ball "Yes, Sir, That's My Baby," *Mademoiselle*, December 1991.

Susan Brenna "Family Traditions: The Power of Knowing Who You Are," *McCall's*, April 1990.

Philip S. Gutis "What Is a Family? Traditional Limits Are Being Redrawn," *The New York Times*, August 31, 1989.

Patricia Horn "To Love and to Cherish," *Dollars & Sense*, June 1990.

Nan D. Hunter "Sexual Dissent and the Family," *The Nation*, October 7, 1991.

Irving Kristol "Reflections on Love and Family," *The Wall Street Journal*, January 7, 1992.

Robert W. Lee "High Court Attack on Families," *The New American*, December 3, 1991.

Elizabeth Leonard "What Happened to the Family?" *Newsweek*, special issue, Winter/Spring 1990.

Christine Winquist Nord and Nicholas Zill "American Households in Demographic Perspective," June 1991. Publication no. WP5, available from the Institute for American Values, 1841 Broadway, Suite 211, New York, NY 10023.

Robert H. Rimmer "Sex, Marriage, and the 21st-Century Family," *The World & I*, November 1990.

Paula Rinehart "Adopt-a-Family," *Moody*, February 1990.

William Sayres "What Is a Family Anyway?" *The World & I*, September 1989.

Jean Seligmann "Variations on a Theme," *Newsweek*, special issue, Winter/Spring 1990.

Jill Smolowe "Last Call for Motherhood," *Time*, special issue, Fall 1990.

Elizabeth Stone "Love and Bigotry," *Glamour*, February 1992.

How Does Divorce Affect the Family?

Chapter Preface

The United States has one of the highest divorce rates in the world. Demographers project that 60 percent of first marriages in the United States will end in divorce, and half of those will involve children under age eighteen. Already, more than one million children see their parents divorce each year in America. Since the divorce rate began its climb in the 1960s, scholars have puzzled over the reasons for this increase and how divorce has affected the American family.

Researchers such as Constance R. Ahrons and Roy H. Rodgers cite dramatic economic and social changes in recent decades as reasons for the rise in divorce. As increasing numbers of women entered the labor market in the 1960s and 1970s, they became less economically dependent on men and marriage for financial security. Many women in unhappy marriages found that they could divorce and still support themselves. These economic changes were accompanied by social changes: divorce became more acceptable and liberalized divorce laws made divorces easier to obtain.

Some experts believe that these economic and social changes have been accompanied by Americans' higher expectations of marriage. These experts hypothesize that people today think the primary purpose of marriage is to fulfill emotional needs. In the past, many marriages were made for practical reasons such as companionship or financial security. Today Americans may be more likely to end a marriage when their emotional needs are not being met. As Ahrons and Rodgers state in their book *Divorced Families*, "Unless the relationships created by the marriage and birth of children satisfy the needs for love, caring, and emotional support, the marriage is not considered a successful one."

How these social and economic changes affect the divorce rate and the family is a question of much concern. The authors in the following chapter debate both the short- and long-term effects of America's "divorce epidemic."

"The current rates of divorce are a logical response to societal trends."

Divorce Is Normal

Constance R. Ahrons and Roy H. Rodgers

The authors of the following viewpoint believe divorce is a normal response to fundamental changes in American society. They argue that in the past, people married for economic reasons, while today people marry for love and companionship. Divorce is normal when these emotional needs go unfulfilled, the authors conclude. Constance R. Ahrons is professor of sociology and associate director of the marriage and family therapy program at the University of Southern California in Los Angeles. Roy H. Rodgers is professor of family science at the University of British Columbia in Vancouver, Canada.

As you read, consider the following questions:

1. How did industrialization affect the family, according to the authors?
2. How did urbanization affect the family, according to the authors?
3. What are the effects of feminism on the family, according to Ahrons and Rodgers?

Excerpted from *Divorced Families: Meeting the Challenge of Divorce and Remarriage* by Constance R. Ahrons and Roy H. Rodgers. New York: Norton, 1989. Copyright 1989 by Constance R. Ahrons and Roy H. Rodgers. Reprinted with permission.

We are strong proponents of the view that the North American family is very much alive and well and that the changes in form and purpose are evidence of the family's capacity to adjust to societal flux. In addition, we assert that the problems of children and families that are receiving so much attention today have been present in society for a long time. Incest, child abuse and neglect, alcoholism, and delinquency are not new problems, nor can we be certain that they have increased disproportionately to the increase in the population. The fact that society is addressing itself to these problems, rather than keeping them closeted in the family, is rooted in the vast societal changes of the 19th and 20th centuries.

Bureaucratic Change and Industrialization

There is no question that *recorded* problems have increased. This is a result of several factors. First, modern society simply keeps better records on such things. Bureaucracy is a modern fact and one of the major features of bureaucracy is the keeping of records. Thus, crime, school records, and all sorts of health information are much more widely available than in the past. . . .

North American society *has* changed, but families have been affected by those changes far more than they have been responsible for them. Beginning in the late 19th century and continuing into the 20th, industrialization and urbanization changed the place of the family in the social structure. Families became consumers of goods produced in the expanded industrial system, rather than producers of their own requirements—often with some surplus which was used in barter or sale. Family members became sources of labor for industry and commerce, with the husband and father leaving the home to pursue work. . . .

Urbanization

We add to this the impact of urbanization, a concomitant of the buildup of the industrial system, which forced families to move from the more intimate and supportive communities of rural areas and small towns to cities. . . .

While it is now clear that our idealized image of several generations living under the same roof is not supported by the data, there was still a more continuous and supportive kin contact in the rural and small town environment. Life in cities and suburbs meant that families were much more on their own. When they could not meet their needs, they were much more dependent upon private and public agencies for help. While, especially in suburbia, there might be some close relationships with one or more others families in the neighborhood, help was not as readily available. Further, the norm of privacy made it much more difficult to know what might be happening in the house next door. This had the effect of increasing the focus on the value of the nuclear family for its members. The anonymity of urban life reduced the community and friendship networks and, to some extent, the extended family resources that provided emotional meaning in individual lives. In a very real sense the family took on a major, almost exclusive, role in the emotional support arena. Failure of the family in this area became a major inadequacy.

The Normalization of Divorce

When we consider the lifetime experience of all married persons, at least one third and perhaps as many as one half will experience at least one divorce.

Given these statistics, divorce has become a "normal" experience, which occurs to many persons, and which touches virtually all families either directly or indirectly. A generation ago, getting a divorce was accompanied by the psychological stain attached to being involved in a "deviant" and a stigmatized activity. Today, with the exception of some atypical subcultures such as fundamentalist religious groups, getting a divorce is not considered an unusual occurrence, nor is it necessarily a source of stigma and shame. In the 1950s, the divorced were a deviant minority, and they were faced with restricted options; in the 1980s, the divorced constitute a substantial and growing minority, and they enjoy a proliferation of socially acceptable life style alternatives.

Jean E. Veevers, *Journal of Divorce and Remarriage*, vol. 15, nos. 1/2, 1991.

So, did family values change—or did the structure and values of the society change, thus having their impact on the family? We favor the latter explanation. Blaming the victim is often a way of dealing with a problem. . . . And there is a good deal of nostalgic belief, not supported by very strong evidence, that things in families were "better back then." We do not want to overemphasize the impact of industrialization and urbanization on all aspects of social life. We simply want to observe that these major developments in all of western society were not a result of changing family structure and modified family values, but, more likely, a cause of them. Indeed, in some ways, family values have continued to be quite strong in spite of this major dual revolution in societal organization. . . .

The feminist writings of the past two decades have been instrumental in uncovering the myths of the ideal of the traditional American family. The inequality of worth of women's work, both in the home and in the marketplace, is a well documented characteristic of sex-role segregated societal structures. Challenging assumptions of appropriate gender behaviors has caused a reexamination of women's and men's roles in the family.

The well-documented increase of women entering the labor force has resulted in heated debates about the consequences of this social change for the stability of the family. Some argue that a move toward equality is synonymous with a move toward individualism which will essentially undermine the value of the family in society. Others argue that more gender equality in family roles will result in more satisfaction within intimate relationships. Still others argue that more equality will improve the quality of parenting and hence be beneficial to children. . . .

These societal changes do affect both the function of marriage and attitudes toward marriage and divorce. As women become more independent economically, their need for marriage as their source of economic support lessens. As they strive for more equality in society, their need for marriage as a source of status also lessens. Finally, when women may choose to have sexual relations without the fear of pregnancy and societal scorn, their need for marriage as their only acceptable route to sexual satisfaction is reduced as well. With the lowered pressure of these traditional "advantages" of marriage, women are freer to choose whether marriage meets their emotional needs, and if it does not, then they have the option to choose not to remain married.

The Divorce Reform Movement

In the past two decades we have witnessed major changes in divorce legislation which reflect the changes we have noted in the institutions of marriage and the family. If a major, perhaps the key, reason for marriage today is love, companionship, and emotional support, then a key justification for terminating marriage becomes the failure of the marriage to meet these objectives. Thus, the "incompatibility" grounds for divorce became more commonly cited in the increasing numbers of actions filed. In more recent years, "no fault" divorce legislation, often using such terms as "breakdown in the marital relationship" or "irreconcilable marital differences" has recognized explicitly that there is no assignable "marital offense" in such situations. Rather, two people have simply failed to achieve the goals upon which marriages are primarily based. Indeed, some of the former marital offenses, viz., adultery and desertion, are now often seen as symptoms of the breakdown in the emotional quality of the marriage. Many marriages have survived adultery because the basic emotional quality of the marriage was seen to be good and worth preserving.

Even with this shift in attitudes toward the role of marriage, the prevailing views of divorce are still steeped in the presumption of social deviance. Lynne Halem, in tracing the evolution of the ideology of divorce and its relationships to the history of divorce reform, states: "Yet because we, as a nation, operate within the context of a 2000-year-old heritage, we still regard divorce as a problem of momentous consequence, a pathological event that threatens not only the institution of the family but also social cohesiveness and order."

Lifetime Commitments Obsolete

Industrialization, with all of its technological developments, has allowed us to produce a highly urbanized society. The characteristics of an urban society—especially anonymity; the tendency to displace primary relationships with secondary ones in the form of membership in organizations; the breakdown of traditional authority in all areas of life; the secularization of religion; the debunking of the old ways of doing things; the emphasis on achievement rather than ascribed positions; the expectation of constant social change; mobility; and the focus on hedonism, materialism, and short-term contractual relationships—all militate against lifetime commitments of any sort, including marriage.

James M. Henslin, *Marriage and Family in a Changing Society*, 1989.

It is interesting to note that even though we are in the midst of the "divorce revolution," we still cling to the long-held notion that divorce is inherently pathological. In the 1970s, statutory reform in the form of no-fault legislation removed the law's punitive function in divorce. Surprisingly, however, this divorce reform movement began, not as an expression of liberalized social attitudes, but as an essentially conservative effort. The intent behind the new laws was concern for the social pathology that resulted from the breakdown of the traditional institution of marriage. . . .

Although no-fault legislation removes the issue of blame or fault from the legal arena, divorce is still being blamed for such social problems as delinquency, crime, alcoholism, and welfare dependency.

Redefining Child Custody

Child custody issues have become part of this divorce reform movement. The history of child custody decisions reveals that the custody of children has changed along with prevailing social trends. Before the 19th century women and children were the property of men. Although divorce was rare, the issue of custody was clear: children belonged to fathers. As industrialization and urbanization developed, with the associated shift from the instrumental to companionate notion of marriage and its emphasis on the importance of motherhood, maternal custody became the presumption of the courts. With the traditional nuclear family as the ideal, women were clearly accorded sole responsibility for the rearing of children. The issue of custody was clear: children belonged to mothers. It was only in rare cases, when the mother was proven to be "unfit" due to mental illness or adultery, that custody was awarded to fathers.

Now that we are in the midst of redefining gender and family roles the issue of custody is being redefined as well. Current legislation reflects this societal shift toward equality of women's and men's roles by removing the presumptive attitude toward either parent. Custody may not be determined on the basis of sex. But, rather than clearly defining how custody should be awarded, the laws instead provide only for how custody awards should *not* be determined. This egalitarian legislative change has resulted in a more ambiguous, and hence more controversial, custody situation. Heated debates and increasing custody litigation mark the last decade. It should not be surprising, in light of changing societal attitudes toward gender roles, that joint custody should emerge as a solution. However, how parents manage to share custody and childrearing after marital dissolution is not as clear as the new mandates. As the history of custody reveals, the determination of custody based on the children's needs is more myth than reality. Child custody decisions have changed in accordance with the changes in societal attitudes toward the family.

Although we have set forth the view that the current rates of divorce are a logical response to societal trends, attitudes toward divorce are still imbued with pathology. We still cling to the long-held belief that marriage implies an "until death do us part" ideology. Any departure from that image has been labeled pathological. The clinical notion of pathology stems from the belief that divorce is the product of individual neuroses formed in childhood and played out in adult life. It follows that, if marriage is still regarded as a lifelong commitment, the decision to terminate the marriage is a result of the failure of the partners to sustain a committed relationship. This, then, implies a defect in one or both partners.

These two perspectives, individual pathology and social deviance, have guided the research and clinical writings that have emerged in the past three decades. . . .

Skewed Research

It is important to note that the prevailing attitude that divorce is deviant and reflects pathology has influenced our current knowledge base about divorce. Prior to 1972, almost all of the research was formulated to look for the pathological consequences of divorce on children and adults. Hence, in psychological research almost all studies were conducted on subjects drawn from clinical settings, and in sociological research the focus was on studying the relationship between social deviance and the breakdown of the nuclear family. When the findings of these research studies are examined in a total context, they are seen to be inconclusive and often contradictory.

These trends have resulted in a new appraisal of divorce. Challenges to traditional sole mother custody awards, the proliferation of joint custody legislation, and the liberalization of the divorce laws have focused our attention on the *process* of divorce, rather than on the event and its outcomes. We are in the midst of defining divorce as an enduring societal institution much in the same way as we have viewed marriage in our culture. . . .

A New Assessment of Divorce

The gradual shift in ideology—from viewing divorce as pathology to viewing divorce as an institution—is clearly having an impact on the study of divorce. The study of divorce is no longer narrowly defined within a deviance perspective. Instead, we are able to begin to identify which of the many complex factors associated with divorce result in negative consequences for the participants. As a necessary concomitant, we are beginning to identify which of these factors result in healthy functioning. But even now, as we are moving in our attitudes toward normalizing divorce in our society, we still have difficulty ridding ourselves of the pathological model. We still tend to think in terms of pathology, looking for the absence of pathology rather than focusing on the normal family patterns that result from divorce. . . .

We believe that divorce is both normative and, for many couples, nonpathological in character. Each of these ideas requires some elaboration.

Norms, in sociological language, are expectations for behavior. Divorce is based on the belief that marriage should meet very important needs of the spouses. If this does not occur, the expectation is that the marriage should be terminated—a basic norm related to marriage and divorce in our society. However, we do not have well-developed norms about how divorced couples ought to deal with each other and with their children, their kin, their friends, and the community—or how these people should relate to the divorced couple. There is a very definite lack of clarity in the norms surrounding postmarital behavior—a condition labeled *anomie* in sociology. If spouses should not continue a marriage which is unsatisfactory, how should former spouses behave toward one another and how should others behave toward them once they have severed their marital ties? . . .

Furthermore, if these norms concerning marriage prevail, sev-

ering an unsatisfactory marriage should not be seen as pathological. Many marriages have conflict and serious differences.
Marriage partners fight, argue, discuss, and negotiate over these
differences. They often reach mutually agreeable solutions. On
the other hand, others find it impossible to come to such agreements. Viewing them as "sick" or "bad" or labeling them in
other pathological ways lacks basic validity. It is true that some
spouses are emotionally disturbed and incapable of meeting basic expectations for behavior both in and out of marriage.
However, many more marital partners simply find it impossible
to develop the kind of marriage which meets their expectations.
While in former times they would have been expected to "grin
and bear it," they are no longer under such pressure. Therefore,
we do not see divorce as a symptom of pathology in marriage
and the family. At the most it may involve individuals with
pathological characteristics acting out their sickness in the marital setting. Most divorces, however, involve persons well within
the range of normality acting on norms that reject remaining in
an unsatisfactory marriage.

Painful Process, Successful Outcome

None of this is to say that divorce is not painful, stressful, cri-
sis-producing, and often infused with conflict. Nor is it to say
that divorced couples and their families necessarily find themselves better off than they were before the divorce. We are not
"in favor" of divorce as compared to marriage. Obviously, most
of us would prefer to have happy and successful marriages. But,
failing that, we believe that divorce can be successful and that it
can lead to better life situations for all concerned.

"*Divorce's romanticized image as a harmless quick fix is a lie.*"

Divorce Is Abnormal

Fred Moody

In the following viewpoint, Fred Moody argues that divorce harms everyone: individuals, the family, and society. He believes people abandon marriage too quickly, not realizing divorce causes more problems than it solves. Moody is a staff writer for *Seattle Weekly* in Washington.

As you read, consider the following questions:

1. What problems was no-fault divorce reform supposed to solve, according to the author?
2. According to Moody, how does divorce affect the father-child relationship?
3. What should be the purpose of marriage and divorce education, according to the author?

Adapted from "Divorce: Sometimes a Bad Notion" by Fred Moody, *Utne Reader*, November/December 1990. This article originally appeared in the November 22, 1989 issue of *Seattle Weekly* and is reprinted with the author's permission.

Divorce, along with high-school graduation, marriage, and death, is now an established American rite of passage. Everyone, either directly or indirectly, is touched by it. A first marriage undertaken today stands (avert your eyes, squeamish reader) a 66 percent chance of ending in divorce. For the first time in history, an American marrying now is more likely to lose a spouse through divorce than through death.

Divorce most often is portrayed as liberating. The ease with which we divorce is regarded as a proof of the individual freedoms Americans enjoy. It is one more means we have of achieving self-fulfillment—the *raison d'etre* of the baby-boom generation. When no-fault divorce was ushered in 20 years ago, it was hailed as a quick and easy solution to relationships gone sour. Now, a generation later, legions of divorced parents and their children are emerging to paint a far different picture: one of financial travail, psychological devastation, and endless emotional turmoil. Study after study documents so much discontent surrounding divorce that it now appears to be an even greater source of disillusionment than marriage is.

Economic Consequences

Divorce is particularly disillusioning for women and children. No-fault reforms have robbed women of alimony, and no-fault's lax child-support enforcement has allowed men to default on their obligations to the point where many divorced women and children are reduced to poverty. Instead of reducing inequality between the sexes, no-fault divorce has widened the gap in status between men and women, and is the leading cause of the well-documented feminization of poverty in America.

There's no question that the fundamental right to divorce should be available to anyone; the ability to divorce a monster or an addict, or to get out of a marriage that is an incurable mistake, is a humane and civilized right. But the notion that every unhappy marriage is a bad one, or that individuals are morally as well as legally entitled to place their own pursuit of happiness above the well-being of their offspring, is ruinous. Opting for divorce before having exhausted every effort at preserving a relationship is self-destructive.

Progressive Weakening of Marriage

We need to re-examine our motives and consider reforms— from marriage education to legal representation for children in divorce proceedings. But first we need to look more closely at the path we have taken from the strict protection of marriage as a social institution to its severe weakening by our now-inalienable right to divorce.

In England, birthplace of the American legal tradition, divorce didn't even exist until 1857, and not until 1900 had most of the United States legislated, under stringent guidelines, grounds and procedures for divorce. From then on, so gradually that no one noticed for nearly 40 years, the divorce rate crept steadily upward. After World War II it took a huge leap, then crept up gradually again until the mid-1960s, when it took off on a sharp upward curve that is still rising. In 1965, there were 10.6 divorces for every 1,000 married women in the United States; by the early 1980s, that number had nearly doubled, to 22.6 per 1,000.

"Oh Marcie! Isn't it divine? I'm getting divorced in the same dress my mother was divorced in!"

Until the early 1970s, divorce in nearly all instances was universally acknowledged as a horrible event. Divorce proceedings were ugly, detailed airings of connubial crimes, as husband and wife squared off in court to fight over money, children, and one another's morals. Then came the 1970 advent of no-fault divorce in California, followed by its almost instant acceptance nationwide.

With no-fault, couples had only to declare their marriage irretrievably broken, reach an agreement over division of assets, custody of children, and child-support payments, and have the agreement ratified by a court. Proponents even asserted that it would reduce the nation's rising divorce rate, for by eliminating the issue of guilt from marital disputes, no-fault divorce would facilitate reconciliations. People would use divorce proceedings as a forum for solving problems rather than exacerbating or creating them. Reasoning like this led such conservative groups as Christian fundamentalists and the Catholic Church to join liberals in supporting California's proposed no-fault laws.

In theory, divorce was supposed to be liberating for men and women alike as well as demonstrably better for children than living with unhappily married parents—another milestone on America's most-traveled road, the path to self-fulfillment.

Alas, none of those hopes has been realized. Even with the nationwide adoption of no-fault legislation, the American divorce rate continues to rise at the same rate. In all likelihood, nothing could have slowed the divorce rate's climb, but it would have been interesting to see what might have happened had California lawmakers agreed to fund a proposed "family court," in which divorce issues would have been debated and sometimes resolved. Without that feature, the court system became a mere rubber-stamp reviewer of agreements hammered out between spouses and their lawyers.

Emotional Devastation

The emotional fallout of divorce is easy to see. Legions of divorced people, their attorneys, their therapists, their children, and their children's therapists have learned that divorce is shattering.

"Quite often, divorce is much more devastating than people who go into the process anticipate," says Seattle psychiatrist Dr. Herbert Wimberger. "They are surprised by how painful it is, by how long the pain lasts. Divorce very often is a serious loss, bringing on a severe grief reaction." Adds Seattle psychotherapist Diane Zerbe, "Everybody knows somebody five years later who is still emotionally invested in their failed marriage, still angry at their ex-spouse, and their bitterness is a major part of their life. They haven't been able somehow to come to terms with what happened and go on to find a more satisfying relationship.". . .

Marriage in our society is a swamp too mysterious to be charted by lawyers, judges, and legislature. Particularly given our uniquely American preoccupation with the self, a married couple's individual psychological needs are at odds with their common need. "Some sociologists argue," says [sociologist Diane] Lye, "that the American ideology of love is completely incompatible, and clashes head-on, with continued self-fulfillment."

Says Wimberger, "Marriage in some ways can be described as an impossible proposition to begin with. There are these divergent needs: People want companionship, closeness, and so on, but at the same time they want to be themselves, so they are constantly negotiating." The negotiation is made all the more tense, in Wimberger's view, by a society in which everything is transitory. In the past, a person's innate fears about the changes such negotiations would entail could be overcome by the need to make a marriage livable, for he or she had no other choice. In the no-fault present, married people often find it easier simply to flee the marriage. Spouses are disposable.

Much of Wimberger's counseling work is with couples, and over the years he has seen certain distinct patterns take form in one marriage after another. American marriages are so imbued with romanticism that most people enter into them blissfully blinded to practicality. "So many people take marriage for granted," he explains. "You tie the knot and everything is supposed to go happily ever after. People don't realize that relationships need a lot of work. Then when things start to go sour, they don't know what's wrong, because they don't know how to talk to each other, and they don't have any support from an extended family."

As marriages deteriorate, couples tend to think more wistfully of divorce than a reconciliation. As Zerbe sees it, "It's such a pleasant fantasy if you're having problems in your marriage. To think that you can go out and find somebody better and have dates and have all that excitement. And that if only you were free to find the right person, who would appreciate how great you are. . . . Each partner assumes that the problem is with the other partner."

Recognized early enough, these patterns can be broken. Too often, however, couples are too lost in their anger by the time they seek help. Where once they might have recognized that they had workable emotional problems, now one or the other is simply convinced that he or she is no longer in love.

Adverse Effects on Children

Divorce brings with it a whole new set of problems—particularly if the divorcing couple has children. While research until very recently has implied that children of divorced parents are better off than children of unhappily married parents, new studies, such as those cited in Judith Wallerstein's book *Second Chances* (Ticknor & Fields, 1989), suggest the opposite. Wimberger is convinced that the adverse effects of divorce on children are grossly understated. "I think the literature is a little bit slanted," he says. "Too many of the researchers perhaps are divorced and trying to make the best of things. Even when children accept sort of superficially that their parents are divorced and that they might be better off after divorce, they usually continue to have the fantasy of Mom and Dad getting back together. Children of divorced parents have a much higher incidence of divorce. And, of course, a great deal depends on what their relationship is with the parent who leaves after a divorce. If a child loses a parent, that is a loss that people don't get over."

A Psychologist Recants

In my private practice as a marriage counselor and psychologist, I've helped plenty of struggling couples through separation and "liberation." I originally thought that staying together in turmoil was more traumatic than making the break, that striking down taboos about divorce was part of modern enlightenment.

I was wrong. As I shifted my professional focus to divorced individuals, the truth was difficult to avoid: treating divorce as "morally neutral"—an option no better or worse than staying married—was irreparably damaging to the very people I wanted to help.

Diane Medved, *Reader's Digest*, May 1989.

In Zerbe's view, divorce very often robs children of both parents, whatever the custody arrangements. "Part of it," she observes, "is not so much the divorce itself but the fact that both parents are so devastated by it that their parenting abilities are interfered with. So that really the kids are struggling not just with the divorce but with the fact that they've lost both parents' emotional availability."

When fathers are often physically absent (since mothers more often get full or primary custody), there emerges one of divorce's most constant and classic patterns. There is something about the lack of continual contact between fathers and children, through routine and traumatic moments alike, that dramatically heightens the child's feelings for the father and just as dramatically dulls the father's feelings for his child. In her 10-year study of 60 middle-class divorced families, Wallerstein sees this terrible pattern played out everywhere, in nearly every divorce. "One of the great tragedies of divorce is that many fathers have absolutely no idea that their children feel rejected," she writes in *Second Chances*. "Although the fathers seem indifferent or uncaring, this may not be the case at all. I have talked with many fathers who genuinely think that they have good re-lationships with their children, while the children feel rejected and miserable."

Burdens on Society

This rampant paternal blindness adds to one of our society's most profound problems: the emotional and financial neglect of children. Fathers, unable to see their children's need for their love and their lucre, may simply default on both counts, leaving the state and the schools to try to pick up the pieces. As a result, as Seattle University economics professor Peter Nickerson points out, "the taxpayers pay a tremendous burden. In this state, more than half a billion dollars are paid out in AFDC [Aid to Families with Dependent Children] payments, and as much as half of that may be going to children of divorce. And that doesn't include the fact that the schools are so screwed up—kids there are hungry and ornery and their parents are fighting."

What little is being proposed in the way of solutions to this mess generally falls into two approaches, one seeking to buttress the family and the other seeking to replace it. In Washington, state senator Ellen Craswell, noting that 26,000 Washington marriages each year end in divorce, and that 14,000 of those divorces involve children, introduced a bill that would have elimi-nated no-fault divorce. Her reasoning was simple: If divorce is harder to get, there will be less of it, and more families will opt to find a way to remain intact.

Legal Reform Is Not Enough

But it is probably impossible to turn back the clock, as the conservative Craswell has proposed. Washington's divorce rate, save for a brief blip immediately after the 1973 introduction of no-fault divorce, has risen along a steady curve from the mid-1960s to the present, which suggests that no-fault was more a recognition of reality than its cause. "When we think about fam-ilies," says Diane Lye, "we have to think about the diversity of family life in America. Whatever we might like, and however much we feel that the family is the best place for children, the reality is that that is not what's happening. We need not so much to force families to stay intact as to separate out the nega-tive consequences of divorce. Ours is not a problem of rising di-vorce rates—it's a problem of inadequate financial support for mothers and children."

The Washington legislature implemented a new child-support program in 1988 designed not merely to help children subsist, but to preserve their standard of living after divorce. Divorcing parents fill out detailed income forms that have led to payments far higher than what courts had been ordering in the past; more importantly, it serves as a guideline that judges must follow instead of using their discretion in setting a payment amount.

Clearly, far more sweeping reforms are called for. At the very least, courts need enough time and money to study divorce decrees and determine whether they adequately provide for women and children. As things stand now, they simply rubber-stamp agreements reached between people who are in no shape to keep their children's best interests in mind.

There should also be lawyers representing children in divorce hearings, as they do in child-abuse hearings. A child's lawyer should be able to argue on behalf of the child's best interests—that the divorce be denied, that parents undergo further counseling, that children be compensated for the emotional and material damage divorce will bring down on them.

Rampant divorce is dangerous not only to children—it also harms, often permanently, the husbands and wives who suffer through it. It lowers the moral tone of the entire nation, as society seconds the motion that we are entitled to look first of all after ourselves. Since the mid-1960s, divorce has had almost unremittingly good press, and the better divorce's public image, the greater priority many people give to self-fulfillment over obligations to others. Those who shape and mold opinion in this country—writers, reporters, moviemakers, and advertisers, to name a few—need to de-romanticize divorce.

Deromanticize Divorce

Young people need to be made aware of the dire consequences of marriages carelessly undertaken: Marriage and divorce education is as critical to our society's health as sex education. Divorce's romanticized image as a harmless quick fix is a lie. That fantasy has led legions of naive and discontented people into even greater unhappiness than they had suffered in their marriages.

Since the advent of no-fault, one of the fundamental truths about divorce has been discounted: that love or marriage may be fleeting, but divorce is forever. Those contemplating divorce should understand that it often affords not a new beginning, but only a new form of anguish. "You never get divorced for real," says one woman, who left her husband six years ago. "You never get rid of that person." Another woman concurs: "I thought divorce would be like jumping through a hoop," she says. "But it's not a hoop—it's a tunnel."

"Divorce was the single most important cause of enduring pain and anomie in [children's] lives."

Divorce Harms Children

Judith S. Wallerstein and Sandra Blakeslee

In the following viewpoint, researcher Judith S. Wallerstein and author Sandra Blakeslee argue that divorce is traumatic for the developing child. Wallerstein's fifteen-year study shows that many children continue to experience anxieties, fears, anger, and guilt related to divorce throughout adolescence and into adulthood. Wallerstein is the founder of the Center for the Family in Transition in Corte Madera, California. Blakeslee is a freelance science and medical writer and a regular contributor to *The New York Times* science news department.

As you read, consider the following questions:

1. What is the role of the overburdened child, according to Wallerstein and Blakeslee?
2. What proportion of children felt rejected by one or more parents, according to the authors?
3. According to the authors, which age group of children seemed to have adjusted best ten years following divorce?

From *Second Chances: Men, Women, and Children a Decade After Divorce* by Judith S. Wallerstein and Sandra Blakeslee. New York: Ticknor and Fields, 1990. Reprinted with permission.

As recently as the 1970's, when the American divorce rate began to soar, divorce was thought to be a brief crisis that soon resolved itself. Young children might have difficulty falling asleep and older children might have trouble at school. Men and women might become depressed or frenetic, throwing themselves into sexual affairs or immersing themselves in work.

But after a year or two, it was expected, most would get their lives back on track, at least outwardly. Parents and children would get on with new routines, new friends and new schools, taking full opportunity of the second chances that divorce brings in its wake.

These views, I have come to realize, were wishful thinking. In 1971, working with a small group of colleagues and with funding from San Francisco's Zellerbach Family Fund, I began a study of the effects of divorce on middle-class people who continue to function despite the stress of a marriage breakup.

That is, we chose families in which, despite the failing marriage, the children were doing well at school and the parents were not in clinical treatment for psychiatric disorders. Half of the families attended church or synagogue. Most of the parents were college educated. This was, in other words, divorce under the best of circumstances.

Our study, which would become the first ever made over an extended period of time, eventually tracked 60 families, most of them white, with a total of 131 children, for 10, and in some cases 15, years after divorce. We found that although some divorces work well—some adults are happier in the long run, and some children do better than they would have been expected to in an unhappy intact family—more often than not divorce is a wrenching, long-lasting experience for at least one of the former partners. Perhaps most important, we found that for virtually all the children, it exerts powerful and wholly unanticipated effects. . . .

We planned to interview families at the time of decisive separation and filing for divorce, and again 12 to 18 months later, expecting to chart recoveries among men and women and to look at how the children were mastering troubling family events.

Unexpected Results

We were stunned when, at the second series of visits, we found family after family still in crisis, their wounds wide open. Turmoil and distress had not noticeably subsided. Many adults were angry, and felt humiliated and rejected, and most had not gotten their lives back together. An unexpectedly large number of children were on a downward course. Their symptoms were worse than they had been immediately after the divorce. Our findings were absolutely contradictory to our expectations.

Dismayed, we asked the Zellerbach Fund to support a follow-up study in the fifth year after divorce. To our surprise, interviewing 56 of the 60 families in our original study, we found that although half the men and two-thirds of the women (even many of those suffering economically) said they were more content with their lives, only 34 percent of the children were clearly doing well.

Troubled Children

Percent of children ages 3-17 who have ever had an emotional or behavioral problem that lasted 3 months or more or required psychological help, by the family structure.

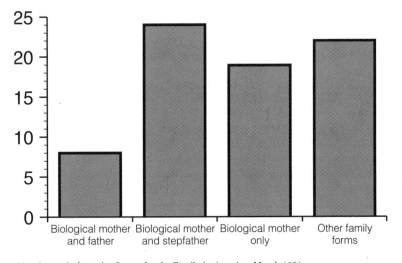

New Research, from the Center for the Family in America, March 1991.

Another 37 percent were depressed, could not concentrate in school, had trouble making friends and suffered a wide range of other behavior problems. While able to function on a daily basis, these children were not recovering, as everyone thought they would. Indeed most of them were on a downward course. This is a powerful statistic, considering that these were children who were functioning well five years before. It would be hard to find any other group of children—except, perhaps, the victims of a natural disaster—who suffered such a rate of sudden serious psychological problems.

The remaining children showed a mixed picture of good achievement in some areas and faltering achievement in others;

it was hard to know which way they would eventually tilt. . . .

It was only at the 10-year point that two of our most unexpected findings became apparent. The first of these is something we call the sleeper effect. . . .

The Sleeper Effect

We saw a pattern that we documented in 66 percent of the young women in our study between the ages of 19 and 23; half of them were seriously derailed by it. The sleeper effect occurs at a time when these young women are making decisions with long-term implications for their lives. Faced with issues of commitment, love and sex in an adult context, they are aware that the game is serious. If they tie in with the wrong man, have children too soon, or choose harmful life styles, the effects can be tragic. Overcome by fears and anxieties, they begin to make connections between these feelings and their parents' divorce:

"I'm so afraid I'll marry someone like my dad."

"How can you believe in commitment when anyone can change his mind anytime?"

"I am in awe of people who stay together."

We can no longer say—as most experts have held in recent years—that girls are generally less troubled by the divorce experience than boys. Our study strongly indicates, for the first time, that girls experience serious effects of divorce at the time they are entering young adulthood. Perhaps the risk for girls and boys is equalized over the long term.

When a marriage breaks down, men and women alike often experience a diminished capacity to parent. They may give less time, provide less discipline and be less sensitive to their children, since they are themselves caught up in the maelstrom of divorce and its aftermath. Many researchers and clinicians find that parents are temporarily unable to separate their children's needs from their own.

The Overburdened Child

In a second major unexpected finding of our 10-year study, we found that fully a quarter of the mothers and a fifth of the fathers had not gotten their lives back on track a decade after divorce. The diminished parenting continued, permanently disrupting the child-rearing functions of the family. These parents were chronically disorganized and, unable to meet the challenges of being a parent, often leaned heavily on their children. The child's role became one of warding off the serious depression that threatened the parents' psychological functioning. The divorce itself may not be solely to blame but, rather, may aggravate emotional difficulties that had been masked in the marriage. Some studies have found that emotionally disturbed parents within a marriage produce similar kinds of problems in children.

These new roles played by the children of divorce are complex and unfamiliar. They are not simple role reversals, as some have claimed, because the child's role becomes one of holding the parent together psychologically. It is more than a caretaking role. This phenomenon merits our careful attention, for it affected 15 percent of the children in our study, which means many youngsters in our society. I propose that we identify as a distinct psychological syndrome the "overburdened child," in the hope that people will begin to recognize the problems and take steps to help these children, just as they help battered and abused children. . . .

In truth, few children can rescue a troubled parent. Many become angry at being trapped by the parent's demands, at being robbed of their separate identity and denied their childhood. And they are saddened, sometimes beyond repair, at seeing so few of their own needs gratified.

Since this is a newly identified condition that is just being described, we cannot know its true incidence. I suspect that the number of overburdened children runs much higher than the 15 percent we saw in our study, and that we will begin to see rising reports in the next few years—just as the reported incidence of child abuse has risen since it was first identified as a syndrome in 1962.

The sleeper effect and the overburdened-child syndrome were but two of many findings in our study. Perhaps most important, overall, was our finding that divorce has a lasting psychological effect on many children, one that, in fact, may turn out to be permanent.

Children of divorce have vivid memories about their parents' separation. The details are etched firmly in their minds, more so than those of any other experiences in their lives. They refer to themselves as children of divorce, as if they share an experience that sets them apart from all others. Although many have come to agree that their parents were wise to part company, they nevertheless feel that they suffered from their parents' mistakes. In many instances, conditions in the post-divorce family were more stressful and less supportive to the child than conditions in the failing marriage.

Effects on Boys

If the finding that 66 percent of the 19- to 23-year-old young women experienced the sleeper effect was most unexpected, others were no less dramatic. Boys, too, were found to suffer unforeseen long-lasting effects. Forty percent of the 19- to 23-year-old young men in our study, 10 years after divorce, still had no set goals, a limited education and a sense of having little control over their lives. . . .

112

In the decade after divorce, three in five children felt rejected by one of their parents, usually the father—whether or not it was true. The frequency and duration of visiting made no difference. Children longed for their fathers, and the need increased during adolescence. Thirty-four percent of the youngsters went to live with their fathers during adolescence for at least a year. Half returned to the mother's home disappointed with what they had found. Only one in seven saw both mother and father happily remarried after 10 years. One in two saw their mother or their father undergo a second divorce. One in four suffered a severe and enduring drop in the family's standard of living and went on to observe a lasting discrepancy between their parents' standards of living.

Social and Personal Ills

Beyond the deprivations of poverty, children living without their fathers are more vulnerable to a number of social and personal ills less often found among children living with both parents. Compared to children living with both parents, children living in single-parent households are more likely to fail in school, to suffer poorer physical and mental health, to suffer abuse or neglect, to commit crimes or to be victims of crime, to bear or beget children out of wedlock, to use alcohol or drugs, and to be unemployed as young adults. Even suicide among teens and young adults appears traceable to parental divorce.

Bryce J. Christensen, *The Family in America*, vol. 5, no. 9, September 1991.

We found that the children who were best adjusted 10 years later were those who showed the most distress at the time of the divorce—the youngest. In general, preschoolers are the most frightened and show the most dramatic symptoms when marriages break up. Many are afraid that they will be abandoned by both parents and they have trouble sleeping or staying by themselves. It is therefore surprising to find that the same children 10 years later seem better adjusted than their older siblings. Now in early and mid-adolescence, they were rated better on a wide range of psychological dimensions than the older children. Sixty-eight percent were doing well, compared with less than 40 percent of older children. But whether having been young at the time of divorce will continue to protect them as they enter young adulthood is an open question.

Our study shows that adolescence is a period of particularly grave risk for children in divorced families. Through rigorous analysis, statistical and otherwise, we were able to see clearly that we weren't dealing simply with the routine angst of young people going through transition but rather that, for most of them, divorce was the single most important cause of enduring pain and anomie in their lives. The young people told us time and again how much they needed a family structure, how much they wanted to be protected, and how much they yearned for clear guidelines for moral behavior. An alarming number of teen-agers felt abandoned, physically and emotionally.

For children, divorce occurs during the formative years. What they see and experience becomes a part of their inner world, influencing their own relationships 10 and 15 years later, especially when they have witnessed violence between the parents. It is then, as these young men and women face the developmental task of establishing love and intimacy, that they most feel the lack of a template for a loving relationship between a man and a woman. It is here that their anxiety threatens their ability to create new, enduring families of their own.

As these anxieties peak in the children of divorce throughout our society, the full legacy of the rising divorce rate is beginning to hit home. The new families being formed today by these children as they reach adulthood appear particularly vulnerable. . . .

A Changing Society

It is time to take a long, hard look at divorce in America. Divorce is not an event that stands alone in children's or adult's experience. It is a continuum that begins in the unhappy marriage and extends through the separation, divorce and any remarriages and second divorces. Divorce is not necessarily the sole culprit. It may be no more than one of the many experiences that occur in this broad continuum.

Profound changes in the family can only mean profound changes in society as a whole. All children in today's world feel less protected. They sense that the institution of the family is weaker than it has ever been before. Even those children raised in happy, intact families worry that their families may come undone. The task for society in its true and proper perspective is to strengthen the family—all families. . . .

Like it or not, we are witnessing family changes which are an integral part of the wider changes in our society. We are on a wholly new course, one that gives us unprecedented opportunities for creating better relationships and stronger families—but one that also brings unprecedented dangers for society, especially for our children.

"The experience of divorce . . . is one of the processes that best equip us to be healthier in our relationships in the future. "

Divorce May Not Harm Children

Diane Fassel

In the following viewpoint, Diane Fassel acknowledges that the pain of divorce can cause children to suffer in the future. However, she is convinced that adult children of divorce can also develop positive behaviors as a result of their experience. Fassel is a family counselor in Colorado who specializes in divorce and child custody cases.

As you read, consider the following questions:

1. How does divorce make children more independent, according to the author?
2. According to the author, how can parents undergoing divorce benefit their children by expressing emotions?
3. Some reports have found that ACODs seek professional therapy more frequently than children of non-divorcing families. Why does Fassel believe this can be a positive trait?

Having seen the pain of many ACODs [adult children of divorce], it would be tempting to reach the conclusion that divorce is "bad." But after scores of interviews with ACODs, I am still certain that divorce itself is a neutral act. It is the process of divorce that affects children and results in their being problem-afflicted ACODs. Nevertheless, I was heartened by the many ACODs who were quick to point out that divorce had its positive aspects, as well. In fact, in a large number of stories, the divorce was far preferable to staying together through years of dysfunction. . . .

Independence and Resilience

Many ACODs found themselves on their own as a result of their parents' divorce. Many times they were denied financial support for higher education, and the divorce lowered their standard of living. They began working at an early age, and they realized they had to take responsibility for themselves.

In divorced families, as the custodial parent (usually the mother) is working and rebuilding a social life, children take on greater responsibility in the household. They learn to cook, clean, and do chores. . . .

There is another way that these ACODs are independent. They are independent of the feelings of others. They are not so enmeshed in others' troubles. . . . ACODs who saw divorce as positive seem to have a healthy sense of themselves as separate from others. They are not isolated from others. They are possessed of a sense of self. They want to make their own decisions and are willing to take the consequences of their mistakes. They do not refuse help when it is offered, and they have developed a sense of self-reliance such that they would not be helpless if others were not available to them.

I considered naming [one] characteristic "toughness," for ACODs sometimes do develop an exterior that hides great vulnerability. Still, I think "resilience" is more appropriate. ACODs, themselves, comment wonderingly about their ability to bounce back. They feel that they witnessed things in their families that were deeply disturbing, yet they find that they go on. . . .

Access to Feelings

This characteristic, more than any other, distinguishes the positive outcome of divorce from the negative for the ACODs. Scores of ACODs grew up with frozen feelings. It was unsafe to feel in their dysfunctional, divorcing families because there was no one there who could provide safety. Consequently, ACODs reach adulthood completely out of touch with feelings, or they may have only one feeling—anger.

In families where divorce was positive, ACODs had different

experiences. They saw their parents expressing feelings, and in many cases the feelings were not directed inappropriately onto the children, but they were not hidden, either. As children, these ACODs were encouraged to feel, and feelings were not judged. . . .

Children Adjust with Third-Party Support

The situations in which divorced youngsters were doing fine had one characteristic in common: There was a third party. Somebody acted as the third leg of the stool, giving it stability. It could be a friend, a coworker, more often a relative: the mother's mother, sometimes her mother-in-law. But the most effective, most powerful stabilizing third party was the father, the ex-husband. If he still hung in there, not just in relation to his children but in relation to that family; if he was there to spell the mother; if in an emergency she could call his number; if he dropped by to ask, "Are things OK?"—then nothing terrible happened so far as the children were concerned. Mom may not have been particularly happy, but the kids were able to hack it.

Urie Bronfenbrenner, *Marriage and Family in a Changing Society*, 1989.

Another aspect of this characteristic among ACODs is that they have access to a wide range of feelings, not just one or two. Some ACODs complain that they know sadness or fear, but are otherwise numb. Not so the ACOD whose parental divorce experience was positive. They feel a range of emotions. They know frustration, irritation, depression, grief, anger, concern, loving, joy. There are more nuances to their feelings. They do not need an explosive feeling to knock them over the head to know they are alive. Again, these ACODs received two messages from their divorcing parents. One was that it was safe to feel during the divorce process. It was normal to feel. The second was that their own parents had feelings, and they shared them. Feelings were a legitimate part of the divorce process, and not to be controlled out of existence. . . .

Suffering Is Not Romanticized

There is a decided lack of the dramatic among ACODs for whom parental divorce was a positive experience. They watched their parents come to the conclusion that the marriage was not a healthy option, and with that realization, they saw them take firm action. This is not the case in families where parents "stayed together for the sake of the kids." Many of these ACODs can create suffering out of the most trivial relationships. They believe you don't care if you don't suffer. . . .

Divorce forces change. It alters every aspect of children's existence; which adults will be in their lives, where they will live, where they will spend holidays, what schools they will attend, what friends they'll have, whose faces will be in the family portraits. Divorce, perhaps more than any other event except death, teaches that life is a process.

ACODs who are positive about their experience of their parents' divorce say they were initially wrenched by the changes that the divorce produced. They mourned the loss of their security. At the same time, their worlds broadened, and they began to see that their perspective was not the only perspective. . . .

These ACODs are flexible in the face of differences. They experienced various styles of living in multiple families. They know their preferences. They have learned that the world is diverse, for their own little universe is teeming with differences. Although initially wary in relationships, they are not shocked to find someone acting other than they expected. "I just try to roll with the punches," mused one ACOD rather philosophically. "You never can predict how things will be. It's just easier to take them as they come."

Whether sought or resisted, change has been a constant in the lives of all ACODs. Those who resisted are troubled today with the fallout from their controlling behavior. Those who accepted change seem to go through life with a noticeable ease, perhaps even a serenity. They have learned to let go. As a consequence, their lives are less restricted and the world is not a fearful place. They walk more effortlessly through life's events. They say they learned how as a result of the divorce. . . .

Experience Different Styles of Child Rearing

Books on divorce are filled with admonitions to parents to maintain consistency in rules as children go between parents. Many of the ACODs I interviewed felt that even in the most consistent environments, they still perceived great differences in how their parents cared for them, and overall, they found the experience of these differences was positive for their own development. . . .

Divorce gives children an experience of different styles in almost every aspect of family life. As they go between families, they form opinions of what works and what does not. Early in life, the opinions are self-centered. Later, children appreciate certain values and carry these forward into their families. . . .

Divorce gave ACODs a wide range of options when it came to lifestyles. At the very least, Mom's and Dad's were the first two separate lifestyles after divorce, but in many cases there were more. Many ACODs had parents who divorced more than once. With each new partner came an explosion of new grandparents and relatives. ACODs' flexibility was often tested to the limit in the changing form of the family, and as they participated in ever new arrangements. . . .

Leaving Unhealthy Relationships

With crystal clarity, children of divorce learn this lesson above all else: They can walk away from unhealthy relationships. The ability to leave a dysfunctional relationship is a distinguishing characteristic of the ACOD who experienced divorce positively. Many ACODs have not resolved their relationship issues and perpetuate their family patterns in all their relationships, but some learn this basic lesson through the divorce process: When it is unhealthy, you can leave. . . .

ACODs for whom divorce was positive have a realistic estimate of their own strengths and weaknesses. In many cases, facilitators helped families talk through their differences. During divorce, parents encouraged their children to seek therapy, if it would help them. ACODs approach therapy not with a sense that they are crazy but with a sense that they need special support during a time of crisis. This, it seems to me, is a healthy response, not a sign of instability. . . . Those who experienced divorce as a positive solution say they first acknowledged their need for help during the divorce process. Without the divorce, they would neither have sought nor received the assistance that has made a noticeable difference in their lives. . . .

Children of divorce entered adulthood with new eyes about relationships, suffering, choices, and change. They achieved independence and resilience and knew enough to know when they needed help. In our society, we have tended to pity the children of divorce, believing that somehow they missed out on something essential. They were handicapped. But if, indeed, divorce is a process, and a process that is integrally related to a wider societal process, could it be that ACODs are developing exactly the survival skills needed for this new era? It is true that some ACODs are bitterly unhappy about the events of their childhood. The process surely went awry. Still, many others learned valuable lessons. Rather than being handicapped, they feel more astute about life and family. For all we know, they are the forerunners of new family forms. ACODs say they have divorce to thank for their awareness. How ironic if the experience of divorce, an experience most of us would wish to avoid, is one of the processes that best equip us to be healthier in our relationships in the future. For at least a segment of ACODs, this has been the case. Divorce has positive outcomes; those ACODs who could see the possible positive opportunities do not regret it.

"U.S. census data show a direct link between divorce, the increase in female-headed families, and the 'feminization of poverty.' "

Divorce Laws Harm Women Economically

Lenore J. Weitzman

In the following viewpoint, sociologist Lenore J. Weitzman argues that, while a man's income increases after divorce, a woman's income plummets. She believes that this disparity is a result of an unjust legal system, which she argues must be reformed. In spite of the fact that Weitzman's study was completed in 1985, her research continues to be influential today. Weitzman is an associate professor of sociology at Harvard University in Cambridge, Massachusetts.

As you read, consider the following questions:

1. According to the author, why does an equal division of property between divorcing spouses still benefit the husband more than the wife?
2. How are a woman's employment prospects limited by responsibilities to her minor children, according to Weitzman?
3. What changes does the author suggest to improve divorce laws?

In 1970, California launched a legal revolution by instituting the first no-fault divorce law in the United States. The new law not only changed the rules for divorce, it also changed the rules for dividing property and awarding support. This seemingly simple move pioneered sweeping reforms that quickly spread to other states. While not all states adopted the California law (and totally abolished "fault"), today every state allows some form of no-fault divorce.

Under the old fault-based divorce, one party had to be judged guilty of some marital fault, such as adultery or cruelty, before a divorce could be granted. Moreover, the guilty party was typically punished in the divorce settlement by having to pay alimony or forfeit marital property. Although alimony was awarded much less frequently and in lesser amounts than the press about celebrated divorcees like Joanna Carson and Ivana Trump would have us believe, still only an "innocent wife" could be awarded alimony. Thus, the financial terms of the divorce were closely linked to the findings of fault.

Unintended Consequences

The no-fault reforms were designed to eliminate the acrimony and hostility generated by fights about fault and to create more equity in divorce settlements. But the changes in the law have had unintended consequences; they have created substantial inequalities between divorced men and women and, as my research demonstrates, have led to the impoverishment of many divorced women and their children.

Why are women suffering under laws that were meant to create more equity and fairness in divorce? The answer lies in the four components of divorce laws:

1) how the law defines marital property;
2) how marital property is divided;
3) the standards for awarding alimony; and
4) the rules for awarding and enforcing child support.

How the Law Defines Marital Property

In a modern industrial society, the major property acquired during marriage is rarely the family farm. Today, husbands and wives increasingly invest in careers, most particularly in the husband's career and earning capacity. *Career assets* is the term I coined to refer to the "tangible and intangible assets acquired as part of either spouse's career or career potential." There are two types of career assets:

1. investments in human capital (one's education, on-the-job training, and ability to earn a living in the future), and
2. the benefits and entitlements of employment (such as pension and retirement benefits, medical and hospital insur-

ance, and entitlements to company goods and services.)

When we examined the value of traditional forms of property (such as cars and TV's) by researching divorce cases in court records, we found that the average divorcing couple in California had only $20,000 worth of assets. Yet, the average couple was able to earn more than $20,000 *in just one year*. This comparison suggests that the value of the couple's career assets—in fact, the value of their earning capacities alone—are worth much more than the value of their physical property. But the courts have resisted recognizing these new forms of property and dividing them at divorce.

Earning Capacity as an Asset

These facts have important policy implications. If one partner builds his or her earning capacity during the marriage, while the other is a homemaker and parent, the partner whose earning capacity has developed during the marriage has acquired the major asset of the marital partnership. If that earning capacity, or the income it produces is not divided upon divorce, the two spouses are left with very unequal shares of their joint assets. This is one of the major sources of the impoverishment of women and children after divorce. For example, consider one case from our research sample:

> We married at 21 with no money. When he was a graduate student, I worked as a secretary and then typed papers at night to make extra money. . . . [Then] I retired to raise our children, but I never stopped working for him . . . [for thirty years of marriage]. . . . It's not that I regret my life or didn't enjoy what I did, *but it's supposed to be a partnership—a fifty-fifty split*. It isn't fair for the court to treat it as his. . . . *I earned it just as much as he did.*

The "it" that this woman is referring to is her husband's career and their joint investments in his earning capacity. I have recommended changing the law in California to explicitly recognize these career assets as marital property (and to require judges to include them in the property to be divided upon divorce).

The Division of Property

One of the major innovations of California's no-fault reforms was the institution of a fixed rule for dividing property. It *required* judges to divide marital property *equally*, half to the husband, half to the wife. The equal division standard was seen as fair because it guaranteed each spouse one half of their joint assets.

The startling finding of my research—when we compared 1,000 divorce cases from court records under the old law with 1,500 divorce cases from court records after no-fault was instituted—is that the equal division rule *reduced* the wife's share of marital property in California. This is because wives were usually the innocent plaintiffs under the old fault-based divorce law, and they were, therefore, typically awarded more than half (60%) of the marital property. In practice, most of these awards allowed the wife to keep the family home. Under the new law, without the lever of fault, the wife's share of property dropped to 50%.

Losing the Family Home

The major impact of the equal division rule has been to force the sale of the family home. The court records reveal that the number of cases in which the judge ordered the family home sold tripled after the law changed, and 66% of the couples who were forced to sell their homes had minor children.

The loss of a family home is more than a financial loss. It creates disruption and dislocation in the lives of children who have to change schools and lose friends and neighbors at the very time when they (and their mothers) most need continuity and stability. An example from my interviews illustrates the emotional upheaval of the forced sale of the home:

> I begged the judge. . . . All I wanted was enough time for Brian [her son] to adjust to the divorce. . . . I broke down and cried on the stand . . . but the judge refused. . . . It was the most unjust experience of my life.

To avoid these unnecessary hardships I advocated a change in the California law to require judges to preserve the family home for minor children. This is, in fact, the law in England.

The Standards for Alimony: The Short Goodbye

Alimony, more than any other aspect of divorce law, reflects the change in the position of women under the divorce reforms of the 1970's. The traditional divorce laws assumed that husbands remained responsible for supporting their former wives after divorce. In contrast, the reformers thought divorced women should now be treated "equally" and be equally responsible for supporting themselves (and their children) after divorce.

In theory, under the new law, alimony was still supposed to be available for older housewives and parents caring for children after divorce. But in practice—and the essence of my research was to discover *what was actually happening in practice*—judges are not awarding enough alimony to either group of women. The court dockets we examined show that under the old law 62% of the alimony awards in California were "permanent." Under no-fault, in contrast, "permanent" awards dropped to 31%, while the new alimony awards were limited to fixed-term transitional awards for an average of only two years.

Thus while older women and middle-class women are still

awarded alimony (and, in fact, *the percentage* of awards to older women actually increased slightly), the real dollar value of the awards declined dramatically because they are cut off after two years.

While it is reasonable for the law to consider the wife's ability to support herself in determining alimony, it is shocking to see how judges apply the law. Women with no job prospects or minimal employment histories are routinely denied spousal support because judges decide that they have "the ability to be self-supporting."

The Plight of Older Homemakers

How realistic is it to assume that an older housewife with minimal or no employment record will easily find a well-paid full-time job and become self-supporting within two years? (Just think about how hard it would be for a man who had not been employed for 20 or 25 years. . . .) Most of the older housewives we interviewed found the task impossible. As one said:

> No training can recapture twenty-seven years of my life. . . . I'm too old to start from the beginning and I shouldn't have to.

When we compared the post-divorce incomes of long-married husbands and wives, we found that minimal alimony awards left wives with much less money and much worse off economically than their former husbands. For example, wives married 18 years or more with predivorce annual family incomes of $20,000 to $30,000, have on the average a median income of $6,300 after the divorce. Their husbands, in contrast, enjoy a median annual income of $20,000. The result is that post-divorce income of these wives is 24% of the previous family income, while their husbands' is 87%.

It is no wonder that the older homemaker feels the most betrayed by the current legal system. She was promised by both her husband and our society that marriage was a partnership and that her husband would share his income with her. Instead, from her point of view, we have changed the rules on her after she fulfilled her share of the bargain and can no longer choose another life course. As one woman said:

> You can't tell me there's justice if someone uses you for twenty-five years and then just dumps you and walks out scot-free. . . . It's not fair. It's not justice. It's a scandal.

As we noted above, in theory, alimony is also supposed to be available for women with custody of young children. However, my research found that alimony awards to mothers of children under six had dropped more than to any other group of women since 1970. Today, only 13% of the California mothers of preschool children are awarded alimony.

124

In recommending policy changes, I argue that because it is harder and more expensive to raise children as a single mother, a woman's own job opportunities and work schedule (i.e. her availability for overtime, training, and travel) are often restricted after divorce. It is therefore vital to provide her with enough alimony to allow her to maximize her long-term employment prospects. Investing in her earning potential will "pay off" not only for her and her children, but also for her former husband because she will have more money to share the costs of child support.

For the older housewife, however, the goal of self-sufficiency should itself be challenged. It is both unrealistic and unfair. Women who divorce at 45 or 55 or 60 need rules that require judges to make alimony awards that divide the husband's post-divorce income so that the older housewife continues to share the standard of living she helped to build.

Child Support Awards

Although divorce courts are supposed to order sufficient support to provide for the needs of minor children after divorce, in California, according to the court records, the average child support award was less than the average cost of day care alone, not even considering food, housing, and clothing. These findings are typical of the United States as a whole: U.S. census data report average child support awards of $200 per month.

Yet it is very rare for any court to order more than 25% of a man's income in child support or more than 32% in combined child support and alimony. Even where 32% of the man's income is allocated to his children and former wife, he is nevertheless left with two-thirds of his income for himself.

Children Suffer

Despite these low awards, only half of the fathers ever pay the child support the court orders (according to the U.S. Census). By the end of 1989, census data show that $18 billion in accumulated unpaid support was owed to 16 million American children. For many children in single-parent families, the lack of child support payments leads to dependence on welfare. One in four American children under the age of 18 now lives in a single-parent family, and one in five children lives in poverty.

Despite Congressional legislation designed to enforce child support (1984 and 1988), few states have invested in the computer system required for tracking delinquent parents through income tax and credit card records. (Yet, many of these same states have managed to install lottery ticket computers.) The fact is that few states are serious about enforcement, and fathers often get the message that child support is discretionary. So mothers, who are the primary custodial parents in 90% of the divorces, are left with the major burden of supporting their children after divorce.

The Larger Economic Consequences of Divorce

The net effect of the present rules for property, alimony, and child support is severe financial hardship for most divorced women and their children. They experience a dramatic decline in income and a drastic drop in their standard of living. In the California sample, we found that just one year after divorce, women and children experienced a 73% decline their standard of living, while the men to whom they were married experienced a 42% increase.

On a societal level divorce increases female and child poverty. U.S. census data show a direct link between divorce, the increase in female-headed families, and the "feminization of poverty." Contrary to popular perception, most female-headed, single-parent families in the United States are *not* the result of unwed parenthood; they are the result of marital dissolution. Only 18% of the nearly 10 million female-headed families in the U.S. are headed by an unwed mother. Over 50% are headed by divorced mothers, and the remaining 31% by separated mothers. All this has been well documented elsewhere.

What has not been well documented—and not even acknowledged—is the direct link between the terms of the divorce decrees and the feminization of poverty. When courts fail to divide property equally, and when courts deny divorced mothers the support and property they need to maintain their families, the legal system itself contributes to their poverty.

It is essential to recognize that the current hardships are not inevitable consequences of divorce. They can be altered dramatically by the changes in the law and legal practice that have been suggested throughout this viewpoint.

Epilogue: 1992

It is now seven years since my book *The Divorce Revolution* was published. It therefore seems appropriate to add a brief note on what has happened since then.

First, and most gratifying, was the California Senate's response to the book. They established a Blue Ribbon Task Force on "Family Equity" to consider my findings and to recommend new legislation to correct the inequities of the legal system of divorce. The task force recommended 21 new laws. As of 1991, 14 of these bills had become law. Hopefully, this signals the beginning of a new era of fairness in divorce in California.

Second, (and most frustrating), was the response from those who misunderstood my findings and/or recommendations. For example, the journalist Susan Faludi, in an otherwise excellent book, selected several incomplete and misleading bits of infor-

126

mation out of context to support her thesis. Consider these examples:

1. Faludi argues that we should not tell women that divorce is economically difficult because they will be "frightened" and stay in unhappy marriages. This argument is an insult to women's intelligence. I believe we should always tell the truth and that people are always better off making decisions based on the truth. *Further, the message of my book is that divorce does not have to bring economic hardship because we can change the laws*. This is a positive message because it means that something should and can be done to remedy the current unfairness.

2. Faludi contends that other researchers, Gregory Duncan and Saul Hoffman, using a national sample, found a decline in divorced women's living standards of "only 30%," less than in my California sample. But their data are not based on real divorces. They include people who lived together and never legally married and couples who married but never legally divorced. (My data, in contrast, are based on *court records of actual divorces*.) Obviously a sample which includes never married cohabitors and couples who never divorced can not tell us about the effects of the legal system of divorce.

But even if women and children experienced "only a 30% decline" in their standard of living after divorce, would that suggest that we should ignore the hardships they were facing?

Results Replicated

In fact, since my book was published, my results have been replicated by research based on court records in seven other states: Alaska, Connecticut, Illinois, Maryland, New York, Oregon, and Vermont. All of these studies report the same overall results—i.e., unequal division of property, short-term and inadequate alimony awards, low child support with inadequate enforcement, and economic hardships for the women and children after divorce.

Nor are these results limited to the United States. In a major new book on worldwide changes in divorce, Harvard sociologist William J. Goode reports that women and children suffer economic hardships after divorce in most countries with similar legal regimes. The few exceptions, such as Sweden and Denmark, have already instituted many of the reforms suggested above.

3. In some cases Faludi simply misreads my results. For example, she erroneously criticizes me for not analyzing cases under the old law—ignoring the court docket research which compared 1,000 divorce cases *before* the no-fault law with 1,500 divorce cases *after* no-fault was instituted.

Similarly she criticizes my "small" sample, claiming that I only interviewed 228 people (which is a substantial sample for in-depth 4 hour interviews)—by ignoring the interviews with 169 attorneys, 44 judges, and the lengthy analysis of 2,500 divorce cases from court dockets over a ten-year period—to say nothing of the research that followed.

4. Faludi claims that my data show that older women are better off under no-fault, citing the rise in the *percentage* of longer married women who are awarded some alimony. But she ignores the fact that these awards are for *fewer* years. Alimony that lasts only two years instead of fifteen, clearly represents a net loss for older housewives.

Lessons for the Future

But most important are the implications and recommendations for the future. Faludi argues that the most effective way to change the inequities of the present system (and she must believe the inequities are real if she wants to change them) is to correct pay differences between men and women. While pay equity is a vital goal, why should we let the legal system off the hook? We can help divorced mothers much more quickly by changing the law. For example, divorced women would be much better off if we changed the laws on how property is defined and divided and the ways alimony and child support are awarded and enforced.

Similarly, Faludi recommends that we focus on "educating judges" and "urging divorced men to be responsible." While such efforts are important, there is a much more effective way to assure more fairness now. We can change the laws to remove judicial discretion and to instead *require judges* to divide career assets as property, and to *require judges* to reserve the home for minor children. The same may be said of efforts to urge men to pay child support. How many people would pay their taxes if they were merely "urged" to do it? What we need is strict laws and strict enforcement of these laws if we are really serious about creating equal results for men and women after divorce.

The issue today is no longer whether we should have fault or no-fault divorce laws. As of 1992, all 50 states had some form of no-fault divorce. The challenge we now face is that of making the current legal system of divorce—and the specific rules for dividing property, awarding alimony, and providing child support—a fair system that produces equality of results for men and women and children.

The major lesson of my research is that the divorce laws have real-life effects. If we want to change some of those effects, the best place to start is with the laws themselves.

"The real source of divorced women's woes can be found not in . . . divorce legislation but in the behavior of ex-husbands and judges."

Divorce Is Not the Cause of Women's Economic Hardships

Susan Faludi

Susan Faludi is a Pulitzer Prize-winning author and reporter for *The Wall Street Journal*. In the following viewpoint, Faludi argues that blaming divorce for women's impoverished status is inaccurate and harmful to women. She contends that if women believe divorce leads to economic catastrophe, they will be frightened into staying in unhappy marriages and traditional oppressive roles. Faludi suggests that flawed research and uncritical media reports encourage the belief that divorce has catastrophic consequences for women.

As you read, consider the following questions:

1. What role did feminists play in divorce-law reform, according to Faludi?
2. According to Faludi, what are the economic effects of divorce reported in Hoffman and Duncan's *5,000 Families* study?
3. What must be done to lift divorced women out of poverty, according to the author?

In the 1970s, many states passed new "no-fault" divorce laws that made the process easier: they eliminated the moralistic grounds required to obtain a divorce and divided up a marriage's assets based on needs and resources without reference to which party was held responsible for the marriage's failure. In the 1980s, these "feminist-inspired" laws came under attack: the New Right painted them as schemes to undermine the family, and the media and popular writers portrayed them as inadvertent betrayals of women and children, legal slingshots that "threw thousands of middle-class women," as a typical chronicler put it, "into impoverished states."

Perhaps no one person did more to fuel the attack on divorce-law reform in the backlash decade than sociologist Lenore Weitzman, whose 1985 book, *The Divorce Revolution: The Unexpected Social and Economic Consequences for Women and Children in America*, supplied the numbers quoted by everyone assailing the new laws. From Phyllis Schlafly to Betty Friedan, from the *National Review* to the "CBS Evening News," Weitzman's "devastating" statistics were invoked as proof that women who sought freedom from unhappy marriages were making a big financial mistake: they would wind up poorer under the new laws—worse off than if they had divorced under the older, more "protective" system, or if they had simply stayed married. . . .

This is Weitzman's thesis: "The major economic result of the divorce-law revolution is the systematic impoverishment of divorced women and their children." Under the old "fault" system, Weitzman writes, the "innocent" party stood to receive more than half the property—an arrangement that she says generally worked to the wronged wife's benefit. The new system, on the other hand, hurts women because it is too equal—an evenhandedness that is hurting older homemakers most of all, she says. "[T]he legislation of equality actually resulted in a worsened position for women and, by extension, a worsened position for children."

Feminists Did Not Initiate Reform

Weitzman's work does not say feminists were responsible for the new no-fault laws, but those who promoted her work most often acted as if her book indicts the women's movement. *The Divorce Revolution, Time* informed its readers, shows how forty-three states passed no-fault laws "largely in response to feminist demand." A flurry of anti-no-fault books, most of them knock-offs of Weitzman's work, blamed the women's movement for divorced women's poverty. "The impact of the divorce revolution is a clear example of how an equal-rights orientation has failed women," Mary Ann Mason writes in *The Equality Trap*. "[J]udges are receiving the message that feminists are sending."

Actually, feminists had almost nothing to do with divorce-law reform—as Weitzman herself points out. The 1970 California no-fault law, considered the most radical for its equal-division rule, was drafted by a largely male advisory board. The American Bar Association, not the National Organization for Women, instigated the national "divorce revolution"—which wasn't even much of a revolution. At the time of Weitzman's work, half the states still had the traditional "fault" system on their books, with no-fault only as an option. Only eight states had actually passed community property provisions like the California law, and only a few required equal property division.

No Economic Windfall for Men

Contrary to one widely cited analysis, divorce causes economic hardship for men as well as women. In a critique of *The Divorce Revolution* by Lenore Weitzman, legal scholar Jed Abraham challenges Weitzman's assertion that "men experience a 42 percent improvement in their postdivorce standard of living, while women experience a 73 percent decline." Although Abraham agrees that divorce is "a serious financial trauma for many women and for the children in their custody," he exposes a feminist bias in Weitzman's statistical analysis, especially in her characterization of divorce as an economic windfall for men. Abraham observes that after divorce "men in particular experience losses . . . that are not easily quantifiable." He points out that in many cases divorced men "will have left single-family homes for small apartments. They will have exchanged home-cooked meals for fast-food fare."

The Family in America, December 1989.

Weitzman argued that because women and men are differently situated in marriage—that is, the husbands usually make more money and, upon divorce, the wives usually get the kids—treating the spouses equally upon divorce winds up overcompensating the husband and cheating the wife and children. On its face, this argument seems reasonable enough, and Weitzman even had the statistics to prove it: "The research shows that on the average, divorced women and the minor children in their households experience a 73 percent decline in their standard of living in the first year after divorce. Their former husbands, in contrast, experience a 42 percent rise in their standard of living."

These figures seemed alarming, and the press willingly passed them on—without asking two basic questions: Were Weitzman's statistics correct? And, even more important, did she actually show that women fared *worse* under the new divorce laws than the old?

In the summer of 1986, soon after Lenore Weitzman had finished testifying before Congress on the failings of no-fault divorce, she received a letter from Saul Hoffman, an economist at the University of Delaware who specializes in divorce statistics. He wrote that he and his partner, University of Michigan social scientist Greg Duncan, were a little bewildered by her now famous 73 percent statistic. They had been tracking the effect of divorce on income for two decades—through the landmark "5,000 Families" study—and they had found the changes following divorce to be nowhere near as dramatic as she described. They found a much smaller 30 percent decline in women's living standards in the first year after divorce and a much smaller 10 to 15 percent improvement for men. . . .

Contradictory Studies

What baffled Hoffman and Duncan most was that Weitzman claimed in her book to have used *their* methods to arrive at her 73 percent statistic. . . .

Duncan and Hoffman tried repeating her calculations using her numbers in the book. But they still came up with a 33 percent, not a 73 percent, decline in women's standard of living. The two demographers published this finding in *Demography*. "Weitzman's highly publicized findings are almost certainly in error," they wrote. Not only was the 73 percent figure "suspiciously large," it was "inconsistent with information on changes in income and per capita income that she reports." The press response? The *Wall Street Journal* acknowledged Duncan and Hoffman's article in a brief item in the newspaper's demography column. No one else picked it up. . . .

Explanation of Inconsistencies

How could Weitzman's conclusions have been so far off the mark? There are several possible explanations. First, her statistics, unlike Duncan and Hoffman's, were not based on a national sample, although the press widely represented them as such. She drew her cases exclusively from Los Angeles County divorce court. Second, her sample was remarkably small—114 divorced women and 114 divorced men. . . .

Finally, Weitzman drew her financial information on these divorced couples from a notoriously unreliable source—their own memories. "We were amazed at their ability to recall precisely the appraised value of their house, the amount of the mortgage, the value of the pension plan, etc.," she writes in her book. Memory, particularly in the emotion-charged realm of divorce, is hardly a reliable source of statistics. . . .

To be fair, the 73 percent statistic is only one number in Weitzman's work. And a 30 percent decline in women's living standard is hardly ideal, either. Although the media fixed on its sensational implications, the figure has little bearing on her second and more central point—that women are *worse* off since "the divorce revolution." This is an important question because it gets to the heart of the backlash argument: women are better off "protected" than equal.

Yet, while Weitzman's book states repeatedly that the new laws have made life "worse" for women than the old ones, it concludes by recommending that legislators should keep the new divorce laws with a little fine-tuning. And she strongly warns against a return to the old system, which she calls a "charade" of fairness. "[I]t is clear that it would be unwise and inappropriate to suggest that California return to a more traditional system," she writes.

Needless to say, this conclusion never made it into the press coverage of Weitzman's study. A closer reading explains why Weitzman had little choice but to abandon her theory on no-fault divorce: she had conducted interviews only with men and women who divorced after the 1970 no-fault law went into effect in California. She had no comparable data on couples who divorced under the old system—and so no way of testing her hypothesis. . . .

Alimony Statistics Compared

Nonetheless, Weitzman suggests she had two other types of evidence to show that divorcing women suffered more under no-fault law. Divorcing women, she writes, are less likely to be awarded alimony under the new legislation—a loss most painful to older homemakers who are ill equipped to enter the work force. Second, women are now often forced to sell the family house. Yet Weitzman fails to make the case on either count.

National data collected by the U.S. Census Bureau show that the percentage of women awarded alimony or maintenance payments (all told, a mere 14 percent) is not significantly different from what it was in the 1920s. Weitzman argues that, even so, one group of women—long-married traditional housewives—have been hurt by the new laws, caught in the middle when the rules changed. Yet her own data show that older housewives and long-married women are the *only* groups of divorced women who actually are being awarded alimony in greater numbers under the new laws than the old. The increase that she reports for housewives married more than ten years is a remarkable 21 percent.

Her other point is that under no-fault "equal division" rules, the couple is increasingly forced to sell the house, whereas under the old laws, she says, the judge traditionally gave it to the wife. But the new divorce laws don't require house sales and, in fact, the authors of the California law explicitly stated that judges shouldn't use the law to force single mothers and their children from the home. If more women are being forced to sell the family home, the new laws aren't to blame. . . .

Judicial Enforcement Is Needed

The real source of divorced women's woes can be found not in the fine print of divorce legislation but in the behavior of ex-husbands and judges. Between 1978 and 1985, the average amount of child support that divorced men paid fell nearly 25 percent. Divorced men are now more likely to meet their car payments than their child support obligations—even though, for two-thirds of them, the amount owed their children is *less* than their monthly auto loan bill.

Capitalism, Not Divorce, Causes Poverty

When it is argued that the feminization of poverty places all or most women at risk, including middle- and upper-middle-class women, a very important observation is made that does not apply to women across social classes. The often-made statement, "most women are just a man or a divorce away from poverty," reflects the conditions of existence of most *propertyless* women whom the capitalist organization of production and reproduction makes dependent on marriage and/or employment for economic survival.

Martha Gimenez, *Social Justice*, vol. 17, no. 3, Fall 1990.

As of 1985, only half of the 8.8 million single mothers who were supposed to be receiving child support payments from their ex-husbands actually received any money at all, and only half of that half were actually getting the full amount. In 1988, the federal Office of Child Support Enforcement was collecting only $5 billion of the $25 billion a year fathers owed in child support. And studies on child support collection strategies are finding that only one tactic seems to awaken the moral conscience of negligent fathers: mandatory jail sentences. As sociologist Arlie Hochschild has observed, economic abandonment may be the new method some divorced men have devised for exerting control over their former families: "The 'new' oppression outside marriage thus creates a tacit threat to women inside marriage," she writes. "Patriarchy has not disappeared; it has changed form."

At the same time, public and judicial officials weren't setting much of an example. A 1988 federal audit found that thirty-five states weren't complying with federal child support laws. And judges weren't even upholding the egalitarian principles of no-fault. Instead, surveys in several states found that judges were willfully misinterpreting the statutes to mean that women should get not one-half but *one-third* of all assets from the marriage. Weitzman herself reached the conclusion that judicial antagonism to feminism was aggravating the rough treatment of contemporary divorced women. "The concept of 'equality' and the sex-neutral language of the law," she writes, have been "used by some lawyers and judges as a mandate for 'equal treatment' with a vengeance, a vengeance that can only be explained as a backlash reaction to women's demands for equality in the larger society."

In the end, the most effective way to correct the post-divorce inequities between the sexes is simple: correct pay inequality in the work force. If the wage gap were wiped out between the sexes, a federal advisory council concluded in 1982, one-half of female-headed households would be instantly lifted out of poverty. "The dramatic increase in women working is the best kind of insurance against this vulnerability," Duncan says, observing that women's access to better-paying jobs saved a lot of divorced women from a far worse living standard. And that access, he points out, "is largely a product of the women's movement."

Distinguishing Between Fact and Opinion

This activity is designed to help develop the basic reading and thinking skill of distinguishing between fact and opinion. Consider the following statement: "One million children in America each year see their parents divorce." This is a factual statement because it could be checked by looking at divorce statistics published by the U.S. Department of Health and Human Services in its *Monthly Vital Statistics Report*. But the statement "The emotional trauma of divorce leads to juvenile delinquency" is an opinion. Many people may not consider divorce emotionally traumatic. Others might argue that even if rates of juvenile delinquency are rising, divorce is not the cause.

When investigating controversial issues it is important that one be able to distinguish between statements of fact and statements of opinion. It is also important to recognize that not all statements of fact are true. They may appear to be true, but some are based on inaccurate or false information. For this activity, however, we are concerned with understanding the difference between those statements that appear to be factual and those that appear to be based primarily on opinion.

Most of the following statements are taken from the viewpoints in this chapter. Consider each statement carefully. *Mark O for any statement you believe is an opinion or interpretation of facts. Mark F for any statement you believe is a fact. Mark I for any statement you believe is impossible to judge.*

If you are doing this activity as a member of a class or group, compare your answers with those of other class or group members. Be able to defend your answers. You may discover that others come to different conclusions than you do. Listening to the reasons others present for their answers may give you valuable insights into distinguishing between fact and opinion.

O = opinion
F = fact
I = impossible to judge

1. In the 1970s, "no-fault" legislation allowed couples to divorce without placing blame for the failure of the marriage.

2. For the first time in history, an American marrying now is more likely to lose a spouse through divorce than through death.

3. In 1965, there were 10.6 divorces for every 1,000 married women in the United States; by the early 1980s, that rate had nearly doubled, to 22.6 per 1,000.

4. If divorce is harder to get, there will be less of it, and more families will find a way to remain intact.

5. A first marriage undertaken today stands a 66 percent chance of ending in divorce.

6. The average child-support award covers less than half the cost of raising a child.

7. The rise in divorce has been the major cause of the increase in teen suicide in America.

8. Divorced men experience less day-to-day stress than their ex-wives, and have greater freedom to build new lives and new families after divorce.

9. The impact of the divorce revolution is a clear example of how an equal-rights orientation has failed women.

10. In 1988, the federal Office of Child Support Enforcement collected only 20 percent of the $25 billion fathers owed in child support.

11. Only one in seven children of divorce sees both parents happily remarried after ten years.

12. Divorce is far preferable to staying together through years of dysfunction.

13. Families have been affected by social change far more than they have been responsible for it.

14. Legal grounds and procedures for divorce did not even exist in most states until 1900.

15. The court system has become a mere rubber-stamp reviewer of divorce agreements hammered out between spouses and their lawyers.

16. Children suffer more stress from divorce than they do from living with parents who are having marital problems.

17. Incest, child abuse and neglect, alcoholism, and delinquency are not new problems; their apparent increase is due to better record keeping and widespread reporting.

Periodical Bibliography

The following articles have been selected to supplement the diverse views presented in this chapter.

Andrew J. Cherlin et al.
"Longitudinal Studies of Effects of Divorce on Children," *Science*, June 7, 1991.

Bryce J. Christensen
"Taking Stock: Assessing Twenty Years of 'No Fault' Divorce," *The Family in America*, September 1991. Available from The Rockford Institute, 934 N. Main St., Rockford, IL 61103-7061.

Robert H. Coombs
"Marital Status and Personal Well-Being," *Family Relations*, January 1991.

Linda L. Creighton
"Silent Saviors," *U.S. News & World Report*, December 16, 1991.

Eric Felton
"Divorce's Atom Bomb: Child Sex Abuse," *Insight*, November 25, 1991. Available from PO Box 91022, Washington, DC 20090-1022.

Barbara Kantrowitz and Pat Wingert
"Step by Step," *Newsweek*, special issue, Winter/Spring 1990.

Barbara Kantrowitz et al.
"Breaking the Divorce Cycle," *Newsweek*, January 13, 1992.

Lawrence Kutner
"Parent and Child," *The New York Times*, January 16, 1992.

Michael Lerner
"Does Work Cause Divorce?" *Utne Reader*, November/December 1990.

Art Levine
"The Second Time Around: Realities of Remarriage," *U.S. News & World Report*, January 29, 1990.

Jane Marks
"We Have a Problem," *Parents*, June 1991.

Susan Moller Okin
"Economic Equality After Divorce: 'Equal Rights' or Special Benefits?" *Dissent*, Summer 1991.

Marla K. Richards
"When It's Not Apparent You're a Parent," *U.S. Catholic*, May 1991.

Betty Vos
"Practicing a Love Ethic for All Families," *The Christian Century*, November 13, 1991.

Karl Zinsmeister
"Growing Up Scared," *The Atlantic*, June 1990.

How Are Two-Career Parents Affecting the Family?

Chapter Preface

Women have entered the work force in unprecedented numbers. As a result, more American children today live in families in which both parents work. Whether these dual-career couples adversely affect their children is a highly emotional issue. Individual parents deal with this issue on a personal level: Are they spending enough time with their children? Experts ponder the broader impact of this trend on society: Will children of two working parents develop more emotional and social problems and consequently present problems for society in the future?

Critics such as columnist Phyllis Schlafly argue that children are harmed and families weakened by two working parents because such parents may spend less time with their children. Schlafly maintains that two-career couples add "a significant level of extra distress and conflict to the all-important infant-mother-father relationship." Schlafly concludes that the added stress of managing family and career has led parents to neglect their children and that this, in turn, will weaken society.

Conversely, others argue that in many families both parents simply must work—two incomes are a financial necessity. In addition to this practical need, many family experts agree that careers satisfy emotional and psychological needs for many parents, who may be more fulfilled by productive work and consequently may be happier. People who support the two-career family trend argue that children are affected positively when their parents have fewer money worries and more chances for fulfillment.

Sweeping generalizations cannot adequately express the effect working parents have on the family when so many variables —the amount of time spent at work, the type of work, the type of child care, and the emotional and financial needs of the children and the adults involved—come into play. The authors in the following chapter address these issues.

"Time spent outside the home can renew a woman's sense of vigor and widen her interests, so that she has more to offer her family."

Working Mothers Benefit the Family

Robin Parker

Women who choose both career and family are happier, healthier people and thus better parents, argues Robin Parker in the following viewpoint. She suggests women with multiple interests and busy lives are better role models for children and more interesting marriage partners. Parker is a writer, editor, and mother in Washington, D.C.

As you read, consider the following questions:

1. How does Parker contrast the health and happiness of working mothers and fathers today with parents in the 1950s?
2. According to Parker, how does society harm families by raising women to believe their place is in the home?
3. Why might working mothers have better relationships with their teenagers than full-time mothers, according to the author?

Adapted from "Superwoman: Myth, Reality—or What?" by Robin Parker. This article appeared in the May 1990 issue of, and is reprinted with permission from, *The World & I*, a publication of the Washington Times Corporation, © 1990.

She's amazing! Last night she and her husband invited your family for dinner. Although she works forty hours a week, volunteers for a teen hotline, is acting president of the PTA, does aerobics, and takes a weekly art appreciation class, she is calm and together. Her house is tidy, her three children are obedient and well-behaved, and she looks great—not a hair out of place.

Contrary to the popular "superstressed modern mom" theory, the more activities a woman opts to involve herself in, the happier, healthier, and more interesting she frequently appears. According to recent surveys, women who play multiple roles (not all of them necessarily professional) feel better physically, have a higher sense of self-esteem, and say they enjoy life more.

Working Mothers Are Happier

In the '50s, married women who pursued a career were rarities. It was a man's world. He headed the family, and his wife was his dependent. In the late '50s, a team of researchers at the University of Michigan's Survey Research Center interviewed more than 2,500 men and women to find out how happy they thought they were. When it came to marriage, more than half of the married people they interviewed said that their unions were unhappy. And almost all of those unhappily married were the women. Most of the men reported that they were extremely satisfied with their marriages.

Several studies indicate that a shift has occurred—that women are, by and large, the happiest people now, especially married women who work outside the home. "Married, employed parents—the busiest women—are in the best physical health," says Lois Verbrugge, research scientist at the University of Michigan. Citing a study of 700 Detroit men and women, she also found the converse true: It was the widowed, unemployed, and childless who were in the poorest of health. Two conclusions were indicated: Either being busy and occupied maintained good health, or good health empowers women to do more in their lives.

In a study of her own, Verbrugge analyzed the health of thousands of women over a period of twenty-five years. Her conclusions showed that the health status of women who did less declined, while that of women involved in many roles showed no such signs.

Two other studies, one of a group of 197 women and another of 96 women, were carried out by researchers at Columbia University's School of Medicine and Boston University's Department of Psychology to explore how women were coping with their life choices. Those who had chosen the multiple roles of wife, mother, and working woman were happiest and healthiest. They seemed to thrive on their busy, stress-filled lives.

Then, in descending order of physical and emotional health, came single working women, married women who stayed at home, and, finally, single women who stayed at home.

Working Men Want More Family Involvement

The contrast between the findings of these surveys of women and those of a survey by the American Management Association of 2,800 top male business executives is striking. A startling number of these men—83 percent of them—reported that they were not happy with their lives. They spoke of wanting a chance for more self-expression, of wishing they could be more involved with their families, of yearning to fulfill their potential.

Working Mothers Are a Positive Influence

Both the daughters and the sons of wage-working mothers have been found to have a more positive view of women and less rigid views of sex roles; the daughters (like their mothers) tend to have greater self-esteem and a more positive view of themselves as workers, and the sons, to expect equality and shared roles in their own future marriages. We might well expect that with mothers in the labor force *and* with fathers as equal parents, children's attitudes and psychologies will become even less correlated with their sex. In a very crucial sense, their opportunities to become the persons they want to be will be enlarged.

Susan Moller Okin, *Justice, Gender, and the Family,* 1989.

In an analysis of this study, psychologist Dr. Joyce Brothers concluded that it was less that these men hated their work than that their work was no longer enough for them. No longer were they willing to be consumed by work. They wanted to be free to channel their energies in other directions that they considered more emotionally rewarding. These top male executives were saying, "There must be more. This is not enough."

In a way, these men are like the wives in the '50s who had embraced homemaking and child rearing with enthusiasm and dedication, only to find they craved more. The pendulum has indeed swung.

Dangers of Underload

But what about the women who complain that they are overworked, overstressed, and can't take it anymore? Rosalind Barnett, senior research associate at Wellesley College's Center of Research on Women, believes the media only focus on isolated stories of women who claim they are overburdened and can't cope. She believes that underload is just as dangerous as overload, meaning that people who have little to do and don't interact with many people are plagued with boredom and lack challenges in their life. That is, having fewer responsibilities may actually cause or exacerbate psychological and physical problems. She says, "Studies prove that the more people do, the better off they are. Not only do they derive health benefits and have variety in their lives, but it is a way of being connected to others and a way to grow and change."

Psychiatrist Dorothy Holmes perceives the difference between the happy busy woman and the miserable busy woman is that the former is truly devoted to her tasks without conflict. Holmes has a full-time practice in Washington, D.C., is associate professor at Howard University's Department of Psychiatry, teaches at the Baltimore-Washington Institute for Psychoanalysis, is married, and is the mother of two daughters. "I've been able to resolve any conflicts that came up and I'm committed to my responsibilities. I love them. They are energizing."

Some women shy away from competition; challenge terrifies them. Others feel that another member of the family is more important than they, so they should sacrifice their interests for them. Still others deny the notion that they deserve to be successful and self-fulfilled. "These people are in conflict and have difficulty being productive," says Holmes. "They usually feel overstressed and unhappy and rationalize their predicament by saying no one can do all the things they are trying to do."

Also, much depends on social and cultural values. If a woman's upbringing tells her that her place is in the home, she may find that developing her potential is difficult. According to Holmes, some women are comfortable with this life-style and can live in this role without conflict; but others may find this way of life uncomfortable and become unhappy, depressed, or alcoholic. Because they are in conflict, they can't be entirely available to their children, their husbands, or even to themselves. A third type of woman determines angrily that she will not give in to what she regards as a sexist stereotype and will substitute the feminist group for the family.

Don't Expect Perfection

There are other reasons women are unable to shoulder a variety of responsibilities. Many try to juggle too many activities. They are often perfectionists and become terribly frustrated. Rae Forker Evans, vice president of International Affairs for Hallmark Cards, also a wife and the mother of two, says, "The art is not in the speed or deftness of juggling but in knowing that it is impossible to keep them all up at once. My husband will say jokingly, 'What hit the floor today?'"

Evans often holds candid discussions with her children. She

will say, "Let's take a moment and talk about what Mommy did today. How could you have helped so we could spend more time together?" She and her husband have set rules in order to try to avoid the tyrannical goal of perfection. Since they were trying to raise children, they decided not to do business entertaining at home. Friday night is family time. And at least one parent is always home each weekday night.

"It's uniformly understood among my friends that the Superwoman myth is a fallacy," Evans says. "We know it's a myth when we see the look on our kids' faces if we miss a kindergarten sing along." She offers one suggestion for the careeraholic Mommy who is going through mid-life crisis: Don't allow yourself to be forced to perfection. . . .

Working Women Are Healthier

Women who work outside the home enjoy better health than women who stay home, according to a long-term study by UC San Diego researchers.

The study showed that working women had significantly lower risk of heart disease, the nation's leading killer of women, than homemakers or women who could not find steady work.

Alan Abrahamson, *Los Angeles Times*, January 28, 1992.

After interviewing dozens of the most eminent women of the past decade for her book *The Successful Woman*, psychologist Joyce Brothers says, "The most important advice I can give a woman when it comes to juggling career and marriage is to put herself first." She emphasizes that this is not being selfish. "When I say 'put yourself first,' I am talking about what psychologist Abraham Maslow called self-actualization: Making the most of yourself and your abilities." Self-actualizers know what they want out of life, feel responsible for both themselves and others, and radiate self-esteem. They are guided by their own standards rather than those of others. They are here-and-now oriented, not there-and-then; they do the very best they can at the moment, while also keeping their longer-term goals in sight. They find life a challenge and a pleasure.

Better Mothers

When asked if women with interests outside the home are better off, Brothers replied, "Not necessarily, if they are getting paid for it. But if they are involved in community work, volunteer work—they become better mothers." Time spent outside the home can renew a woman's sense of vigor and widen her interests, so that she has more to offer her family. If her attention is focused solely on her own family, she may tend to cling too tightly to her children, especially when they're teenagers seeking their own independence.

Positive Attitudes

Patricia Harrison, president of the National Women's Economic Alliance, cofounder of the E. Bruce Harrison public relations firm, mother of three, editor of the book *America's New Women Entrepreneurs*, and member of many service organizations, feels that it is critical to be involved in activities outside the home. But she also recognizes that many women have viable excuses for being overloaded; they may be single parents, have financial burdens, and have no choice in the matter. . . .

Genuine friends, a sense of humor, and a set of priorities other than herself, such as volunteer community work, are the equipment in Harrison's "mental spa." "We wouldn't be as frazzled if we built up the internal parts of ourselves." She also suggests indulging in enjoyable, nonwork-related activities that force you to be alone, because "you should like your own company for more than ten minutes at a time."

If you feel trapped, you will be trapped. It's a self-fulfilling prophecy. Doors don't open until you put your hand on the doorknob. "My life turned around when I stopped whining and complaining," says Harrison. "To be successful, you must give up having people feel sorry for you. Things started looking up when I started to look at things differently." You have to focus, Harrison says, on being the "best person you can in this life."

> "No sitter, no day-care program, no early-childhood-development expert can give our little son what I, his mother, can give."

Working Mothers Harm the Family

Juli Loesch Wiley

There is no child-care system that can replace a mother's care at home, argues Juli Loesch Wiley in the following viewpoint. Full-time maternal care, Wiley believes, best benefits children from infancy through adolescence. She suggests that most mothers work out of choice, not necessity, and that if working mothers really cared for their children, they would quit work and stay at home. Wiley is a free-lance writer based in Johnson City, Tennessee.

As you read, consider the following questions:

1. What do most families actually give up when they choose to live on a single income, according to the author?
2. According to Wiley, how can maternal deprivation affect children?
3. How does Wiley advise women who *want* to work?

Juli Loesch Wiley, "Babies Need Their Mothers at Home," *U.S. Catholic*, August 1990. Reprinted with permission from U.S. Catholic, published by Claretian Publications, 205 W. Monroe St., Chicago, IL 60606.

At my six-week postpartum checkup, the nurse asked me, "Have you gone back to work yet? Or are you still just tending the baby?"

"I'm a full-time nursing mother . . . and . . ." And what? A little defensive?

Do I need to add, ". . . and I do a little writing and speaking"? Perhaps that would establish me as being a *productive* person, not a female underachiever schlepping around the apartment with a baby on my shoulder, not—ah, to put it delicately—a nurturant zombie.

Why is it that putting one's prime time into nurturing one's child is now "the love that dare not speak its name"? Why are so many of my female friends being driven back into the wage-labor market while their children are still very young?

I hear phrases like "today's economic realities," "financial necessity," "getting bills paid"—but it ain't necessarily so. Mona Charen of the *Chicago Tribune* cites statistics showing that middle-class fathers whose wives stay at home with the kids earn about the same salaries as fathers whose wives work.

That means some families are simply choosing to get along with less money so that mama (or papa) can stay home.

Financial Necessity Redefined

As a first-time mother, I don't have enough experience to be a Great Authority; and my own life is such a fracas that I'm in no position to tell other women how to run their lives. But I've seen time and time again that when women like me opt for working and day-care centers, it's not, *in most cases*, dictated by outright financial necessity. We do have choices.

The family budget is as much a moral document as a papal encyclical. And you can choose two cars, a high mortgage, a certain amount of regular splurging on clothes and food and entertainment—on two incomes, of course—or you can choose one income and mothering.

My husband and I are, I recently discovered, officially in the "bottom third": the 30 percent of U.S. families with kids who get by on an income of less than $20,000. One paycheck.

That means that, for the time being, we're renting small instead of buying big. We go in for banjo, not video. We select the cheaper cuts of macaroni. It's the life we've chosen. Why?

Maybe an old ad jingle will make it clear. Remember the Nestlé's Chocolate tune? Our version of it goes like this:

M-O-T-H-E-R-S
Mothers make the very best
MI-ILK.

It's also important for nonnursing mothers to stay at home with their babies; but, in many ways, my decision to nurse our baby is the central fact in our decision for me to be a stay-at-home mother. No sitter, no day-care program, no early-childhood-development expert can give our little son what I, his mother, can give: optimal nourishment, intimate observation, and consistent, round-the-clock, loving discipline.

© Schwadron/Rothco. Reprinted with permission.

It goes beyond breast-feeding; but that's, so to speak, the main course. Mother's milk is like Chinese food: my baby stuffs himself, and in an hour or two he's hungry again. Because of the frequency and intimacy of contact between a nursling and his or her mother, an irreplaceable relationship blossoms that forms the basis of all subsequent training, teaching, and caring.

Some of my friends who go off to jobs and who are away from their babies eight or ten hours every day say that what little ones need is quality time. Right. As Mary Ann Cahill of La Leche League says, kids do need quality time: large quantities of it.

Research Confirms Need for Mother's Care

Even academia—the Harvard research under Dr. Burton White—acknowledges the importance of a full-time mother in a child's first two or three years for his or her optimal emotional development. Dr. John Bowlby's book, *Separation*, goes into the greatest detail describing the sometimes psychopathic effects on a child when prematurely separated from his or her mother.

It's something Sigmund's psychoanalyst daughter Dr. Anna Freud discovered decades ago when she started a nursery for babies and toddlers in England. As she became increasingly aware of the destructive effects of maternal deprivation—psychosomatic illnesses; grieving behavior; and emotional disturbances, such as withdrawal and aggression—she concluded that it would be better for each of her staff to take a couple of kids home and close the nursery.

Inadequate Substitutes

Every mother knows in her heart that her little child's intense need to be with her is as basic as his or her need for food.

If you had a busy life and felt you weren't spending enough time with your husband, would you go out and hire another woman to love him for you?

Okay, it's a ridiculous question. But isn't that what a lot of mothers are doing to their kids? As one mother told me, "I saw Natalie (a neighbor who tended her toddler during the day) become the real 'mommy' while I was just the evenings-and-weekends 'baby-sitter.' We were all unhappy about it."

What did she do?

"I talked to my husband about it, we refinanced our major bills, and—we took the plunge. I quit my job.

"Sometimes," she admits, "it feels almost self-indulgent to have the pleasure of raising my own child. And it's hard work—but I know it's right. I'm glad I 'let myself' do it."

So far I've been writing about the little kids. What about older children? Does mama have to be there constantly until the son or daughter is accepted into graduate school?

It's hardly that bad. Most families find that if they allow children to be children—to be dependent, even clingy—when they are 2 or 3, by the time they're 4 or 5 they'll be secure enough to be friendly and outgoing. Kids who were unstintingly mothered through toddlerhood are more likely to be leaders in school, both more sociable and less peer-dependent.

But older kids still need their parents—plenty. And I would urge both mothers and fathers to reassess their job commitments periodically right up through their kids' teenage years to see whether they are helping or hindering a close, hands-on relationship with their children.

Professions Versus Vocations

I don't think that full-time mothering of young children is inconsistent with women's high achievement in every other field.

Sandra Day O'Connor will be remembered in history as the first woman on the Supreme Court. What is equally important is that when her children were young, she stepped back from her law career to concentrate on being a mother. Obviously her time away from law did not limit her ultimate job opportunities.

The Wisdom of Sequencing

Women can have it all—but not all at the same time. As we roll into the 21st century, millions of women will learn the wisdom of sequencing—organizing their lives so that they can move in and out of the paid-labor market and enjoy being full-time mothers in the years when such mothering is irreplaceable.

Opportunities are expanding, too, for remunerative work within the home. The traditional women's home industries—child care, music instruction, needlework, crafts, catering, and running typing services—are still excellent choices. They can provide significant income and an outlet for creativity while fitting in well with home living.

The linkup of telephone and computer technology provides even more extensive possibilities for home employment. Editing and publishing, marketing and sales, research, journalism, technical design, real estate and financial transactions, and even many management functions can be done at home with the aid of a modem and a home computer.

Every kind of profession is now, thank God, open to women. But there is one vocation—one relationship—in which a woman is not only valuable but virtually irreplaceable: the nurturing of the physical, intellectual, and spiritual development of her own precious sons and daughters.

Yes, I'm still "just tending the baby." Because mothers make the very best mothers.

"The 'profamily workplace' is gaining ground in boardrooms around the nation."

Businesses Are Meeting the Needs of Two-Career Parents

Sylvia Ann Hewlett

In the following viewpoint, Sylvia Ann Hewlett argues that businesses are faced with labor shortages and increased competition in the 1990s, and so must attract workers and increase productivity. In order to accomplish these goals, businesses are initiating policies such as child-care benefits that help both employees and management, she states. Hewlett, an economist and author, writes and lectures on work and family issues with a focus on child welfare.

As you read, consider the following questions:

1. How do the stresses of two-income families affect business, according to the author?
2. How do employers benefit from family-support programs, according to Hewlett?
3. What criticism does Hewlett level at corporate emergency child-care centers?

Adapted from "Good News? The Private Sector and Win-Win Scenarios" by Sylvia Ann Hewlett, in *Rebuilding the Nest: A New Commitment to the American Family*, David Blankenhorn, Steven Bayme, and Jean Bethke Elshtain, eds. Milwaukee: Family Service America, Inc., 1990. Reprinted with permission.

Once upon a time, women anchored a domestic and familial support system that enabled male breadwinners to focus on their jobs for at least 40 hours a week. They raised the children, looked after the house, took the clothes to the dry cleaner, and visited Grandma in the hospital. This home-based support system began to recede a generation ago and is now more the exception than the rule. Seventy percent of women with children between the ages of 6 and 17 are now in the labor force, either full or part time, as are more than half of women with children younger than one year old.

This new reality has produced enormous stress in family life. Almost every day, working parents are faced with wrenching dilemmas: Who will take care of the three-year-old who is running a temperature? Can the seven-year-old be trusted to look after herself between 3:30 and 6:00 P.M.? Who will let the plumber in so that the leak in the bathroom can finally be fixed?

For employers, these stresses translate into lower productivity, poor concentration on the job, high rates of absenteeism, and increased labor turnover. It is very easy for worries about a latchkey child or a bedridden parent to get in the way of an employee giving his or her best energy to the job. For individual working parents, particularly women, these strains translate into costly career interruptions and lower lifetime earnings.

The Corporate Bottom Line

These are the demographic facts of life of the 1990s: prospective labor shortages with burgeoning numbers of overburdened working parents. It should come as no surprise that the evidence is mounting that an employer's family-support policies directly affect the corporate bottom line. One of the best-documented studies is the National Employer Supported Childcare Project, a nationwide study of 415 industrial, service-sector, and governmental organizations. In this report employers highlight the following "payoffs" to family benefits: improved recruitment (cited by 85% of the respondents in this project and ranked as the most important benefit in virtually all studies); reduced turnover (65%); reduced absenteeism (53%); increased productivity (49%); and enhanced company image (85%). Harder-to-quantify improvements were also reported in such areas as morale, loyalty to firm, and reduced tardiness. To illustrate, consider a few of the companies that have analyzed in detail the costs and benefits of specific family-support policies.

Merck & Company has demonstrated impressive returns to its parenting-leave policy. The price tag attached to replacing an employee at this large pharmaceutical firm is $50,000. But by permitting a new parent to take a generous six-month child-care leave—at a cost of $38,000, which includes partial pay, benefits, and other indirect costs—the company succeeds in retaining almost all of its new-mother employees and, in so doing, achieves a net savings of $12,000 per employee. In addition to its parenting-leave policy, Merck offers a child-care center, child-care referral services, and a flexible time option that has increased productivity up to 20% in some departments. . . .

Johnson & Johnson

In early 1989, Johnson & Johnson announced an extremely broad work-and-family initiative that builds upon earlier, more modest company programs in this area. The expanded program includes family-care leave (up to one year of unpaid leave with benefits and job-back guarantees), resource and referral services for child and eldercare, dependent-care accounts (to make it possible for employees to pay for child care on a pretax basis), adoption benefits, flexible benefits programs (to allow individualized family coverage), flexible hours, a compressed work week, and on-site child care.

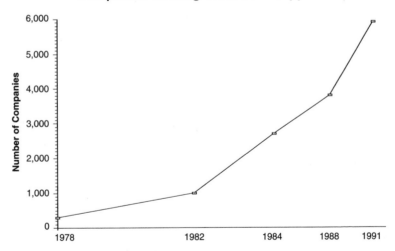

Companies Offering Child-Care Support

Source: Families and Work Institute, 1991.

The enhanced program at Johnson & Johnson was prompted by an in-house study that showed the proportion of women workers at the company rising from 51% in 1989 to 60% at the turn of the century. According to this study, prepared by a task force of senior managers, family supports are increasingly needed if the company is "to attract and retain the top-quality employees it needs to remain competitive."

For more than a decade, IBM has steadily increased its efforts to adapt to family needs. In the early 1980s it pioneered child-care and eldercare assistance programs. A national resource and referral network put together by IBM in 1984 now serves 900,000 employees in more than 25 companies. Today, most employees have the option of beginning or ending their working day an hour earlier or later.

In addition, IBM employees, 30% of whom are women, can take a three-year break from full-time employment—with part-time work available in the second and third year—to care for young children or elderly relatives. With the exception of the part-time component, this "career break" is unpaid, but health and retirement benefits continue while workers are on leave and IBM guarantees a full-time job at the end of the three-year period. More recently the company has added work-at-home options and has also introduced family-issues sensitivity training for more than 25,000 managers and supervisors.

Other Corporate Initiatives

AT&T recently negotiated a contract with two of its unions that establishes a dependent-care referral service and provides for leaves of up to one year, with job-back guarantees, for new parents and for workers with seriously ill dependents. Apple Computer operates its own employee-staffed child-care center and gives "baby bonuses" of $500 to new parents. In 1989 Allstate Insurance Company created a new package of family-support policies called "Work and Family Connections." The package includes special (pretax) employee spending accounts for dependent care, family-illness allowances, and options for job sharing, part-time, and flexible work schedules. DuPont has helped to establish child-care centers in Delaware with contributions of money and space. Eastman Kodak has adopted new rules permitting part-time work, job sharing, and informal, situational flextime. For reasons that are economic and strategic, "these and scores of other businesses are building work environments that let people give their best to their jobs without giving up the pleasures and responsibilities of family life."

Family-support policies can boost productivity for working dads as well as working moms. Both DuPont and AT&T report that male workers are experiencing significant and increasing child-care problems that affect job performance. Surveys at the Los Angeles Department of Water and Power have uncovered the fact that male employees have even more problems with child care than do female employees. According to this company, these "father-oriented" child-care problems are expensive, costing more than $1 million in absenteeism during 1987.

Given this kind of data, it comes as no surprise that the "pro-family workplace" is gaining ground in boardrooms around the nation. According to the Conference Board, as of January 1990, close to 5,000 employers had some kind of systematic child-care and parenting assistance as part of their benefits package, up from 600 in 1982. Dana Friedman, Co-President of the Families and Work Institute, describes recent progress as "phenomenal, particularly since the new initiatives comprise a complete package rather than a token policy or two." Companies are increasingly offering a range of family supports: parenting leave, child care, eldercare, at-home and part-time work, flexible hours, and job sharing. As one analyst has put it, "Enlightened executives see family-sensitive policies as giving them a competitive edge in the tight labor markets of the 1990s. . . . Firms slower to react will pay a price" in that they will fail to attract or keep high-quality workers, thus creating built-in obstacles to profits and growth.

In sum, as we move into the 1990s, the pressure on firms is building. Employees' demand for a family-friendly workplace is clearly growing as working parents are empowered by labor shortages. It now makes economic sense for business to recognize that their employees are also family members. . . .

The Family Bottom Line

From the perspective of family well-being, what does all of this corporate activity amount to? The corporate bottom line and the family bottom line are two distinctive notions of what is ultimately important. They may at times overlap, but they are not identical. For example, if the new corporate policies will enhance both corporate productivity and female earning power, will they also contribute to the well-being of children and the quality of family life? Can the new workplace flexibilities actually ease the strain that permeates the lives of so many employed parents and their children?. . .

What does a family-friendly workplace mean for the well-being of children?

Most corporate supports for working parents do promote the interests of the child. The generous parenting-leave policies of companies such as Merck and Johnson & Johnson make an important difference in the critical first months of life. Job sharing, part-time work, compressed work weeks, staggered hours—all those flexible options now offered by companies such as American Express and IBM—are clearly good for children in that they free parents to spend more and better time with their children. Mothers working full time can experience so much stress in their daily lives that "quality time" for the children seems like a bad joke.

Finally, on-site child care, or subsidies that permit a parent to opt for higher-quality child care, can upgrade the quality of out-of-home care available to children. This is clearly a step in the right direction. Today, many parents are forced to put their infants or toddlers in third-rate, unlicensed, and even dangerous day care because they simply cannot afford anything better.

Possible Negative Effects

But we shouldn't fool ourselves that the interests of the working parent—or the interests of the corporation—are identical to those of the child. Some working parents may be more interested in getting promoted than spending time with little Johnny. Moreover, companies are mostly interested in easing the lives of working parents so that these employees can devote more "quality time" to the firm. For quite understandable reasons, corporate America is more interested in better workers than it is in better spouses or parents.

More Women in the Work Force

The last 20 years have brought dramatic shifts in the American workplace as women make up larger and larger proportions of the work force. This trend is expected only to intensify; in fact, for the remainder of the twentieth century, the majority of new entrants into the work force will be women. This development—coupled with the cultural trends towards fathers' greater involvement in child rearing and the aging of the American population, with more and more older Americans requiring care from their younger relatives—demands that the workplace respond to the changing needs of its workers. The future efficiency of our work force depends upon our willingness and ability to confront these changes.

Barbara Blum, Statement made during hearings held before the Subcommitte on Children, Families, Drugs and Alcoholism of the Senate Labor and Human Resources Committee, January 24, 1991.

Because of this divergence of interest, at least some of the new corporate policies, even those labeled "family supports," are not particularly good for children. A few may actually harm them. For example, out-of-home emergency or sick care for children might reduce absenteeism for the firm and boost earning power for the individual working parent, but such a solution may seem singularly unattractive to a child who wants to be home with Mom or Dad.

[In 1989] Wilmer, Cutler & Pickering, a prominent Washington law firm, set up an on-site child-care center for emergencies—times when a child is sick or a regular babysitter fails to turn up. Despite the fact that this facility proved to be expensive (start-up costs were in the $300,000 range), the law firm expects the center to more than pay for itself. The reason is that (high-priced) female lawyers are now much more available to work late into the night and on weekends.

This idea makes sense for Wilmer, Cutler & Pickering. It may even make sense for individual women lawyers, who are freer to work toward partnerships by logging 14-hour workdays, just like their male colleagues. But even if the center has a cute name and is described as a "family support," is it actually good for the children, who now spend even less time with their mothers?

Edward Zigler, Professor of Psychology at Yale University and long-time children's advocate, has problems with these kinds of emergency arrangements. He points out that children who are ill often want to be with their parents, not with strangers. "Over the long term," Zigler says, "we need a solution like the one in Sweden where mothers have a certain number of days off when their children are sick."

Increase Time Together

Time is the crucial issue here—or more specifically, what one analyst calls "the family time famine." Parents today are working more and spending less time with their children and with each other. According to one estimate, the amount of total contact parents have with their children has dropped 40% since 1965. According to a survey commissioned by Massachusetts Mutual Life Insurance Company, Americans today believe that "parents having less time to spend with their families" is the most important cause of fragmentation and stress in contemporary family life.

Accordingly, new corporate policies that empower parents to spend more time with their families are truly "pro-family" and in the best interests of children. The same cannot be said, however, of those new policies—sick-child care being one example—that seek solely to free parents from parental obligations so that they can spend more, not less, of their time and energy at work.

Yet despite this important qualification, it does seem that most of the new policies . . . are genuinely win-win scenarios: good for the company, good for the worker, good for family life. By the end of the century it is very likely that business will be reaching out to help up to half of all working parents in this country, and in most cases this help will also improve the life prospects for children. The looming labor shortage has tilted the balance of power in society toward skilled labor. Working parents, particularly mothers, are prime beneficiaries of this shift.

"An inflexible and traditional workplace has become a significant factor in creating dysfunctional families."

Businesses Are Not Meeting the Needs of Two-Career Parents

Jan Fletcher

In the following viewpoint, Jan Fletcher argues that expanded child care and flexible work schedules are cosmetic reforms that enable business to operate as usual while ignoring the real needs of families. She advocates more radical policies that give working parents discretion to enter and leave the work force as needed, and she believes parents will work harder to keep companies profitable when they are given such extra flexibility. Fletcher, a mother of three, owns and runs a publishing business from her home in Seattle, Washington.

As you read, consider the following questions:

1. Why does Fletcher believe flextime is not beneficial to families?
2. According to the author, why should benefit packages be extended to all workers regardless of the number of hours they work?
3. How can workers encourage their companies to initiate reforms, according to Fletcher?

Jan Fletcher, "The Common Covenant," *Mothering*, Summer 1989. Reprinted with permission.

The impact of the workplace on families is generating a great deal of concern, and for good reason. As we enter the nineties, the stress on families trying to cope with an inflexible and traditional workplace has become a significant factor in creating dysfunctional families.

As one of many factors currently challenging families, the impact of business was a topic discussed during a three-day conference in November 1988 in Baltimore, Maryland. The "Families in the Nineties" conference brought together 80 participants from various cultural sectors to brainstorm on ways to help our social institutions become more responsive to family needs. I attended the program, with particular interest in ways to help businesses create a more supportive atmosphere for families.

During the conference, my fellow "brainstormers" and I agreed that business is making changes to accommodate families. Some of these changes—such as more opportunities for telecommuters, more job-sharing openings, and more part-time professional positions—appear to be positive and helpful to families. But other changes may well be detrimental in the long run. More and more corporations and midsize companies, for example, are offering workers on-site child care and flexitime. Because these innovations contain inherent hazards and because they represent a major policy decision within corporate America and the federal government, they pose a serious threat to family cohesion and health.

The Hidden Costs of Child Care and Flexitime

On the surface, both on-site child care and flexitime appear to be welcome changes. After all, for two-income families in which both parents work full-time away from home quality child care is a major concern. And for parents overwhelmed by the many scheduling conflicts inherent in family and workplace life, the ability to work flexible hours adds a sense of relief.

In reality, however, these changes are merely concessions offered to keep talented, committed workers in the traditional workplace and to soothe pressure groups who are now crying out for more and better quality child-care provisions. These pressure groups provide significant amounts of drumbeating. An editorial by Joan Beck, columnist for the *Chicago Tribune*, refers to President Bush's proposal of a child-care credit for low income families, with this observation: "At least Bush didn't sign on to that simplistic and worrisome equation that support for families equals more daycare. It takes political courage not to fall into that trap. And the pressures on the president and Congress are getting harder to resist."

Flexitime, as it turns out, is more beneficial for singles—workers without family considerations. This way, they can avoid traffic jams, have early afternoons or late mornings for personal errands, and still manage to cope with a 40-hour work week. For families, flexitime within the context of a 40-hour work week means a demanding schedule with little time left over for family activities. A workday that starts or ends at a different time does not create more time for family togetherness.

No Support for Dads

A survey by Catalyst, a New York-based research group, showed that 114 companies offered unpaid leave to new fathers. But when those companies were asked what amount of time is reasonable for fathers to take off, 41 percent said men shouldn't take off any time.

Cindy Skrzycki, *The Washington Post National Weekly Edition,* November 26- December 2, 1990.

We now face a workplace of the future in which institutionalized child care and flexitime may be accepted standards. Here, children will be warehoused on-site or in nearby federally funded centers so their parents can continue to work a structured 40-hour week. New parents may encounter mounting pressure to use the company daycare facility and quickly return to full-time work after the birth of their baby. Harried parents will continue to fit 40 hours of work within one week through "flexible hours." And scheduling a family's workday activities will continue to be an exercise in true frustration.

Fundamental Policy Change Is Needed

What makes this scenario so threatening to families is precisely what makes it such an enticing alternative for business. Whereas businesses can appear very generous and profamily by instituting these changes, in reality they leave the underlying structured workplace intact. *Innovations such as these do not require firms to alter their basic corporate philosophy in fundamental ways.*

What is needed is more than a cosmetic change—more than quick solutions that temporarily cure the immediate child-care crisis or the workers' scheduling conflicts. What is needed is a true challenge to business: deep and far-reaching changes in the corporate culture. Only fundamental alterations can facilitate the creation of a workplace that is truly supportive of family needs.

Joan Beck offers practical alternatives: "finding solutions other than getting children out of the way might do more to strengthen families than all the day-care bills in Congress. . . . Employers could well be pushed to help keep young parents on career paths while they spend more time with children during their earliest years. Better part-time jobs, shared jobs, at-home work options, flexible hours, stretched-out qualifying periods, extended leaves and reentry programs are all options that are cost-effective to employers."

Building a Common Covenant

Profound resistance to child-care programs and flexitime is only a small step into a healthier future. Society must go further—much further. Businesses and families must develop a new common covenant: a recognition that we are partners, not adversaries, in a complex economic pact. We can no longer take our mutual interdependence for granted. Indeed, we are now entering an age in which what is good for one is good for the other, and what is harmful to one is ultimately harmful to the other.

Developing a common covenant requires both employers and employees to recognize several outdated assumptions and learn new ways of relating to each other. Assumptions that have arisen from 200 years of industrial-age living are counterproductive in today's world. Workers can no longer be seen in terms of production units.

The assumptions that are particularly harmful to families and parents include the following:

• Workers can and should be measured solely by objective criteria: how much formal education they have had, how many on-the-job credentials they have earned, how fast and effectively they have performed on measured tasks, how much on-the-job time they have logged in.

• Business is primarily about competition and operates in a win-lose fashion.

• Only full-time, permanent workers are dependable and dedicated to job performance and should be granted a full constellation of benefits and consideration in job advancement.

• Productive work occurs only within the context of a static structure. Workers cannot be fully productive if they work in an on-again, off-again sporadic manner, dropping in and out of the work force at will, and work cannot be truly efficient if children are present in the work environment. (Until recently, sex segregation and race segregation existed side by side with this form of age segregation in the workplace.)

• Most work takes place in the context of private, for-profit enterprise.

Rebuilding a workplace that both "works" in a profit-based economy and also supports the commitment to family nurturing involves replacing these outdated assumptions with a new vision based on mutual trust and a recognition of joint limitations and strengths. Here are some new, more functional replacements:

162

• *People have many life skills that can be evaluated comprehensively but perhaps not measured objectively.* Home learning, nurturing children, running a household, and time spent off-the-job have an important bearing on work performance and can therefore be considered in hiring and promotion decisions. Furthermore, methods of evaluating work can go beyond mathematical assessment and be based instead on a human resource model.

• *Cooperation, not competition, is the deciding factor in success.* For many businesses, the future will bring massive changes in information flow, in management's relationship with employees and consumers, and in the company's role in a community that works together to resolve specific problems. Consequently, businesses will need to work cooperatively with government, communities, consumers, and one another to foster win-win situations.

Response Is Mediocre

How good a job is corporate USA doing to help its employees balance work and family?

Just mediocre, according to a study released in November 1991 by the Families and Work Institute, a New York organization that promotes corporate work-family programs such as flexible schedules, job sharing and child-care help. . . .

• One-third of companies have few policies and aren't aware of the issues.

• 46% have some policies but still view work-family concerns as women's issues, with child care as the main focus.

• 19% have expanded their focus from child care to other issues. But some employees fear that taking advantage of an official policy will hurt them. Up to 40% say managers allow some employees more leeway than others.

Julia Lawlor, *USA Today*, November 15, 1991.

• *All workers are worthy of a basic benefit package, regardless of the number of hours worked or how those hours are arranged within a given work period.* Because a worker's performance, contribution, and commitment are not related to the time spent at the task, the benefits need not reflect a reward system, but rather a means of protection. A benefit package can be considered a basic expense of doing business—just like paying taxes or obtaining a business license.

• *Productive work occurs in a fluid environment.* A work force that utilizes frequent leave-taking, flexible part-time hours, and age integration can be most productive, and what makes it happen is a human resource management task. The skills needed by managers serving in this capacity are less focused on worker-unit pro-

163

duction and task management and more focused on people as re-sources to be effectively managed within a fluid context of changing hours and personal priorities. This arrangement can offer unseen benefits for small companies. In a March 1989 interview, Pat Farenga, manager of Holt Associates and editor of *Growing Without Schooling*, acknowledged the ability to recruit staff members with compatible interests by offering flexible working conditions: "Being a small company, we don't have a lot of amenities to offer, but we can offer control over your time, which you don't get when you work for a lot of other companies. That's why the whole flextime issue has been one of the saving graces, because we've been able to hire homeschooling parents."

• *Work takes place in a variety of contexts.* A large segment of our society's paid employment is provided by governmental bodies and nonprofit institutions. Another large segment is employed by very small firms (five or fewer employees). Many other workers are self-employed or work as private contractors. As a result, care should be taken to look beyond the "big business" model when forming a common covenant.

Changing Attitudes Is Difficult

Effective changes in the workplace require, first and foremost, effective changes in attitude. Before taking action, we need to step back, look carefully at the frustrations shared by businesses and parent employees, and find nonharmful ways of resolving the difficulties.

More and more businesses, for example, are now offering truly flexible alternatives such as job-sharing, telecommuting, or part-time positions with benefits. However, many employees hesitate to take these opportunities because they fear being stigmatized. Along with their coworkers and bosses, these employees are operating under the assumption that flexible workers are not committed to their jobs. To effectively transform the workplace, we must first transform these destructive attitudes.

Changing these attitudes may not be easy. In *The Responsive Workplace*, Sheila B. Kamerman and Alfred J. Kahn elicited this insightful response from a high-level executive: "It's not the rules we lay down; it's the signals we give employees that really make a difference. This is especially important for family issues in the corporate context. . . . Whether or not middle and lower level managers are carrying out such policies [showing more responsibility toward the problems and needs of employees] should be part of the criteria by which they are evaluated." He also noted that the commitment to policies supporting a changed work force "may be formal, but not deep."

Stepping back, we can see that the greatest common frustration is the profound tendency of current business practices to "get in the way" of family togetherness. How do we go about resolving this difficulty? Do we try to bend business to a socialistic viewpoint, in which employers become even more paternalistic? Or do we advocate simple, inexpensive, and even profitable policies that prevent the workplace from being so intrusive in family life?

Family and Work Spheres Are Merging

One way to resolve the dilemma is to understand how our corporate culture evolved. In the past, the work force operated in one sphere of life while women, children, and the elderly operated in another, taking care of each other during the workday. Family time took place after work hours, was of lesser importance, and was expected to be intruded upon freely should the need arise. We must now challenge the validity of this corporate premise. Work does not occur in a vacuum, and workers are people with full and complex lives.

Corporate Policy Should Support Child Care

As I see it, the challenge we in the corporate world face—is *how* do we *balance* our needs for a skilled labor force with our employee's personal needs.

As women enter the workforce in ever-increasing numbers, childcare will become even more important to a company's ability to compete.

We will no longer be able to afford to tell a large segment of our working age population to stay at home and watch after the children.

Stephen E. Ewing, *Vital Speeches of the Day*, June 15, 1990.

Business policies that do not honor this reality can only continue to isolate the business sphere, frustrate workers, and wreak havoc on family life. We can go a long way toward a healthier workplace by developing policies that are not punitive toward family members and yet do not impose a hardship on business. Here are some specific policy changes that can be adapted to a variety of business models:

• Develop job applications and performance evaluations that take into account not only job experience and formal education, but also life experience.

• When possible, convert job performance evaluations from a time-based measurement to an end-product measurement.

• Involve workers and their families in "extracurricular" company activities, and make a special effort to include off-site and telecommuting workers and their families as well.

• Encourage personnel managers to adopt a flexible, nonpunitive approach toward workers requesting unusual hours, temporary leaves, and reentries due to personal needs.

• Offer workers requiring great flexibility the option of being private contractors working in their homes, and give these "freelance employees" preferential consideration when awarding company contracts.

• Sponsor entrepreneurial community activities to generate a local pool of private contractual talent that can be drawn upon to fulfill human resource needs. Small businesses might cosponsor activities or classes on running a small business, on bidding procedures, or on forming a support network of independent workers.

• Sponsor a number of employees or a number of hours for one employee to take on a community service role for a limited time.

• Recognize that workers are committed to their jobs regardless of their personal decision to use or not use available work options within the company, including corporate childcare or flexitime options.

Family Policies Do Not Penalize Business

Employees and employers are partners in any equation that brings about effective and constructive change for families. Employees can help create a more viable workplace by thinking carefully before making suggestions, realizing that rebuilding the workplace requires a mutual commitment. When employees respect the company's bottom line and fiscal health and consider cost effectiveness of various workplace options, their suggestions will be given much more merit by employers. Bruce O'Hara, founder of Canada's first Work Options Resource Center, offers this advice: "Employers often fear that nonstandard work schedules will cost them money. Itemizing costs and potential savings usually makes it clear that the expense involved is manageable."

Employers can instigate change by understanding the long-term implications of *not* rebuilding the workplace. The ultimate health and productivity of the future generation of workers—today's children—absolutely depend upon the current workplace environment. It is the task of business to reinforce the central importance of strong and healthy families.

"The short supply of high-quality day care is the greatest obstacle to better prospects for America's children."

More Day Care Is Needed to Support Two-Career Couples

Kenneth Labich

Increasing numbers of women in the labor force are a fact of life, argues Kenneth Labich in the following viewpoint, and it is unrealistic to expect women to stop work to raise children. Labich believes business must help families solve the child-care shortage crisis by expanding on-site day-care programs, subsidizing community child-care centers, and improving referral networks to help parents find alternative high-quality care. Labich is a member of the board of editors of *Fortune* magazine.

As you read, consider the following questions:

1. According to the author, how can day care benefit the infants and toddlers of working mothers?
2. What is the increased risk of alcohol and drug abuse by latchkey children, according to Labich?
3. What three criteria are necessary for high-quality day care, according to the author?

Because children are the future, America could be headed for bad bumps down the road. Some of the symptoms are familiar—rising teenage suicides and juvenile arrest rates, average SAT scores lower than 30 years ago. But what is the disease festering beneath that disturbing surface? Says Alice A. White, a clinical social worker who has been counseling troubled children in Chicago's prosperous North Shore suburbs for nearly two decades: "I'm seeing a lot more emptiness, a lack of ability to attach, no sense of real pleasure. I'm not sure a lot of these kids are going to be effective adults."

Not all children, or even most of them, are suffering from such a crisis of the spirit. In fact, some trends are headed in a promising direction. For example, drug use among young people has fallen sharply since the 1970s. But a certain malaise does seem to be spreading. Far more and far earlier than ever before, kids are pressured to take drugs, have sex, deal with violence. In a world ever more competitive and complex, the path to social and economic success was never more obscure.

And fewer traditional pathfinders are there to show the way. Divorce has robbed millions of kids of at least one full-time parent. With more and more women joining the work force, and many workaholic parents of both sexes, children are increasingly left in the care of others or allowed to fend for themselves. According to a University of Maryland study, in 1985 American parents spent on average just 17 hours a week with their children.

A Patchwork System of Child Care

This parental neglect would be less damaging if better alternatives were widely available, but that is decidedly not the case. Families that can afford individual child care often get good value, but the luxury of a compassionate, full-time, $250-a-week nanny to watch over their pride and joy is beyond the reach of most American parents. They confront a patchwork system of informal home arrangements and more structured day care centers. In far too many cases, parents with infants or toddlers cannot feel secure about the care their children get. Says Edward Zigler, a professor of child development at Yale, who has spent much of his career fighting the abuses of child care: "We are cannibalizing children. Children are dying in this system, never mind achieving optimum development."

For older children with no parental overseer, the prospects can be equally bleak. Studies are beginning to show that preteens and teenagers left alone after school, so-called latchkey children, may be far more prone than other kids to get involved with alcohol and illegal drugs.

For some experts in the field, the answer to all this is to roll back the clock to an idyllic past. Mom, dressed in a frilly apron, is merrily stirring the stew when Dad gets home from work. Junior, an Eagle Scout, and Sally—they call her Muffin—greet him with radiant smiles. Everybody sits down for dinner to talk about schoolwork and Mom's canasta party.

For others more in touch with the economic temper of the times—especially the financial realities behind the rising number of working mothers—the solution lies in improving the choices available to parents. Government initiatives to provide some financial relief may help, but corporations could make an even greater difference by focusing on the needs of employees who happen to be parents. Such big companies as IBM and Johnson & Johnson have taken the lead in dealing with employee child care problems, and many progressive corporations are discovering the benefits of greater flexibility with regard to family issues. At the same time, an array of professional child care organizations has sprung up to help big corporations meet their employees' demands.

Satisfaction with Day Care Is High

The most comprehensive survey of the child-care market since the mid-1970s found that employed mothers of preschool children are, for the first time, likelier to place their children in a center than to use any other child-care option. Nine parents out of 10 reported they are satisfied with their child-care arrangements, the survey found.

"That's tremendous news and it tells us that the best policy is to continue to provide access to a wide range of child-care options," says Wade F. Horn, commissioner for children, youth and families in the Department of Health and Human Services, which funded the survey along with the Department of Education and the National Association for the Education of Young Children, a private, nonprofit group.

Paul Taylor, *The Washington Post National Weekly Edition,* November 25-December 1, 1991.

Without doubt, helping improve child care is in the best interest of business—today's children, after all, are tomorrow's labor pool. Says Sandra Kessler Hamburg, director of education studies at the Committee for Economic Development, a New York research group that funnels corporate funds into education projects: "We can only guess at the damage being done to very young children right now. From the perspective of American business, that is very, very disturbing. As jobs get more and more technical, the U.S. work force is less and less prepared to handle them."

The state of America's children is a political mine field, and threading through the research entails a lot of gingerly probing as well as the occasional explosion. Much work in the field is contradictory, and many additional longer-range studies need to be done before anyone can say precisely what is happening.

Moreover, any researcher who dwells on the problems of child care—of infants in particular—risks being labeled antiprogressive by the liberal academic establishment. If the researcher happens to be male, his motives may seem suspect. If he says babies are at risk in some child care settings, he may be accused of harboring the wish that women leave the work force and return to the kitchen. Much valid research may be totally ignored because it has been deemed politically incorrect.

Child-Care Studies

For example: Jay Belsky, a Penn State professor specializing in child development, set off a firestorm in 1986 with an article in *Zero to Three*, an influential journal that summarizes existing academic research. His conclusions point to possible risks for very small children in day care outside the home. Though he scrupulously threw in a slew of caveats and even went so far as to confess a possible bias because his own wife stayed home with their two children, Belsky came under heavy attack. Feminist researchers called his scholarship into question. Says Belsky: "I was flabbergasted by the response. I felt like the messenger who got shot."

Belsky's critics charged, among other things, that he had ignored studies that document some more positive results from infant day care. Since then, for example, a study conducted by researchers at the University of Illinois and Trinity College in Hartford, Connecticut, found that a child's intellectual development may actually be helped during the second and third years of life if the mother works. The study, which tracked a nationwide sample of 874 children from ages 3 to 4, determined that the mental skills of infants in child care outside the home were lower than those of kids watched over by their mothers during the first year, but then picked up enough at ages 2 and 3 to balance out.

Whatever the merits of his critics' assault, Belsky presents a disturbing picture of the effects on infants of nonparental child care outside the home. In a 1980 study he cited in the article, involving low-income women in the Minneapolis-St. Paul area, infants in day care were disproportionately likely to avoid looking at or approaching their mothers after being separated from them for a brief period.

Another study, conducted in 1974, concluded that 1-year-olds in day care cried more when separated from their mothers than those reared at home; still another, in 1981, found that day care infants threw more temper tantrums. To at least some extent, the observations seemed to apply across socioeconomic boundaries. A 1985 University of Illinois study of infants from affluent Chicago families showed that babies in the care of full-time nannies avoided any sort of contact with their mothers more often than those raised by moms during their first year.

An infant's attachment, or lack of it, to the mother is especially crucial because it can portend later developmental problems. In the Minnesota study, toddlers who had been in day care early on displayed less enthusiasm when confronted with a challenging task. They were less likely to follow their mothers' instructions and less persistent in dealing with a difficult problem. Another study, which took a look at virtually all 2-year-olds on the island of Bermuda, found more poorly adjusted children among the early day care group regardless of race, IQ, or socioeconomic status. . . .

Quality of Care Is Critical

What we should take away from the research, says an unrepentant Belsky, is this: "There is an accumulating body of evidence that children who were cared for by people other than their parents for 20 or more hours per week during their first year are at increased risk of having an insecure relationship with their parents at age 1—and at increased risk of being more aggressive and disobedient by age 3 to 8."

Belsky adds several "absolutely necessary caveats": First, the results of all these studies must be viewed in light of the added stress that many families experience when both parents work and of the fact that affordable high-quality day care is not always available. Belsky agrees with some of his academic opponents that the quality of day care matters. His second warning: The results of these studies are generalizations and do not apply to every single child. Third, he says, nobody really knows what causes underlie the findings.

Research on older children who spend at least part of the day on their own is far less controversial, though no less disturbing. A study by the American Academy of Pediatrics focused on substance abuse by nearly 5,000 eight-graders around Los Angeles and San Diego. The sample cut across a wide range of ethnic and economic backgrounds and was split about half and half between boys and girls. The researchers concluded that 12- and 13-year-olds who were latchkey kids, taking care of themselves for 11 or more hours a week, were about twice as likely as supervised children to smoke, drink alcohol, and use marijuana. About 31% of the latchkey kids have two or more drinks at a time; only about 17% of the others do. Asked whether they expected to get drunk in the future, 27% of the latchkey kids and 15% of the others said yes. . . .

Just about everyone in the child-development field agrees that all this adds up to a discouraging picture, but opinions vary wildly as to what ought to be done about it—and by whom. For a growing band of conservative social thinkers, the answer is simple: Mothers ought to stay home. These activists, working at private foundations and conservative college faculties, rail against what they see as the permissiveness of recent decades. They save their most lethal venom for organized child care, blaming it for everything from restraining kids' free will to contributing to major outbreaks of untold diseases. One conservative researcher, Bryce Christensen of the Rockford Institute in Illinois, has likened day care to the drug Thalidomide. Day care, he writes, is "a new threat to children that not only imperils the body, but also distorts and withers the spirit.". . .

Working Is Not a Choice

Most employed women, of course, don't have "careers." They wait on tables, type and file, enter data, clean houses, work in child-care centers or hospitals; in other words, they remain permanently concentrated in low-paying "female" occupations, often with no fringe benefits or opportunities for advancement. They don't have to worry about whether to work after the baby is born; they *have* to. Their daily hardships are magnified many times over by fragile resources and the crunch of poverty. Those are the stories . . . we rarely hear, but most need to if we are serious about understanding and changing women's multiple burdens.

Marge Frantz, *Mother Jones*, January 1988.

Still, the dual-career trend continues. No wonder. Most American families could not afford to forfeit a second income, a fact that renders the conservatives' yearning for a simpler past quixotic at best. Real weekly earnings for workers declined 13% from 1973 to 1990. So in most cases two paychecks are a necessity. Also, about a quarter of American children—and about half of black children—live in single-parent homes. Those parents are nearly all women. Though some receive child support or other income, their wages are usually their financial lifeblood. About half the mothers who have been awarded child support by the courts do not get full payments regularly.

From the standpoint of the national economy, a mass exodus of women from the work force would be a disaster: There simply won't be enough available males in the future. Women now make up over 45% of the labor force, and they are expected to fill about 60% of new jobs between now and the year 2000.

Even if a child's welfare were the only consideration, in many cases full-time motherhood might not be the best answer. Children whose mothers are frustrated and angry about staying home might be better off in a high-quality day care center. And many kids may well benefit from the socializing and group activities available in day care. A mother and child alone together all day isn't necessarily a rich environment for the child.

In the end, the short supply of high-quality day care is the greatest obstacle to better prospects for America's children. Experts agree on what constitutes quality in child care—a well-paid and well-trained staff, a high staff-child ratio, a safe and suitable physical environment. They also generally concur that if those criteria are met, most children will not just muddle through but prosper. Says Barbara Reisman, executive director of the Child Care Action Campaign, a nonprofit educational and advocacy organization in New York: "Despite all the questions that have been raised, the bottom line is that if the quality is there, and the parents are comfortable with the situation, the kids are going to be fine."

But even tracking, much less improving, child care quality is a monumental task. Something like 60% of the approximately 11 million preschool kids whose mothers work are taken care of in private homes. That can be a wonderful experience: Grandma or a warm-hearted neighbor spends the day with the wee ones baking cookies and imparting folk wisdom. Or it can be hellish. Yale's Edward Zigler speaks in horror of the home where 54 kids in the care of a 16-year old were found strapped into car seats all day. Low pay and the lack of status associated with organized day care centers make it tough to recruit and retain qualified workers. A study by a research group called the Child Care Employee Project in Oakland revealed an alarming 41% turnover rate at day care operations across the U.S. One big reason: an average hourly salary of $5.35. Says Zigler: "We pay these people less than we do zoo keepers—and then we expect them to do wonders.". . .

The Role of Business

Business has a crucial role to play in helping employees who are parents cope with their responsibilities. The U.S. Congress is currently considering legislation that would guarantee 12 weeks of unpaid leave in the event of a family illness or the birth of a child. According to a study conducted by economics professors at Cornell University and the University of Connecticut, the costs of allowing such leaves for most workers is less than letting them quit and hiring permanent replacements. Companies can provide big-time relief with smaller gestures as well: making a telephone available to assembly-line workers so they can check up on their latchkey kids, say, or letting office workers slip out for a parent-teacher conference without a hassle.

As the competition for good workers heats up, many companies will be forced to grapple with the problems working parents face, or risk losing desirable employees. Says Douglas Besharov, a resident scholar at the American Enterprise Institute in Washington: "If you need workers, you will do what has to be done.". . .

Child-development experts admire a relatively new and growing company, Bright Horizons Children's Centers of Cambridge, Massachusetts, for the innovative on-site day care it provides for major corporations including IBM, Prudential, and Dun & Bradstreet. Founded in 1986 by Linda Mason and her husband, Roger Brown, both former economic development workers in Africa, Bright Horizons now operates 38 centers up and down the East Coast. In most cases the corporate client donates space for child care in or near its office building, providing Bright Horizons with a handsome cost advantage. Fees can be steep— up to $225 per week for infants—but companies often subsidize the payments for employees low on the wage scale.

Improving Child Care Helps Families and Business

Because the centers are close to the workplace, parents are encouraged to drop in throughout the day. Bright Horizons' teaching staff members earn up to $20,000 per year, far more than most day care centers pay, plus a full benefits package. They can pursue a defined career track and move into management ranks if they qualify. As a result, turnover runs at a relatively low 16% to 24%.

Brown and Mason concede that many children might be damaged by second-rate child care, but they contend that parents rarely have anything to fear from the kind of high-quality attention their centers provide. Says Mason: "It's very much like health care. If you can afford to pay for it, you can receive the best child care in the world in this country.". . .

More companies are finding that they have to help employees cope not just with their children but also with the gamut of life's vicissitudes. Says Roy Howard, BellSouth's senior vice president for corporate human resources: "Business used to feel that you ought to leave your personal problems at home. We can no longer afford to take that view." The psychic welfare of workers—and of their children—is increasingly a legitimate management concern, and companies that ignore it risk their employees' future as well as their own.

"What most mothers want today is the chance to rear their own children in their own homes without jeopardizing . . . equal participation in the labor force."

More Day Care Will Not Solve the Problems of Two-Career Couples

Mothers at Home

Mothers at Home is a Virginia-based nonprofit organization that supports women who choose to rear their children at home. The following viewpoint, a policy paper written by organization volunteers, criticizes those who say that more day care is what working mothers really want. In fact, the authors maintain, working mothers go to great lengths to keep their children out of day care. Instead of increased day care, mothers need public- and private-sector policies that enable them to raise their own children.

As you read, consider the following questions:

1. According to Mothers at Home, how does the Department of Labor inflate estimates of the percentage of mothers working outside the home?
2. Why are so many mothers unable to find satisfactory child care, according to the authors?
3. What is the public perception of mothers at home versus working mothers, according to the authors? How is this perception false?

Adapted from "Mothers Speak Out on Child Care," a paper by Mothers at Home, April 1989. Reprinted with permission.

For the past twenty-five years, almost the only news the American public has heard about mothers is that they are leaving home for the workplace. At the basis of every discussion of the subject are government statistics—indisputable evidence that the number of mothers in the labor force has risen dramatically over the years. However, a general misunderstanding of what these figures actually measure has led to inaccurate and potentially dangerous conclusions about society's need for more child care.

Everywhere from Congressional hearings to local meetings of the PTA, the same cry is heard: Mothers are working, and there is a critical shortage of child care for their children. Leaders from every sector of society are urging immediate action, backing their pleas with government statistics that have become so well known and widely accepted that hardly a reference to motherhood escapes mention of them.

"Those who decry the trend for children to be placed in out-of-home care must accept the fact that American society has changed," stated the American Academy of Pediatrics in February 1988 testimony before Congress. "More than 50% of mothers with children under one year of age are in the out-of-home workforce. Greater than 60% of mothers with children under three are similarly employed." At the same hearing before the House Committee on Education and Labor, the YWCA reported: "Our country is faced with a major child care crisis because the number of children with working mothers has grown tremendously. By 1995, two-thirds of all preschool children will have mothers in the workforce; and four out of five school-age children will have working mothers."

Most likely, the representatives of these organizations based their use of the statistics quoted above on media reports, which invariably combine announcements of the latest government figures with stories of mothers struggling to manage full-time jobs while searching for "quality" child care. Media presentations of this nature give most people the impression that every mother who joins the workforce needs a child care provider or access to child care facilities.

This perception simply is not true. Millions of mothers who are considered by the government to be an active part of the labor force do not need or want substitute care for their children. In fact, a close look at the statistics reveals that a large number of these so-called "working mothers" actually consider themselves "at home."

The U.S. Department of Labor Definition of "Work"

Almost every reference to the number of mothers in the workforce, including the three quoted above, can be traced back to the statistics on women and employment released annually by the U.S. Department of Labor (DOL). These statistics are based on a survey of 60,000 "scientifically selected" households, conducted each March by the Bureau of the Census. Because the objective of the survey is to identify trends by comparing labor force participation from year to year, the DOL has had to devise a standardized definition of "employment.". . . According to spokespersons at the DOL, the 65% of mothers who are usually described as "working outside the home" also includes:

Most Working Mothers Do Not Use Day Care

Children under 5 cared for by:

Mothers	58%
Tag team parents	7%
Other adult relatives	11%
Total in family care	76%
Informal care, non relatives	13%
Group day-care center	11%

Mothers' employment status:

Not employed	54%
Part time	17%
Full time	29%

Sources: U.S. Census Bureau and The Heritage Foundation.

1. *Mothers who work part-time, as little as one hour per week and up.* In a *Newsweek*-commissioned Gallup Poll of 1,009 women (reported in the March 31, 1986, issue of *Newsweek*), over half the mothers interviewed who were working part-time or flexible hours "said they had cut back or changed jobs to be with their kids." In other words, mothers who choose part-time work often do so just to avoid the need for substitute child care. . . . According to the DOL, 16.5% of all mothers worked part-time in 1988. Only 44.4% of the nation's mothers were actually employed full-time.

2. *Mothers who work seasonally, as little as one week out of the year.* Many mothers who work do so while their children attend school and avoid employment during their children's summer vacations. Other mothers work only occasionally during the year, perhaps substitute teaching, selling handcrafts, or helping a business during a high-volume period. These mothers who work seasonally are also calculated into the DOL statistics, although some work as little as one week out of the year. According to DOL tabulations, only 33.1% of all mothers with children under the age of 18 work full-time year round. That

figure drops to 25.9% for mothers whose youngest child is under six years of age.

3. *Mothers who work from their homes.* Whether working for employers or running their own home businesses, many mothers avoid child care by working from home. . . . The DOL, however, makes no distinction between women who work at an office or factory or some other facility and those who work in their own homes. Therefore, an unknown percentage of the DOL's mothers who supposedly "work outside the home" refer to mothers who work with their children around them, literally *inside* the home.

4. *Mothers who provide child care for other mothers.* Both full-time family day care providers and mothers who collect a check for watching a neighbor's child a few hours each day after school are counted in the DOL figures. . . .

5. *Mothers who work without pay for a "family-operated enterprise" at least fifteen hours per week.* Some mothers at home . . . mention participating in a family business. Whether or not they are paid for their work, these women are within the national definition of "working mothers." Yet, most of them are able to do their work from home or to perform their work during hours that allow their children full-time access to "Mom.". . .

6. *Mothers who work full-time but have flexible hours.* Even mothers who are employed full-time can defy the media image of the working mother. By arranging flexible work hours or by having their husbands do so, many women go to great lengths to avoid leaving their children in a day care center or with a sitter. Although they definitely consider themselves working mothers, they are usually home when their children are home. An example is Linda Hayes, a mother of two from Vienna, Virginia, who works the so-called "mother trip" as an airline stewardess. An especially grueling assignment, which condenses a week's worth of work hours into back-to-back flights that can be completed in two days, it is nevertheless so popular that only women with nearly twenty years of seniority are able to request it. Says Linda, "It's just not in me to leave [my girls] so much of the time."

Tag-Team Parents

In some families where both parents are employed full-time, the husband and wife have a "tag team" arrangement: They plan their work schedules so that one of them gets home as the other is leaving for work. Thus, one parent is always available to care for the children. The DOL figures do not include information about child care arrangements; however, the Bureau of the Census (*Who's Minding the Kids?* 1984-85) reports that 7% of the nation's children under age five have "tag team" parental care.

7. *Mothers who are on maternity leave, whether or not they return to their jobs.* Women on maternity leave also are numbered among the working population. . . .

8. *Mothers who are unemployed, but who are looking for work.* Since women who are job-seeking generally do not remain unemployed for long, they are considered an active part of the labor force and are counted as such. In 1988, 6.5% of the DOL's "working mothers" were unemployed.

Inaccurate Estimates of the Demand for Child Care

Thus, the Department of Labor's statistics on working mothers include women who participate in the workforce in a variety of ways—not just full-time employed mothers or those whose job circumstances dictate the need for child care. In fact, the Current Population Survey, from which the statistics are drawn, does not ask respondents any questions about child care; nor can a respondent's need or desire for child care be inferred from answers to other questions.

Yet, the notion persists that every mother who participates in the labor force needs substitute care for her children. This mistaken assumption has led many well-intentioned people—from community leaders to reporters to Congressional Aides—to routinely misuse the DOL statistics as "proof" of the need for more day care. It has even led researchers to project how many children will need day care in the near future by devising formulas based on the faulty premise of how many working mothers have been "counted" by the DOL. In reality, as explained above, many mothers who are considered an active part of the labor force do not need any child care services at all. Therefore, estimates of child care needs based on the DOL's employment statistics on women are both inaccurate and misleading. . . .

It is clear that more mothers than ever before are participating in the workforce in some way. It is equally clear that these mothers are experiencing a deeply emotional crisis concerning the care of their children. Yet, in spite of considerable media coverage, the true nature of this crisis remains largely misunderstood.

The truth is that most people's understanding of the child care crisis is based on the media's perception of the problem. That perception—as portrayed in news stories, on talk shows, in books, on television, and in the movies—is far from what mothers really want and children really need.

Media coverage for the past three decades has almost universally divided mothers into two distinct camps: mothers who are home with their children (pictured as a shrinking minority) and mothers who "work outside the home" (identified as the growing majority). Mothers at home are supposedly politically conservative, married to a high wage earner, and ideologically committed to the view that women belong in the home. "Working mothers," on the other hand, are depicted as educated women pursuing self-fulfillment in the workplace and mothers forced to work for economic reasons.

Home-Based Employees Are More Productive

Naturally, parents who work at home find their labors "frequently interrupted by child, family, and household tasks." Because of their motives for in-home employment, however, most home-based workers (particularly women) say they regard such interruptions "as a positive aspect of working at home." Such interruptions do not prevent at-home workers from making valuable contributions to their employers. Some studies show that home-based employees are actually *more productive* than their office-based counterparts. With growing use of new technology such as personal computers that allow operators to telecommute, home-based employment may grow much more common in the decades ahead.

Bryce J. Christensen, *The Family in America*, November 1990.

The outpouring of letters we have received from mothers of nearly every political, religious, and socio-economic background, completely contradicts this picture. We have heard from single mothers who have managed to stay home, wealthy women who feel they "must" work, political conservatives who have balanced career and family for years, and ardent feminists who quit work as soon as their first child was born. Thus we have learned that mothers simply cannot be categorized by their work/home choice.

If anything unites mothers today, it is not the choices they make concerning the care of their children; it is the exhausting inner turmoil they suffer as they weigh the alternatives. Pulled one way by an intense social and economic pressure to work and pushed another by a dawning realization that they are truly needed by their children, most mothers feel hopelessly torn. In fact, many of them wander in and out of the workforce—seeking from society support at work, then at home—only to find it severely lacking in either place. . . .

We believe that most mothers who cannot find satisfactory child care are not suffering from a lack of "quality" options. In fact, many of them feel they have already experienced the best there can be. We believe these mothers go from sitter to sitter and center to center because they are continually looking for something that no substitute caregiver can ever provide: the same love and care each mother would give her own child in her own home.

Of course, not all mothers struggling with child care problems share identical feelings and situations. However, it is significant that so many women who feel compelled to speak out about the conflicts they feel are describing the same surprising conclusion: there is no adequate replacement in the life of a child for the intimate, full-time guidance of a loving parent. . . .

Interestingly, those who work with children on a regular basis, especially those who provide substitute child care, express especially strong opinions about the importance of having one parent always available to a child:

From Honolulu, Hawaii, a 20-year-old, unmarried day care worker writes: "I am so concerned for children whose mothers work full-time. You see, I've been working in a nursery school and after school program for the past five years. Those kids need individual attention so badly, but they don't get it. Most kids want to go home to be with mommy right after school. They want to hug and kiss their moms . . . talk and show off for their parents. But all they get is me. I try my best, and I love those kids so; but I'm not mommy."

A teacher from California, and a former nanny for a White House Aide, explains: "I was the best they could hire, and they were the ideal employers. They paid me as much as I could have made teaching, and I got along well with both the mother and the children. Still, after that experience I am certain that when I have my own children, I will not work outside the home. There is no one who is going to raise your kids like you would.". . .

What Mothers Want

What, then, do mothers want? Recent studies and surveys are making it increasingly clear: Mothers want more time at home. . . . What most mothers want today is the chance to rear their own children in their own homes without jeopardizing the opportunity for fair and equal participation in the labor force in the future. They want flexibility in the workplace so they can have time at home when their children most need them. . . .

As a society, we have long equated women's progress in the workplace with the struggles of the working mother. In fact, there is fear that giving childrearing a place of importance in a woman's life will somehow forsake the gains in equality that have been made. Yet, women who feel forced to work when they would rather be home are every bit as unliberated as women who feel forced to stay home when they would rather work. It is critical that we move forward by acknowledging that helping mothers put their children first does not have to threaten the full and equal participation of all women in the labor force.

Before any "solutions" are rushed through Congress, it is imperative that the true needs of families be accurately assessed. To date, almost no systematic research has been done to determine what child care arrangements parents most prefer or how to make their top preference readily available. Rather, most studies simply assume that institutional day care (which can be easily regulated for safety and affordability) will become the favored option of the future, and their survey questions reflect that assumption.

Parents and Children

The open and deeply moving expression of feelings we have received from parents across the nation reveals a need to ask questions few researchers seem to have considered: What do parents believe is best for their children? What do they feel their ideal child care arrangement would be? What would have to happen to make that arrangement possible? What kinds of child care options have parents tried in the past and how did they feel about each one? Are there arrangements that parents recognize as "good" for them, but harmful for their children? What requests have parents made of employers in hopes of preventing or reducing the need for substitute child care, and how were those requests received? Would changing a spouse's work situation (i.e. flexibility at work or the ability to work from home) make it possible for a number of families to avoid child care altogether? Would parents prefer this flexibility over "good" substitute care?

There seems to be a significant difference between what the media say about mothers and what mothers say about themselves. Unfortunately, policy makers who depend on and trust the media to provide accurate information may be tempted to take the word of newspaper columnists and television news anchors over the personal experiences of a mother in Kansas City or a factory worker in Baltimore. It is time to carefully and openly review the facts surrounding the child care crisis, and to demand an accurate assessment of the nation's child care needs, as expressed by the mothers and fathers of the nation's children.

"Parents in the United States today spend less time with their children than parents in any other country in the world."

Two-Career Parents Spend Too Little Time with the Family

William R. Mattox Jr.

In the following viewpoint, William R. Mattox Jr. argues that families lack the time to be effective parents, supportive spouses, or good neighbors. People must spend many more hours working than they did a generation ago, he maintains, and children are growing up in isolation. Mattox supports government policies giving families more time together instead of taking over parental functions. Mattox is director of policy analysis for the Family Research Council, a conservative research and education group in Washington, D.C.

As you read, consider the following questions:

1. According to the author, how many hours per week do most working parents spend with their children?
2. What social patterns typical of the 1950s reinforced family-oriented activities, according to Mattox?
3. Why does the author believe the family time famine is not limited only to workers who consider the breadwinner-homemaker model ideal?

Adapted from "Running on Empty: America's Time-Starved Families with Children" by William R. Mattox Jr., an Institute for American Values working paper, November 1991. This paper was commissioned by the Institute for the Council on Families in America and is reprinted with permission.

Parents in the United States today spend less time with their children than parents in any other country in the world. According to Harvard psychiatrist Armand Nicholi, only Great Britain rivals the U.S. in parental absence, a fact which he believes Americans should find troubling:

> If one factor influences the character development and emotional stability of a person, it is the quality of the relationship he experiences as a child with *both* of his parents. Conversely, if people suffering from severe non-organic emotional illness have one experience in common, it is the absence of a parent through death, divorce, time-demanding job, or absence for other reasons.

Parents in the U.S. today devote roughly 40 percent less time to childrearing activities than did parents a generation ago. In 1965, the average parent spent approximately 30 hours a week in direct or indirect contact with children; by 1985, parent-child interaction had declined to just 17 hours a week.

Many Americans share Nicholi's concerns about the rise of parental absence. For example, a recent survey commissioned by the Massachusetts Mutual Insurance Company found that Americans believe "parents having less time to spend with their families" is the single most important reason for the family's decline in our society. The decline in parental time with children is due in large part to an increase in the number of hours families with children devote to paid employment. While the length of the average work week in America has changed little over the last three decades, the fact that so many more families today have two adult earners (65 percent of all married mothers were in the labor force in 1988, up from 28 percent in 1960) means that there has been a substantial increase in the total number of hours two-parent families work for pay. . . .

Economic Pressure and Materialism

One of the supreme ironies of economic developments since the early 1970s is that while America has experienced steady growth in its gross national product, more and more families have found it increasingly difficult to live on a 40-hour-a-week paycheck. Higher taxes on middle-income parents and real wage stagnation (especially for non-supervisory workers and males under age 25) have both contributed to growing economic pressures on families with children. So have increases in the cost of most major family expenses—including housing, health care, transportation, and higher education—which have outpaced the general inflation rate. . . .

Growing economic pressures, however, are not the only reason families spend less time together. Karl Zinsmeister of the American Enterprise Institute believes "unbridled careerism" is also to blame:

> For years, one of the most cogent criticisms of American sex roles and economic arrangements has been the argument that many fathers get so wrapped up in earning and doing at the workplace that they become dehumanized, losing interest in the intimate joys of family life and failing to participate fairly in domestic responsibilities. Now it appears workaholism and family dereliction have become equal opportunity diseases, striking mothers as much as fathers.

Unfettered materialism has also contributed to the reduction in family time. A Pennsylvania State University study found that the rise in two-earner white families since 1960 has been driven more by a preference for a higher standard of living than by economic necessity. "The rising proportion of married mothers entering the labor force since 1960 is largely due to family decisions to earn a second income so that the family may enjoy a higher standard of living," the authors concluded. . . .

"I'm afraid your mother has to work late again tonight. We do however have this video tape of her eating dinner with us last week."

How do different work arrangements affect family time? A study by University of Virginia sociologists Steven Nock and Paul William Kingston shows that two-earner couples not only spend less time together than do breadwinner-homemaker couples, but the time they do spend together is of lower quality since hours not spent on the job are often devoted to chores and errands homemakers typically do during the day (meal preparation, laundry, grocery shopping, etc.).

In addition, two-income households spend considerably less time with their children than do breadwinner-homemaker households. This discrepancy is most pronounced in maternal time with children. Time diary research collected by University of Maryland sociologist John Robinson shows that as hours of maternal employment increase, time spent in "primary child care activities"—dressing, feeding, bathing, chauffeuring, talking to, playing with, helping with homework, etc.—decreases. Accordingly, mothers employed full time spend just under half as much time in primary child care activities as non-employed mothers at home. Moreover, contrary to some published reports, employed mothers do not spend a higher proportion of their total time with children engaged in "high quality" child-centered activities like playing with dolls, going to the park, or reading *Green Eggs and Ham*. Instead, non-employed mothers spend roughly twice as much time as employed mothers in child-centered activities and this 2-1 ratio is also found in comparisons of overall time with children.

While there is a negative correlation between hours of maternal employment and time with children, fathers employed 40-49 hours a week actually spend more time in primary child care activities than do fathers employed less than 40 hours a week. Moreover, even though some traditional families clearly suffer from father absence due to the time-demanding nature of the sole breadwinner's work, Nock and Kingston find that, on average, fathers in one-income households actually spend more time with their children than do fathers in dual-income families. One research review suggested that guilt-ridden employed wives may "push the dads out of the way in their rush to spend time with baby at the end of the day.". . .

Critics Dismiss Time Famine

Despite all these problems, some observers pooh-pooh talk of a growing time famine. They lambaste commonly-cited surveys showing that Americans are working longer, pointing out that more reliable time diary studies show that the average work week has remained fairly stable since the 1940s when the 40-hour work week was standardized. Moreover, they note that since 1965 there has been a 10 percent increase in the amount of time Americans devote to leisure activities. Thus, Robert Samuelson of *Newsweek* argues:

> Just about everyone seems to think that Americans are more harried and short of time than ever before. Well, we aren't. This is a psycho fact. We feel it, and therefore it must be. . . . The sense of an unprecedented time squeeze is partly a generational phenomenon. Baby boomers are raising children, and these years are always crowded. But being self-absorbed as ever, baby boomers think their experiences are uniquely unique.

Gary Burtless of the Brookings Institution is even more pointed in his criticism of those who complain about time pressures:

> In the past 20 years, the amount of time devoted to watching television has climbed faster than the average amount of free time. To judge by their actual behavior, most Americans who complain they enjoy too little leisure are struggling to find a few extra minutes to watch Oprah Winfrey and "L.A. Law."

When America is viewed as a nation of individuals, Samuelson and Burtless are right on the money. At a macro level, reliable time diary data show that Americans today do not work more or play less than Americans a generation or two ago. But when the scope of time measurements is limited to families with children, the picture changes quite dramatically. The average worker may not be working more or commuting considerably longer than in 1965, but since the average family is now much more likely to have two wage earners, families with children today are devoting more time to paid employment and commuting than did families a quarter-century ago. This, combined with the growth in single-parent families, means that parents today have less time with children and less leisure time. In fact, the amount of time fathers of preschoolers devote to leisure activities has declined 25 percent since 1975. For mothers of preschoolers, leisure time has dropped 11 percent during this same time period. . . .

Parents Want More Time with Children

Whatever the "experts" may say, it is clear many parents are concerned about the lack of time they have available for their children. A 1990 *Los Angeles Times* poll found that 57 percent of all fathers and 55 percent of all mothers feel guilty about spending too little time with their children. A 1989 *New York Times* survey found that 83 percent of employed mothers and 72 percent of employed fathers say they are torn by conflict between their jobs and the desire to spend more time with their families. And a 1988 *USA Today* poll found that parents with young children identify "missing big events in their children's lives" as the thing they most dislike about their current day care situation.

While the breadwinner-homemaker model still has considerable appeal among ordinary Americans, it is important to note that concerns about family time are not limited to those who regard this model as ideal. For example, when respondents to the Massachusetts Mutual survey were asked to identify "extremely effective" ways to strengthen the family, nearly twice as many answered "spending more time together" than answered "full-time parent raising kids." Similarly, a 1988 *Parenting* magazine survey found that home-based employment outranked both full-time homemaking and employment outside the home as the most appealing work-family arrangement for mothers and fathers. A 1987 Cornell University study found that two-thirds of all mothers employed full-time would like to work fewer hours so that they could devote more time to their families. As one Baltimore mother employed full time put it:

> I would like to spend more time with my son hugging him and just doing anything where we could be together. . . . I see that there is a lot of hate and confusion and upset in him and just one thing I would like to do is hold my child.

The breadth of concern about America's family time famine may surprise leaders in government, academia, and the mass media who often view efforts to increase family time—particularly those that recognize the strengths of the breadwinner-homemaker model—as an attempt to "turn back the clock" rather than "facing the realities" of modern family life. . . .

No Time Spent Parenting

Cross-cultural studies show that parents in the United States spend less time with their children than parents in any other nation in the world. Working mothers have shouldered most of the blame; fathers have relied on tradition to excuse their absence from the house. Either way, the child suffers the consequences. Statistics show mothers spend between three and five minutes a day on educational activities with their children; fathers log in at zero to one minute. Cornell professor Urie Bronfenbrenner attached microphones to the shirts of small children and found that their fathers spent an average of thirty-seven seconds a day alone with them, less time than they would devote to cooking a soft-boiled egg.

George Howe Colt, *The Enigma of Suicide*, 1991.

Some experts believe our nation's government and business policymakers should respond to America's growing parenting deficit with a massive effort to socialize childrearing—day care for infants and toddlers, mandatory preschool for young children, after-school programs for latchkey kids, longer school days and year-round schooling. Indeed, some steps towards such a brave new world have already been taken.

Thankfully, there is a growing recognition that easing work-family tensions in these ways places a much higher premium on enabling parents to work than on encouraging them to parent. In addition, there is a growing recognition among people across the political spectrum that government programs, however well-designed, are inferior to strong families. As William Galston and

Elaine Kamarck of the Progressive Policy Institute put it in their landmark 1990 report, *Putting Children First*:

> Government cannot, under any set of circumstances, provide the kind of nurturance that children, particularly young children, need. Given all the money in the world, government programs will not be able to instill self-esteem, good study habits, advanced language skills, or sound moral values in children as effectively as strong families. . . . Government will never have the resources or the ability to replace what children lose when they lose supportive families. This suggests that the focus of public policy should be to look for ways to create stable families, not substitute families.

Rather than expanding the scope of government to replace families, policymakers should seek to help parents fulfill their childrearing responsibilities by giving special attention to promoting: (1) pro-child tax relief; (2) home-based employment and other family friendly work policies; (3) life cycle reorganizing; and (4) policies that encourage family stability. . . .

Passing the Front Porch Rocker Test

While there is clearly a need for government and business policies which give parents greater economic autonomy, it would be a mistake to suggest that policy changes are the sole key, or even the primary key, to a greater parent-child interaction. Indeed, no dramatic change in parent-child interaction is apt to take place so long as the predominant cultural message of our time is one which says that family time should take a back seat to career aspirations and material gain.

To be sure, most young people would not object to seeing the work and family pendulum swing back in the direction of home. A 1990 special edition of *Time* magazine on the "twentysomething" generation found that 63 percent of the 18-29 year olds polled hoped to spend more time with their children than their parents spent with them. As Ellen Galinsky of the New York-based Families and Work Institute explains, "These young people have seen their parents come home from work wiped out and not have time for them, and they are saying they don't want to live that way. Not surprisingly, the desire for parental attention and family time is shared by younger children as well. In fact, when 1,500 schoolchildren were asked, "What do you think makes a happy family?", John DeFrain and his colleague Nick Stinnett report that children "did not list money, cars, fine homes, or televisions." Instead, the answer most frequently offered was "doing things together."

There are signs that attitudes are changing, that U.S. parents are increasingly concerned about the lack of time they have available for children. In fact, polls taken by Gallup, Roper, *The Washington Post*, and Yankelovich Clancy Shulman all show that concerns about family time have grown since the mid-1980s. Ultimately, however, it is parental behavior—not parental attitudes—that must pass the "front porch rocker test" First Lady Barbara Bush described in her 1990 commencement address at Wellesley College:

> At the end of your life, you will never regret not having passed one more test, not winning one more verdict or not closing one more deal. You will regret time not spent with a husband, a friend, a child or a parent.

"Just about everyone seems to think that Americans are more harried and short of time than ever. Well, we aren't."

Two-Career Parents Have Enough Time to Spend with the Family

Gary Burtless and Robert J. Samuelson

Gary Burtless is an economist specializing in labor policy at the Brookings Institute in Washington, D.C. In Part I of the following viewpoint, Burtless disputes the assertion that families lack time together. The length of the work week has remained stable since the 1940s, he finds, while technology has reduced the time required for housework. Burtless believes families squander their leisure time watching television rather than using it for family activities. In Part II, Robert J. Samuelson suggests that Americans have always been a hurried, bustling people mistrustful of idle time, who fill their hours with work. Samuelson is an economics editorial writer for *Newsweek*.

As you read, consider the following questions:

1. Why does Burtless suggest that average time spent on the job has actually fallen since 1950?
2. How would more leisure time actually affect the family, according to Burtless?
3. Why is it natural for the baby-boom generation in particular to feel stressed for time, according to Samuelson?

I

Americans have too little time for leisure. That at least is what they tell poll takers sent around by the Harris organization. According to a Harris report, the typical workweek, including the commute to and from work, has risen by six hours—about 15%—since 1975. The amount of time left for leisure has shrunk nearly 10 hours a week, or more than a third.

With a growing scarcity of leisure, Americans are thought to feel more harried than ever. They are too driven by the demands of work to enjoy the wholesome pleasures of healthful recreation and quiet family life. Although I have not yet seen the word "crisis," a spate of newspaper and magazine articles informs me that present trends are a matter for grave concern. Yale psychologist Edward Zigler told *Time* magazine in 1989 that the shortage of leisure means "we're at the breaking point as far as family is concerned."

It is not altogether clear why leisure has suddenly become so scarce. *Time* magazine blames technology, which has sped up the tempo of life, both on and off the job. In "Work Without End," Benjamin Hunnicutt argues that intellectuals, labor leaders and liberal-minded politicians have abandoned the struggle to improve work life through reductions in work hours. In the modern religion of paid work, honest toil is virtuous and leisure disreputable.

The Workweek Is Not Increasing

But the best available evidence flies in the face of the assertion that leisure is diminishing, Harris polls and anecdotal data notwithstanding. While we lack reliable information about how much time our forebears devoted to leisure, we have a fair idea of how long they worked.

In the middle of the last century the typical workweek was 70 hours—a bit more on the farm and a bit less in urban areas. From 1850 until 1900 the workweek declined gradually to about 60 hours. The trend toward shorter weekly hours accelerated in the first four decades of this century, with the typical paid workweek falling to just 40 hours in the 1940s, where it has remained ever since.

While the typical paid workweek has remained stuck around 40 hours, it is not strictly accurate to say that average weekly hours at work have stayed constant over the past five decades. There are many fewer workers, like farmers, who work extremely long hours each week. There are many more workers, like women and students, who work fewer hours. Even among full-time workers, hours spent on the job have fallen as sick leave, paid holidays and vacation benefits have become more generous. Taking all of these factors into account, average time spent on the job has *fallen* more than five hours a week—roughly 13%—since 1950.

Leisure Time Is Increasing

To be sure, work for pay involves far more people in 1989 than it did in 1950. Women typically work fewer than 40 hours a week, bringing down the length of the average workweek. But women are far more likely to work for pay in the 1980s than they were in the 1950s. Over the course of a lifetime, Americans today can probably expect to devote slightly more time to paid work than they did in 1950 because women now spend substantially more hours in paid work even though men spend less.

Do these trends mean that Americans have less time for leisure? Surprisingly, the amount of time devoted to leisure has risen rather than shrunk in recent decades. The best evidence for this comes from careful studies in which respondents fill out time diaries showing exactly how they spend each minute of the day. This painstaking procedure is expensive and unquestionably burdensome to respondents. But there is little doubt that it provides more accurate information than a phone call from Louis Harris asking people how many hours they think were spent on leisure during the preceding week.

Sociologists in the Survey Research Centers at the University of Michigan and the University of Maryland have administered time diary studies using reasonably consistent methods since 1965. These surveys suggest that among working age adults free time is up, while time devoted to work (including commuting and housework) is down.

Among men, a rise in time devoted to housework and family tasks has been more than offset by a dip in time devoted to paid work, including the commute to a job. Among women, the gain in paid employment has been outweighed by a drop in housework and family responsibilities. Between 1965 and 1985 free time among women rose four hours a week, or about 11%, while time devoted to paid and unpaid work fell about six hours, or 10%. Gains in free time and reductions in time devoted to work were also enjoyed by working-age men, primarily because of a trend toward early retirement.

Television Watching Increases

For those who believe leisure is ennobling, I should mention one other finding from these studies. In the past 20 years, the amount of time devoted to watching television has climbed faster than the average amount of free time. To judge by their actual behavior, most Americans who complain they enjoy too little leisure are struggling to find a few extra minutes to watch

Oprah Winfrey and "L.A. Law."

Mr. Hunnicutt argues that labor leaders and politicians have failed in their responsibility to fight for a shorter workweek. This view might be persuasive if we could discover evidence that Americans would prefer to work shorter hours but are prevented from doing so by legal, institutional or technical constraints at the workplace. When asked whether they are satisfied with their hours, however, most workers report either that they are satisfied or that they would prefer to work even longer if additional hours were available at the same wage rate. Only a handful of workers report dissatisfaction because hours are too long. In fact, workers who would prefer longer hours outnumber those who would prefer shorter by more than 4 to 1.

Unrealistic Standards

In his research, John Robinson, director of the Americans' Use of Time Project at the University of Maryland, has found that Americans on the average actually have more free time today than they did 25 years ago. He defines free time as any time apart from work and family obligations or personal needs like cooking, cleaning and sleeping.

Yet there's also ample evidence that Americans feel starved for time, partly because of a plethora of obligations.

"We have a lot more things we believe are vital now"—from fitness and diet to parenting, cultural enrichment and on-the-job success, says Susan Hayward, a senior vice president at Yankelovich Clancy Shulman who studies time. Some of the time pressures are self imposed by people who set unrealistic standards for themselves, whether it's at work, redecorating their homes or arranging extracurricular activities for their kids. Adds Mr. Robinson: "Even the choice to do nothing is stressful" because people feel guilty for making it.

Carol Hymowitz, *The Wall Street Journal*, August 5, 1991.

Those distressed by the shortage of leisure might consider a heretical thought. Perhaps most people in this country actually like what they do in their jobs. Annual hours of work in the U.S. are higher than in most other countries that have a similar standard of living, but workers here seem to prefer it that way.

More Leisure Would Cost Families

Whatever our attitudes toward work, most of us would probably choose to enjoy more leisure if extra leisure had no cost. For nearly all of us, though, additional leisure does have a cost. Those who work for a living would have to give up some time on our jobs and forfeit some wages. Those who cook or work around the house might have to tolerate less palatable meals, less attractive lawns, and less sanitary kitchens. Given these tradeoffs, most of us strike the best bargain we can, compromising our desire for more leisure with our wish to put food on the table (and our need to clean up the mess afterward).

The suggestion that a mandated drop in the workweek eliminates the unpleasant tradeoff between more leisure and less money is fatuous. Shorter hours would leave us with more time but less money to enjoy our leisure. Those who prefer this combination are welcome to choose it. I see no compelling reason to urge political leaders to force it on the rest of us.

II

Just about everyone seems to think that Americans are more harried and short of time than ever. Well, we aren't. This is a psycho-fact. We feel it, and therefore it must be. Feeling and fact are assumed to be the same. If Americans think they're exceptionally harassed, then they are.

It's a myth. There has never been enough time for us. There probably never will be. Our culture is uneasy with idleness—and uneasy with that unease. As de Tocqueville long ago noted, we Americans live in constant fear that something good in life will pass us by. Consider the complaint of Donald Trump. He goes to parties or dinners four or five nights a week, but listen to him gripe. "I hate going out on Sundays," he once said. "I don't like going out on Monday nights . . . I'm not sure I like going out any night."

So stay home, Donald. Of all people, you can afford to relax. What's to miss?

Trump aside, time pressures are genuine. Working parents are squeezed. Traffic congestion is real. People feel hassled. But what's extraordinary about this? Americans have complained about the rat race for years. The only shred of evidence of something new comes from pollster Louis Harris. He reports that since 1973 leisure time has declined 37 percent (from 26.2 hours to 16.6 hours a week), while the average work week has increased 15 percent (from 40.6 hours to 46.8 hours). These statistics are probably faulty—as I will show shortly—but even if true, they wouldn't mean an unprecedented squeeze on leisure time.

We suffer historic amnesia. "Time . . . once seemed free and elastic," says *Time*, the magazine. When was that?

Work Has Always Dominated Time

Not at the turn of the century. "The average working day was in the neighborhood of 10 hours, six days a week," wrote social commentator Frederick Lewis Allen in "The Big Change:

America Transforms Itself 1900-1950." Keeping house was no breeze either. In a recent history of housework, Susan Strasser reports a conversation with an 88-year-old woman who grew up early in the century. The woman did laundry with tubs and washboards, cooked on a wood stove and cleaned kerosene lamps.

"I'd hate to go through it again," she said. "Took us all day to do a big washing."

Well, was this golden age of leisure just after World War II? That's doubtful. Mass retirement—probably the greatest contribution to leisure time of the century—didn't come into its own until the 1960s. In 1947 nearly half of men over 65 worked; in 1960 it was still a third. By 1987 only 15 percent of men over 65 (and 11 percent of all elderly) worked.

Families Have Time Together

In a survey, when parents and children were queried about their relationships, . . . parents report spending a lot of time with their children every week. For example, 70 percent reported their families eat dinner together five or more nights a week. Almost all parents said they know all or most of their children's friends. And 88 percent said they know "all or most of the time" what their children are doing when they're not home.

Linda Feldman, *The Christian Science Monitor*, November 22, 1991.

Indeed, the tip-off that the Harris poll is unreliable comes from the elderly. Though few of them hold jobs, they recorded the largest drop in leisure in the latest survey. And they say they have only about an hour more of daily leisure than working-age Americans. How can this be? It can't. People don't offhandedly know how much free time they have, and Americans are reluctant to admit they spend too much time relaxing. The Harris data come from two questions (taking about a minute) in a 72-question telephone interview on another subject entirely. Asked quickly to estimate something they don't know, people can easily make innocent mistakes.

Look at Accurate Study

A more accurate picture of how people use their time comes from sociologist John P. Robinson of the University of Maryland. He's done extensive surveys in 1965, 1975 and 1985 in which respondents were asked in detail about specific daily activities. He finds:

• Since 1965 sleeping time (about eight hours) and eating time (an hour and a third) have remained stable. Free time—everything excluding work, sleep, eating, shopping, housework and child care—is up about 10 percent to 5.5 hours a day. Two-fifths of that is spent watching television.

• More women have jobs, but actual time at the job is dropping. Since 1965 men's weekly hours have decreased from 49 to 42; women's, from 39 to 31. Robinson speculates that the decline reflects informal ways that employers accommodate family pressures: by allowing flexible start-up times, absences for doctor's appointments or early departure time.

• As more women enter the labor force, they are doing less housework and men are doing more. In 1965 women did nearly six times as much (27 hours versus 4.6 hours a week). By 1985 the ratio was 2-to-1 (19.5 hours versus 9.8 hours). Most of the cutback in women's hours involves less cleaning (dusting, vacuuming and laundry).

Stress Results from Changing Roles

The sense of an unprecedented time squeeze is partly a generational phenomenon. Baby boomers are raising children, and these years are always crowded. But being self-absorbed as ever, baby boomers think their experiences are uniquely unique. Is traffic congestion getting worse? Probably. But people tend to live close to jobs, and companies expand where they can find workers. In 1960, half of all commuting was within central cities. Today, most commuting is suburb to suburb. The average daily commute in 1980 took 20.9 minutes, up a mere minute from 1975.

Of course, there are real and upsetting changes. But they only indirectly involve time. Part of today's sense of squeeze stems from the breakdown of traditional sex roles. Moms have jobs, and dads do housework. People have blurred responsibilities, and naturally there isn't time to do everything. Choices have to be made, and making them is stressful. Is it any wonder, then, that even the term "leisure" is becoming dated? Media and marketing consultants now talk of "discretionary time"—the idea being that if you've made a choice about how to use your time, then it's no longer free and enjoyable.

Is all the rushing about good for us? Who knows? But it's thoroughly American. What's happening today is a new expression of an old condition. Striving and struggling are part of our culture. We're a hustle-bustle society. Maybe that means we're too uptight and unreflective. But time isn't flying. We are.

Evaluating Sources of Information

When historians study and interpret past events, they use two kinds of sources: primary and secondary. Primary sources are eyewitness accounts. For example, a personal journal written by a working mother describing her dual role would be a primary source. A book about the effects of working mothers on their children that used the journal would be a secondary source.

Historians are not the only people who encounter conflicting information, however. Anyone who reads a daily newspaper, watches television, or just talks to different people will encounter many different views. Writers and speakers use sources of information to support their own statements. Thus, critical thinkers, just like historians, must question the writer's or speaker's sources of information as well as the writer or speaker.

While there are many criteria that can be applied to assess the accuracy of a primary or secondary source, for this activity you will be asked to apply three. For each source listed on the following page, ask yourself the following questions: First, did the person actually see or participate in the event he or she is reporting? This will help you determine the credibility of the information —an eyewitness to an event is an extremely valuable source. Second, does the person have a vested interest in the report? Assessing the person's social status, professional affiliations, nationality, and religious or political beliefs will be helpful in considering this question. By evaluating this you will be able to determine how objective the person's report may be. Third, how qualified is the author to be making the statements he or she is making? Consider what the person's profession is and how he or she might know about the event. Someone who has spent years being involved with or studying the issue may be able to offer more information than someone who simply is offering an uneducated opinion; for example, a politician or layperson.

Keeping the above criteria in mind, imagine you are writing a report on the increased need for day care among two-career parents. *Place a P next to those descriptions you believe are primary sources. Place an S next to those descriptions you believe are secondary sources.* Next, based on the above criteria, *rank the primary sources, assigning the number (1) to what appears to be the most valuable, (2) to the source likely to be the second-most valuable, and so on, until all the primary sources are ranked. Then rank the secondary sources, again using the above criteria.*

P or S

Rank in Importance

1. Testimony given before a senate sub-committee by businesspeople who have instituted family-leave policies at their companies.

2. A speech given by the vice president opposing federally mandated day care.

3. A television report on the lives of women who have taken on a wide variety of roles, including jobs and parenthood.

4. Articles in the *New York Times* discussing different kinds of day-care options available to parents.

5. A position paper written by the National Commission on Children advocating that businesses and society institute changes allowing families to spend more time together.

6. Editorials in the *Wall Street Journal* by business executives arguing that instituting family-friendly policies would be costly and unnecessary.

7. The published results of a long-term study of the harmful effects of day care on children.

8. Review of a book by a leading sociologist arguing that government and businesses should help provide day care for working families.

9. An article in *Ms.* discussing women's attitudes toward work and family.

10. A *Newsweek* article discussing the effects of two-career parents on their children.

11. An article in *Business Week* about fathers who are reorganizing their careers to spend more time with their children.

Periodical Bibliography

The following articles have been selected to supplement the diverse views presented in this chapter.

Katrine Ames et al.	"Wanted: Mary Poppins," *Newsweek*, January 27, 1992.
Aaron Bernstein, Joseph Weber, Lisa Driscoll, and Alice Cuneo	"Corporate America Is Still No Place for Kids," *Business Week*, November 25, 1991.
Deborah Edler Brown and Michele Donley	"The Great Experiment," *Time*, special issue, Fall 1990.
Katharine Byrne	"Other Lives: A Report on the Mommy Track," *Commonweal*, May 4, 1990.
Stephen E. Ewing	"Nourish Thy Children," *Vital Speeches of the Day*, June 15, 1990.
Dianne Feeley	"Child Care: Unfinished Agenda," *Against the Current*, May/June 1990.
Theodora Lurie	"Improving the Quantity and Quality of Child Care," *USA Today*, July 1991.
Connaught C. Marshner	"What Social Conservatives Realize," *National Review*, September 2, 1988.
Angela Browne Miller	"Quality of Day Care Uncertain," *Society*, March/April 1991.
New Perspectives Quarterly	"Prodigal Parents: Family vs. the Eighty-Hour Work Week," Winter 1990.
Phyllis Schlafly	"Liberal 'Solutions' Make Problems Worse," *The Phyllis Schlafly Report*, February 1991. Available from the Eagle Forum, PO Box 618, Alton, IL 62002.
Felice N. Schwartz	"Women as a Business Imperative," *Harvard Business Review*, March/April 1992. Available from HBR Reprints, Harvard Business School, Publishing Division, Boston, MA 02163.
Cathy Trost and Carol Hymowitz	"Careers Start Giving in to Family Needs," *The Wall Street Journal*, June 18, 1990.
The World & I	"Symposium: The Family—The Search for Norms," special section, November 1990.

What Government Policies Would Help the Family?

Chapter Preface

Many politicians, social scientists, and others claim the family is in trouble—financially and morally. In addition, American families themselves feel poor and under stress. Some experts blame the family for a variety of social ills ranging from drug abuse to teenage pregnancy. They want the government to do something about these problems, but disagree radically on what the government should do.

Colorado representative Pat Schroeder is the co-chair of the Congressional Caucus on Women's Issues. She maintains that a comprehensive government family policy is needed to solve the problems faced by America's families. Under this policy, the government would fund programs such as day care and family leave policies for parents with new babies or seriously ill children. It would also increase health care benefits for poor families. Schroeder contends that these policies would relieve the stress many families feel:

> Just as the harsh economic conditions of the Depression demanded federal action for individuals in the 1930s, dramatic changes in social and economic life demand federal action for families in the 1980s and 1990s. It's time for a "New Deal" for American families.

Critics disagree with Schroeder's solutions, but agree that something should be done. Chester E. Finn, professor of economics and public policy at Vanderbilt University in Nashville, Tennessee, argues that sweeping government policies would interfere with family life. He and others believe that government policies too often take over the role of a family; rather than depending upon one another for assistance, family members depend on the state. In an address given before the Center for the American Experiment in Minneapolis, Minnesota, Finn stated:

> Immorality and dependency are apt to result from over-generous social programs, and the more the government does with, to, and for children, the more it interferes with the abilities of families to look after their own.

These experts prefer measures that give more money to families directly, leaving decision-making up to individuals. Advocates believe, for example, that families might use this money to keep one parent out of the work force and home with young children. Choosing this traditional family model would improve family and social stability, these experts maintain.

The wide discrepancy in solutions has made it difficult for the government to enact a family policy on which everyone can agree. The viewpoints in this chapter reflect this ongoing debate.

"Policymakers and other leaders have a moral obligation to speak the obvious truth that two-parent families are superior and to adopt policies that promote them. "

The Government Should Support Traditional Families

William R. Mattox Jr.

In the following viewpoint, William R. Mattox Jr. asserts that the government should adopt a variety of policies specifically aimed at strengthening traditional families. Mattox defines traditional families as two-parent families in which one parent works and the other parent stays home to raise the children. According to Mattox, a government-supported return to this family model would help reduce teen pregnancy and chemical dependency. Mattox is a policy analyst for the Family Research Council, a Washington, D.C.-based organization that promotes the traditional family in public policy.

As you read, consider the following questions:

1. Mattox claims that in most two-parent families, both parents work. How does this situation affect the family and society, according to the author?
2. What specific policies does Mattox recommend to promote traditional families?
3. Why does Mattox believe that promoting a return to traditional family values can ease America's social problems?

Adapted from "The Parent Trap" by William R. Mattox Jr. Reprinted with permission from the Winter 1991 issue of *Policy Review*, the flagship publication of the Heritage Foundation, 214 Massachusetts Ave. NE, Washington, DC 20002.

Contrary to the assertions of professional children's advocates in Washington, the number one problem facing American children today is not lack of subsidized day-care centers, nutrition programs, or after-school care for "latchkey" kids. It's not even economic poverty, although 20 percent of American children live below the official poverty line. The biggest problem facing American children is a deficit of another kind—a deficit that is at least as serious as the budget or trade deficits. The biggest problem facing American children today is a lack of time with and attention from their parents.

Parents Need More Time

Parents today spend 40 percent less time with their children than did parents in 1965, according to data collected from personal time diaries by sociologist John Robinson of the University of Maryland. In 1965, parents on average spent approximately 30 hours a week with their kids. By 1985, parent-child interaction had dropped to just 17 hours a week.

This incredible decline in family time can be attributed to increases in the number of single-parent families and in the total number of hours two-parent families devote to paid employment. A true "pro-child" policy would seek to combat the economic and cultural forces behind these trends, rather than trying to replace families with government programs.

A growing number of scholars and policy analysts recognize this. Indeed, pro-family conservatives are hardly alone these days in emphasizing the primacy of the family.

"Government, no matter how effective and how important and how necessary, can never, never substitute for strong families," writes David Blankenhorn, president of the Institute for American Values. "If we want to reinvest and strengthen families, it has to be through families, not simply through government programs as a replacement for what we see as a family failure."

Government Support

In a landmark 1990 report, William Galston and Elaine Ciulla Kamarck of the Progressive Policy Institute echo this sentiment:

> Government cannot, under any set of conditions, provide the kind of nurturance that children, particularly young children, need. Given all the money in the world, government programs will not be able to instill self-esteem, good study habits, advanced language skills, or sound moral values in children as effectively as can strong families. . . . Government will never have the resources or the ability to replace what children lose when they lose supportive families. This suggests that the focus of public policy should be to look for ways to create *stable* families, not *substitute* families.

Despite this increasing awareness of the crucial importance of the family, some professional children's advocates remain fixated on federal programs. Early drafts of a report to be released by the bipartisan National Commission on Children suggest that the commission is apt to portray children as an underfunded client class of the welfare state rather than as unique individuals whose well-being is best served when they are raised in strong families. Moreover, it appears likely that the commission will urge lawmakers to create and expand government programs that both take over family functions and require parents to spend more of their time working to generate enough taxes to pay for these programs.

Freedom from State Control

A family policy for a free people will largely be one involving the creative disengagement of the state and the reconstruction, to the degree possible, of the natural family economy. From nature, the family can claim prior existence to the state and the exercise of prerogatives that no government can rightfully impair. For families in America, the central task of the next decade is to win back the authority and autonomy which are their due. The alternative can be starkly drawn: the continued socialization of families and childrearing, to their ultimate disappearance, and the ongoing destabilizing of a free and responsible people.

Allan Carlson, *Family Questions*, 1988.

This is no way to promote the welfare of American children. If policymakers really want to help our next generation, they should promote stronger "family" policy. They need to recognize that while government cannot strongarm Americans into being good parents, government can promote certain policies that make it easier for parents to give their children more of that increasingly precious commodity—time.

Fast-Track Families

The American family today lives in a time-pressure cooker. "On the fast track of two-career families in the go-go society of modern life, the most rationed commodity in the home is time," observes syndicated columnist Suzanne Fields. Accordingly, today's family schedules are often quite complex. . . .

Whether couples adopt a tag-team arrangement or a same-shift strategy, two-income households spend considerably less time with their children than do breadwinner-homemaker households. (Of course, there are certainly some traditional families that suffer from father absence due to the time-demanding nature of the sole breadwinner's work.) This discrepancy is most pronounced in maternal time with children. In fact, research by University of Virginia sociologists Steven Nock and Paul William Kingston shows that employed mothers of preschool children on average spend less than half as much time with their children as do full-time mothers at home. Some suggest that employed mothers spend a higher proportion of their time on "high quality" child-centered activities like playing with dolls, going to the park, or reading *Green Eggs and Ham*. But Nock and Kingston do not find this to be the case.

Paternal time with children suffers as well. In fact, one study found that fathers in two-income households spend less time with their young children than do fathers in single-earner households, largely because guilt-ridden same-shift wives "essentially push the dads out of the way in their rush to spend time with baby at the end of the day.". . .

Singled Out

Time pressures can be especially daunting for single parents—and especially harmful to their children. Children in single-parent homes usually receive less parental attention, affection, and supervision than other children. Not only is one parent absent from the home (and research by sociologist Frank Furstenberg shows that three-fourths of all children of divorce have contact with their fathers less than two days a month), but the other parent is overloaded with money-making and household tasks. Indeed, Robinson's data show that, on average, single mothers spend one-third less time each week than married mothers in primary child-care activities such as dressing, feeding, chauffeuring, talking, playing, or helping with homework. . . .

The time deficits in single-parent households are aggravated by the devastating emotional effects of divorce on children. It is little wonder that, when compared with children in two-parent families, children in single-parent homes have lower measures of academic achievement and increased levels of depression, stress, anxiety, aggression, mental illness, substance abuse, juvenile delinquency, youth gang membership, and other physical, emotional, and behavioral problems. . . .

Unbridled Careerism

Growing economic pressures aren't the only reason families have less time together. A number of cultural factors have also played a major role.

"Unbridled careerism" is partly responsible for the decline in family time, says Karl Zinsmeister of the American Enterprise Institute. "For years, one of the most cogent criticisms of American sex roles and economic arrangements has been the argument that many fathers get so wrapped up in earning and doing at the workplace that they become dehumanized, losing interest in the intimate joys of family life and failing to participate fairly in domestic responsibilities," he writes. "Now it appears workaholism and family dereliction have become equal opportunity diseases, striking mothers as much as fathers."

The devaluation of mothering stands behind such trends. As Zinsmeister notes, "Today, women are more likely to be admired and appreciated for launching a catchy new ad campaign for toothpaste than they are for nurturing and shaping an original personality." Ironically, this has a detrimental impact on fathering as well. So long as child-rearing is viewed as a low calling for women, it is unlikely that it will take on increased significance for men. . . .

Whereas institutions outside the family—such as schools, the mass media, businesses—once largely reinforced the inculcation of traditional values, today they are often indifferent or downright hostile to family values and the rights of parents to pass on such values to their children. Many parents sense that they are being undercut by larger institutional forces. And they recognize that children who lack the self-esteem that comes from parental attention and affection are especially vulnerable to negative peer and cultural influences.

This helps explain why parents are not marching in the streets for government and business policies—such as socialized daycare—that take over child-rearing responsibilities from families. Understandably, parents are not eager to see their already tenuous role in their children's lives diminished further. They correctly perceive that time with children is essential to child-rearing success, and they are unhappy with the amount of time they currently have available for their kids. . . .

Traditional Families Are Best

Many opinion leaders in government, academia, and the mass media view initiatives designed to increase family time—especially those that recognize the strengths of the breadwinner-homemaker family model—as an attempt to "turn back the clock" rather than "facing the realities" of modern family life. They overlook the fact that concerns about family time are shared by a broad spectrum of individuals, all of whom do not agree on the optimal division of household labor.

A 1989 Cornell University study found that two-thirds of all mothers employed full-time would like to work fewer hours so that they could devote more time to their families. And, when respondents to a 1989 survey commissioned by the Mass. Mutual Insurance Company were asked to identify "extremely effective" ways to strengthen the family, nearly twice as many opted for "spending more time together" than listed "full-time parent raising kids." Clearly, concerns about family time are not limited to those who regard the breadwinner-homemaker family model as ideal. . . .

What, then, can government do to foster more family time and nurture stronger parent-child relationships? Rather than expanding the scope of government to replace families, policymakers should seek to help parents fulfill their child-rearing responsibilities by dramatically reducing the tax burden on families with children. Allowing parents to keep more of their own earned income would give families greater control of their money—and their time.

Government Policies Should Support Parents

The nuclear family remains America's bedrock institution. While it has taken a battering, government should not write it off, nor join the socialist assault. Ambition and need may have taken half of American mothers into the work force, but the best decisions, and the final decision, as to where and how children should be reared, should be left to the parents themselves.

Government should support, not direct, that decision.

Patrick Buchanan, *Washington Inquirer*, July 7, 1989.

There are a number of ways to provide such relief. Policymakers could raise the tax exemption for dependents to $7,000 or extend the Earned Income Tax Credit up the income scale, or greatly expand the Young Child Tax Credit (a refundable tax credit that was created as part of the 1990 child-care bill). Whatever the instrument, tax cuts should be keyed to the presence, age, and number of children. This means lawmakers interested in pro-child tax relief should steer clear of Senator Daniel Patrick Moynihan's proposal to reduce payroll taxes because it fails to take into consideration the presence of children. In fact, under the Moynihan proposal, a childless couple earning $100,000 a year would receive three times the tax savings offered to a median-income family of four. . . .

Homework for Parents

Tax relief, while much needed, can only go so far in promoting family time. America must also seek what Zinsmeister calls a "more fluid, less rigid job market" that gives family-oriented workers significant discretion over when, where, and how many hours they work for pay. Accordingly, policymakers should encourage flexible hours, part-time work, job sharing, and most especially home-based employment opportunities. Not only is homework one of the more promising work-family solutions, but it also has the potential to put a dent in rush-hour traffic congestion, daytime home burglaries, automotive air pollution, and gasoline consumption.

The first step toward making home-based employment a more viable option would be to loosen restrictions on the deductibility of home office expenses. Under current law, taxpayers cannot write off home office expenses unless home office space is used exclusively for income-producing activities. In other words, overhead expenses for a room that doubles as an office and a guest bedroom cannot be claimed. This exclusive-use rule is particularly burdensome to families with children because they have greater demands on household space than do, say, bachelors living alone. Thus, Congress should consider dropping the exclusive-use test for parents.

Reordering Priorities

In addition, government policies should encourage a re-ordering of priorities over the life cycle. Americans tend to work greater hours when they are most apt to have child-rearing responsibilities and fewer hours (if any) during the twilight years of life when they are least apt to have child-rearing responsibilities.

Author Arlene Rossen Cardozo and lawyer Edith U. Fierst believe the solution to this curious arrangement is "sequencing"— seeking to "do it all" over the course of one's life, instead of all at once. Cardozo and Fierst point to Supreme Court Justice Sandra Day O'Connor and former United Nations Ambassador Jeane Kirkpatrick as examples of "sequencers" who took time off from employment when children were young and then returned to their careers after their kids were "well-launched."

Sequencing could be encouraged by calling upon employers to give preference in hiring to parents returning to the labor force after an extended stint at home with children. In essence, parents who leave their jobs after the birth or adoption of a child would be treated much like veterans who leave their jobs to serve in the military: they would be given preference in hiring for any available position for which they are qualified.

Apart from facilitating full-time parental care of young children for extended periods of time, Congress should remove disincentives to old-age employment, or "twilighting." Specifically, Congress should eliminate the Social Security earnings test and allow "twilighters" to receive full benefits rather than have their benefits reduced in proportion to their income. At the same time, Congress should seek to reverse the growing trend toward early retirement by accelerating scheduled increases in the Social Security retirement age. Indeed, given the improving health and life expectancy of Americans, Congress should consider raising the retirement age beyond currently scheduled thresholds.

Educational choice is another policy that could give children more time with their parents. Family time has been seriously eroded by parents' attempts to pay for homes in good school districts. Fortunately, this added economic pressure could be alleviated somewhat through the use of school vouchers.

A free-choice educational system would give parents the opportunity to choose, without penalty, the school best suited to meeting the unique needs of their children, even if that school is a private, sectarian, or home school. Such a system would encourage greater parental participation in the educational process, and stimulate some creative experimentation that just might redefine the concept of parental participation entirely. . . .

Finally, lawmakers should construct family policy that favors two-parent families. While it is appropriate to laud the efforts of those conscientious single parents striving to give all they can to their children, policymakers and other leaders have a moral obligation to speak the obvious truth that two-parent families are superior and to adopt policies that promote them.

The will to take such action has often been lacking, yet the urgency for doing so has never been greater. . . .

There are several steps policymakers could take to discourage divorce and illegitimacy. In response to the problems of no-fault divorce, Michael Schwartz of the Free Congress Foundation has urged states to adopt a "two-track" marriage system in which prospective married couples could opt for either an easily dissoluble no-fault union or a marriage that could be dissolved only after findings of fault. Given the freedom to choose, Schwartz believes most couples would opt for a fault-based arrangement. But even if only a handful of marriages opted for this more-difficult-to-break bond, that would be an improvement over the current system, in which one million children see their parents divorce every year. . . .

Parents Need Government Help

It would be a mistake to suggest that government action alone can solve America's family-time famine. Clearly, major changes also are needed in a number of other areas—in the employment practices businesses adopt, in the cultural messages sent by Hollywood and Madison Avenue, in the attitudes and priorities of career-obsessed parents.

Still, the time for government action is now. Americans believe "parents having less time to spend with their families" is the most important reason for the family's decline in our society, according to a recent survey. And most parents would like to see the work-family pendulum swing back in the direction of home.

"Our most pressing problems are simply not susceptible of resolution through policies directed at families."

Government Support for the Traditional Family Is Unnecessary

Stephanie Coontz

Stephanie Coontz teaches at The Evergreen State College in Olympia, Washington, and is the author of *The Social Origins of Private Life: A History of American Families 1600-1900*. In the following viewpoint, Coontz argues that strengthening the traditional family to solve America's myriad social problems would be ineffective. She maintains that the government should solve underlying problems such as economic inequality and the repression of minorities and women if it wants to decrease social problems. Traditional families, Coontz contends, have contributed to this inequality and repression and therefore should not be strengthened.

As you read, consider the following questions:

1. According to the author, how has the nuclear family contributed to the increase in social problems in the United States?
2. How would government family policies contribute to America's social problems, according to Coontz?
3. According to Coontz, how have social changes that have taken place during the 1960s and 1970s affected society?

Stephanie Coontz, "The Pitfalls of Policy," *Against the Current*, September/October 1989. Reprinted with permission.

The family is one of the hottest new topics for political rhetoric, popular concern and faddish prescriptions. Conservatives attack the women's movement and government regulation for robbing families "of the autonomy that was once theirs"; liberals go back and forth between decrying divorce's "feminization of poverty" and celebrating the new "family pluralism" (occasionally sounding as if single-parent families constitute a wonderful growth experience).

Champions of the Family

Even some feminists and leftists have been sucked into the debate, contending that they are the real champions of "the family." There is thus a temptation to articulate a family policy, endorsing a particular definition of family and making demands on its behalf for state support.

I want to argue against attempts by leftists to formulate such a "family policy," on two grounds. First, the fundamental assumptions behind such an endeavor direct our attention away from the real crisis of our society, of which the family crisis is only a subset. This is a crisis of social obligation that extends far beyond sexual or familial relations.

Second, most efforts to articulate a family policy rest on a misunderstanding of the historical relation between family privacy and the capitalist state. The very privacy that we often conceptualize in opposition to state intervention is as much a product of capitalist development and ruling-class hegemony as is the modern state itself.

Effects of Family Breakdown

Now it is certainly true that the crisis of social obligation and commitment in the United States adversely affects familial relations. The United States has the highest teen pregnancy rates in the world, while ranking 18th in infant mortality; child abuse is high and probably rising; as many as 25 percent of urban newborns have been exposed to drugs in the womb; and even middle-class schools report an extraordinary epidemic of parental neglect.

While many women have benefited from liberalized divorce, escaping abusive or oppressive relationships, others have suffered. Fifty-four percent of single-parent families, almost all of them headed by women, fall below the poverty line. People often talk about the feminization of poverty, since women are more than 60 percent of the poor, but more striking still is the infantalization of poverty. Children have now displaced elders as the age group in America most likely to be poor. One in five U.S. children, almost one in two Black children, lives in poverty.

Legal gains for women in the public sphere have done little to mitigate this situation. Eighty percent of all women workers remain concentrated in just twenty-three of the 200 occupational categories listed in the U.S. census. Despite some gains in middle management and the professions, most women have entered low-paid, sex-stereotyped jobs that pose for them a crisis in childcare: 11 million children under age eleven have no childcare while their parents are at work.

New Kinds of Domination

Developments like these have led some people to wonder if family life was really as oppressive as it seemed in the 1960s and early '70s, or at least to conclude that the reforms and movements of that period may have left many families worse off than before. For many women and children, the break-up of traditional family relations has meant not liberation but new kinds of domination and despair.

The Myth of the Nuclear Family

One of the primary justifications for the stingy, arbitrary and humiliating nature of social welfare in the United States has been the myth of the self-reliant, private family: the idea that a normal, healthy family takes care of its own, stands on its own two feet, and seeks to live a private, autonomous life.

It is this *myth* that the capitalist state has imposed upon the working class.

Stephanie Coontz, *Against The Current*, November/December 1989.

Family disruption has been linked to poor school performance, drug abuse and depression among children. Liberalization of repressive legislation and morality has allowed violent anti-female and child pornography to come out into the open. Rising rates of suicide among teenagers of all classes further contribute to the sense that families need our help rather than our criticism.

It is not surprising, then, that many progressive thinkers have abandoned earlier attacks on the repressive nature of the family. They have begun to try to develop a family policy that can allay popular concerns about the excessive individualism of the modern United States and cut into the new mass base that the right wing seems to have garnered with its "pro-family" rhetoric. Thus the Coalition for Labor Union Women now raises many of its demands for welfare and labor reform in the context of defending the family, while many liberal Democrats espouse programs that put "families first."

Efforts of oppressed national minorities to recapture their own history have demonstrated that under some circumstances families can act as a source of resistance to the dominant culture, a means of coping with poverty or preserving distinctive values, an alternative to rampant individualism. Many community organizers, therefore, now prioritize issues and demands that support the maintenance of such families. Some gay and lesbian couples or parents have demanded that their living arrangements be recognized as stable, "normal," and worthy of the label "family." Whatever their differences in defining family, then, a whole new spectrum of groups defines itself as "pro-family."

Capitalism Causes Chaos

Leftists should not minimize the damage inflicted by many changes in family norms and relations. We should not ignore the crisis of our nation's children, nor pretend that demands on behalf of children are encompassed by a general feminist program.

To recognize that kinship, continuity and small intimate associations are essential parts of existence for all people, and that children need consistent, personally involved caregivers, however, is not to say that we should organize around a program for defending, revitalizing or even redefining families. Nor does it follow that we should formulate our demands on the state in terms of its services to families.

First of all, many of the problems associated with the so-called family crisis are simply old inequalities in a new guise, more visible now that some of them have appeared in the group normally thought of as middle class. Capitalism has traditionally distributed poverty unequally within the working class, both outside family channels—through racial and ethnic divisions, occupational rankings, etc.—and within the family. Women and children bore the burdens of poverty just as heavily, if less visibly, within the "traditional" two-parent family as they do in single-parent families today.

The only route to survival for many 19th-century working-class families, for example, was to send their children into the mills and mines. Indeed, the prolonged innocence of 19th-century middle-class children, whose loss is so bemoaned by the right wing, rested on the early adulthood of working children. It depended especially on the young girls whose domestic labor in other people's homes created a "haven" for the development of true motherhood or whose exploitation in sweatshops created the cheap consumer goods that gave middle-class families an elevated standard of living. (Today, too, youth are the core workers of the fast-food industries that make life a little easier for some two-income families.) . . .

214

Second, emphasis on the "feminization" of poverty and on the fact that divorce is now the greatest single (short-term) predictor of poverty for white women and children tends to obscure other kinds of poverty that cannot be explained by family dynamics or dissolution. Indeed, 54 percent of the growth in poverty in the United States since 1979 has taken place in two-parent families.

Women and Minorities

The ethnic group that has experienced the sharpest increase in poverty during the last ten years is the one that census-takers label "Hispanic." Most of the growth in Hispanic poverty is due to the worsening position of married-couple families, whose poverty rate grew by more than one-half from 1978 to 1987.

A feminization-of-poverty or crisis-of-the-family analysis also diverts attention from a process that has been going on among both white women and minority men: increasing polarization between the privileged few, who have the resources to benefit from the dismantling of legal discrimination by competing successfully for management or higher-education jobs, and the majority who are confined to the lowest levels of the economy and never get a shot at equal treatment or affirmative action.

Third, many problems of modern families are symptoms rather than causes of our social ills, and treating the family rather than the cause is at best ineffective, at worse counterproductive. Part of the problem in starting or maintaining families is the deterioration in men's as well as women's economic position.

Young men's real earnings have dropped by almost one-third in the past ten years, young Black men's by almost 50 percent. In 1963, 60 percent of men aged 20-24 earned enough to keep a family of three out of poverty; by 1984 only 42 percent could do so. These are structural problems, not problems caused by divorce or by the "loss of childhood," though they are certainly likely to make divorce, loss of childhood, and failure to pay child support more prevalent.

Declining Wages

The most critical factor affecting family arrangements and their outcomes has been the erosion of those unionized sectors of the economy that traditionally extended a "family wage" to significant portions of the working class. Two-thirds of all contracts negotiated since 1982 have involved take-backs such as two-tier wage systems or loss of benefits.

Since 1980, steel has shed 40 percent of its work force, the United Auto Workers has lost one-third of its members, textile has been stripped of 25 percent of its unionized labor force and the mineworkers have lost 42 percent of their members. Today only 18 percent of the non-agricultural labor force is unionized, half the percentage of the 1950s.

The fastest-growing sector of the economy has been service work, which is only 5 percent unionized (down from 15 percent in 1970); the fastest-growing part of this sector (indeed of the whole economy) is part-time work, which employs women, youths and elders. Demand for cheap female labor is so great that in the 1982 recession, for the first time, male unemployment topped women's.

Such structural factors far outweigh the impact of family rearrangements in affecting the spread and distribution of poverty in the United States today. Even if there had been no changes in the age, race and gender of household heads since 1950, the poverty rate in 1980 would have been only 23 percent lower than it was. This overstates the effect of change in family arrangements by including race and age factors that are not caused by family dissolution, but even so it leaves 77 percent of poverty associated with structural, not familial, factors. Since 1980, a majority of the increase in childhood poverty has occurred in two-parent households.

Mutual Responsibility

Our vision of a better world must include a sense of how we might re-establish interdependence and social responsibility without recreating its earlier repressive aspects. We must consider how a future society could provide social services without engaging in the kind of social engineering or bureaucratic control that has understandably made people suspicious of many plans for a "brave new world." At the same time, in opposing such social engineering we must avoid romanticizing a notion of personal privacy and family autonomy that is equally alienating.

Stephanie Coontz, *Against the Current*, November/December 1989.

These problems are not answered by a policy geared to supporting "families." Obviously, one side effect of a social policy that addressed some of these problems would be to make families more viable for those who wish to remain in them. But our most pressing problems are simply not susceptible of resolution through policies directed at families. The family-wage system to which conservatives are so attached—to the extent that it existed at all—relied, James Coleman points out, "on both dependents and incomes being distributed across households.". . .

Finally, attempts by the left to capitalize on an understandable but romanticized nostalgia for a more stable personal life represent an abandonment of one of the major insights of the feminist analysis of the 1960s. Whatever their role in compensating for or even softening other types of oppression, families are restrictive. Most family systems, whether extended or nuclear, have been based on the private control of female productive and reproductive powers by the household head. The family may be a necessary means of survival for the working class, but it is one that has been based upon the subordination of women and the highly unequal division of its meager benefits among family members.

Women Take the Burden

Families also tend to substitute the private exercise of social obligation by women—care of the young, the aged, the ill, for example—for public responsibility in this arena. Women as a gender rather than people as a community have been forced to shoulder the social dependencies that are inevitable for all individuals at various stages of life. The fact that liberalized divorce and sexuality have highlighted rather than solved the problems of how to meet social obligations and care for dependents doesn't mean that we should go back to the older family, which denied obligation everywhere else in society by forcibly imposing it on women. . . .

Even aside from the analytical problems in focusing on family protection, what kind of policy would we demand that the state adopt toward families, and what kind of unit would we direct that policy toward? Many liberals favor the *Journal of Home Economics* approach, which defines the family as any unit of intimate and transacting persons who share some resources and commitment to each other over time. As a local Democrat in Washington State puts it, family can be a man and woman, two kids and a dog, or simply two friends living together.

Such a definition, however, represents a capitulation to the idea that families are the only appropriate units for intimacy, resource-sharing and—by implication—state support. Clearly, a family has to be more than one. Yet single households are the fastest-growing sector of the population. Should they receive fewer benefits and rights than families?

Besides, a family is also less than something, a way of restricting aid and obligation, setting boundaries. It is safe to predict, given the realities of political power in the United States, that the state will choose a restrictive unit to support or intervene in, however nimbly we choose to define families for ourselves. The state also tends to impose class-biased, sexist and ethnocentric definitions of family norms, putting working-class, minority, or gay individuals at considerable disadvantage in legal disputes about family rights.

Privacy Can Be Dangerous

The pathologies of family life simply cannot allow any concern for "privacy" to override the need for protection of abused family members. A national poll by the *Los Angeles Times* in August 1985 found that 22 percent of Americans had been victims of child abuse, the vast majority of it committed inside families, by relatives. Fifty-five percent of the incidents involved sexual intercourse.

John Demos points to studies showing that abusing families tend to be marked by "constant competition over who will be taken care of." This suggests that abuse is an extension of demands for intimacy, nurturing and individual fulfillment that are part of the 20th-century ideal of family privacy. (Colonial families, without such ideals, did not seem to have such corruptions of them either.)

Colleen McGrath points out that battering occurs "in the most 'private' areas of the house . . . in places that are especially isolated and closed off from outside intervention"; it is the other side of the nurturing intensity that occurs in this "psychological hothouse." In this period of soaring child-abuse and wife-battering cases, any program organized around the sanctity of families is surely unacceptable. . . .

Whatever the limits of 1960s feminism, its great contribution to socialist thought lay in its identification of *both* family and state with patriarchy and repression and its implicit suggestion that neither one can reform the other. Rather, mutual obligation and interdependence must be built into both work relations and personal relations, extending beyond the family and alongside, independent of, the state—including the so-called socialist or workers' states. . . .

Pressuring the State

Feminists and socialists should be discussing what kinds of demands we can raise that put pressure on the state to help those in need while simultaneously projecting a vision of self-organization and mutual support. Concentration on a family policy can only distract us from that task.

"Federal legislation is necessary to ensure that leave benefits are extended to all people."

The Government Should Mandate Family Leave

T. Berry Brazelton and Patricia Schroeder

The following viewpoint is in two parts. Part I is by T. Berry Brazelton. Pediatrician Brazelton is one of America's leading authorities on child development. He has written many books on the subject, including *Working and Caring*. He has also founded Parent Action, a grass-roots parental advocacy organization. Part II is by Patricia Schroeder. Schroeder has been a member of the House of Representatives from Colorado since 1972. She is a member of several congressional committees, and is the co-chair of the congressional Caucus for Women's Issues. In this viewpoint, the authors argue that the government should pass a law requiring employers to provide unpaid leave for new or adoptive parents and guaranteeing their jobs upon their return. This policy, known as family or parental leave, would provide a much-needed benefit for parents, the authors maintain.

As you read, consider the following questions:

1. How would family leave benefit families, according to the authors?
2. According to Schroeder, what damage has the lack of a family leave bill caused?

I

Under the Family and Medical Leave Act, employees of businesses with more than 50 employees would be guaranteed 12 weeks annually of protected leave to care for parents or new children. It is a relatively modest plan: Group health coverage would continue, but no pay would be attached for employees on leave. The cost to employers is estimated at $7 annually per employee. Working couples could share the time, or stagger it to be at home for a total of six months with a new baby. Their benefits and their jobs would be protected.

Family Stress

Making this bill law would help Americans with a serious problem underrated in our society: family stress. There is every indication that families in the U.S. are trying to handle more than they can alone. No one is listening. This stress is affecting our children.

This is something I have witnessed for years in my work as a doctor. I have also seen it during a two-year stint traveling around the country as part of the president's National Commission on Children. We assessed the plight of families, and can report that they are not doing well.

The facts are simple. The clearest one is our embarrassing infant mortality rate—at 13.5 per thousand it is worse than that of some Third World countries. Another serious symptom is the family breakdown and its effect on our children. The divorce rate is rapidly climbing. Some 25% of children under six years of age are in single-parent families, and 57% of all children will spend a significant part of their lives living with one parent. The term "nuclear family" as we knew it in the 1950s now describes less than 25% of families.

Poverty and drugs play a role here. About 15%-20% of babies in city hospitals are being born to addicted women. These newborns are disorganized and vulnerable to the environments to which they must return. Such a disordered generation is ominous.

We need to concentrate, though, on a form of desperation that doesn't make the headlines—that of middle-class families. The tension created by the necessity for both parents to be in the work force pervades their lives. The parents feel there is not enough time left for caring for their children. The family as a nurturing environment for children seems to be disintegrating. We watch the television pictures of children in Romania's "orphanages" with long-distance pity. But we are cheating our own children of their childhood as surely as did Nicolae Ceausescu when he set up "orphanages" in Romania.

My work over the years at Boston's Children's Hospital has involved children in precisely the age groups that would benefit from the Family Leave Act. At Children's Hospital, we have found new evidence pointing to the importance of the first three months of a baby's life. To form stable attachments and get a good start in life, a baby must pass with its parents through four stages.

In the first seven to 10 days of the baby's life, the parents (with the baby's cooperation) must learn how to help the newborn maintain an alert state and pay attention to its surroundings. In the second stage, babies learn to smile and vocalize in return for attention from parents. In the third stage (ages two to three months), the child learns to expect different reactions from each parent and to tell the difference between parents and strangers. In the fourth stage (somewhere around four months) the baby is sure enough of himself and his care-givers to take the lead in building relationships. We have found that the baby "knows" his or her parents by the age of four months and can therefore "know" that they will return after disappearing for the working day.

The parents, too, need the time this leave provides. Post–partum depression in the new mother is sometimes regarded as mundane, but it is a serious and common reaction to labor, delivery and the stresses of a new baby. Colicky crying every evening in the first three months occurs in about 80% of babies. Working parents need the first three months to recover and to regain equanimity as a family if they are to brighten the baby's future. Without this time together, parents suffer the danger of later depressions—and their employers the cost in productivity for that depression in the workplace.

Biases Against Family Leave

Why do some Americans resist the Family Leave Act? Three biases are at the basis of this resistance. The first is the feeling that families should be self-sufficient. Any invasion by government policy is likely to weaken their structure and deprive them of their autonomy. Hence, no family legislation.

The second bias is a self-defeating one. Americans feel that mothers should be at home, and if they are not, their children will suffer. Hence, they let the mother "pay" by allowing no attempt to supplement out-of-home care for children of women who must work.

The third bias is more social: Americans have trouble taking up the question of poverty. Americans dislike poor people and we hate failure. As a result, we ignore failure in our underprivileged classes. We refuse to support them toward success.

Biases are powerful as long as they are unconscious. Once we face them as a nation, there are solutions available. The report of the National Commission on Children recommends changing prenatal health care, ensuring income security for families, improving the role of family in education and improving support systems for families who must work. In this report, we emphasized the importance of introducing a national policy for protected parental leave at the time of a new baby or an adoption.

There are, of course, other steps to take. In the U.S., on-site or available child care, shared job opportunities and flextime are other options. In any case, the results will be positive. The Family and Work Institute, a nonprofit research corporation in New York, recently evaluated businesses in four states that have instituted a Family Leave Act. The businesses found that instituting family policies increased recruitment and retention of trained employees, thereby cutting costs in the long run. The Child Care Action Campaign even studied small businesses that had instituted family leave policies. They have not suffered the financial setbacks predicted by the U.S. Chamber of Commerce. On the contrary, they claim that it has been more than worth it to them in recruitment and retention of family-oriented employees. Women and men both showed strengthened allegiance to their firms.

This is a time in our history when many young families, including their children, feel unnoticed and unwanted. Why not, at the very least, make family leave American law so it can back them up.

II

In his nomination speech at the Democratic convention in 1932, Franklin Delano Roosevelt promised a "New Deal" to the "forgotten man at the bottom of the pyramid." An economic depression had been paralyzing the American economy and impoverishing its citizens. Roosevelt saw it was time for the federal government to step in to enhance the welfare and security of regular folk, literally to "deal" them a new hand that included employment opportunities, improved working conditions, and retirement security.

Parents Need Parental Leave

In most other countries (all rich nations and many poor nations) childbirth receives prominent treatment in the law, and is the subject of elaborate legislative support. When Brazil rewrote its constitution in 1988 one of the provisions was the right of all Brazilian women to paid leave when they gave birth to a child.

The notion of paid parenting leave becoming a constitutional right boggles the American imagination. We cannot even get unpaid leave, for restricted groups of workers, onto our statute books. While there are powerful groups pushing for a constitutional amendment to protect the flag, no one has suggested that the constitution concern itself with protecting pregnant women or newborn babies.

Sylvia Ann Hewlett, *When the Bough Breaks*, 1991.

Just as the harsh economic conditions of the Depression demanded federal action for individuals in the 1930s, dramatic changes in social and economic life demand federal action for *families* in the 1980s and 1990s. It's time for a "New Deal" for American families.

Working women and men are struggling daily to balance the demands of jobs and families. No longer does the typical family contain a husband-breadwinner and a wife-homemaker taking care of the children in the privacy of her home during the day. Most families—even those with very young children—now include employed mothers. In fact, because of high rates of divorce and births out of wedlock, the fastest growing family form is the single-parent family headed by a woman. Many of these families are poor, and an increasing number are homeless.

However, government and employers have not kept pace with these changes. Rather than supporting the diverse range of families that characterize contemporary America, we continue to penalize those that do not fit the old "Ozzie and Harriet" mold. I think it is time to stop punishing families and instead offer them a "New Deal" that ensures their economic security and general health and well-being, no matter what form their family takes. By strengthening the lives of families and individual family members, we will strengthen our economy, our political system, and our national security. All of these depend on the continued commitment and productivity of people, whose health and well-being begins in families.

Throughout my tenure in Congress, I have been working toward this goal by developing a national family policy agenda, one that recognizes the diversity of American families and provides flexibility in meeting their economic and social needs. . . .

Working Women

For the first time in our history, the majority of American women in their childbearing years are also working outside the home. The decision to start a family or have another child is no longer simply a private one between husband and wife; it also involves their bosses. An expectant mother must consider whether she can take leave to have her baby, whether the leave will be paid, whether she will continue to receive health insurance, and, most important, whether there will be a job for her when she is ready to go back to work.

These concerns are real because job protections are not guaranteed to all employees who need temporary leave to care for a newborn or newly adopted child or to care for a sick parent. In the United States, we depend on employers to voluntarily provide parental and sick leave benefits, and it is estimated that only about 40% of employed women receive maternity leave with partial pay and a job guarantee. As the proportion of mothers with young children in the labor force increases (and as the proportion of elderly individuals in the population also increases), the need for flexibility in caregiving is salient.

Slow Response to Families

Both government and private industry have been slow to respond to this need. In fact, the United States is one of the few industrialized nations in the world that does *not* have a national maternity leave policy (South Africa is another). The Pregnancy Discrimination Act, mandating that pregnancy be treated like any other temporary disability, did not become law until 1978. Until then, employers did not have to include pregnancy under a disability insurance plan, nor did an employer-sponsored health plan require coverage of maternity-related medical conditions. Even though the law corrected these inequalities, it did not direct employers to reinstate women in their jobs after they recovered from childbirth, nor did it provide them with disability benefits other than those provided to other employees. The reality for women was that having a baby meant they lost their job.

When thinking about how to extend job protections to pregnant women in the years following the passage of the Pregnancy Discrimination Act, it became evident that a maternity leave policy would not be the best solution because it would exclude fathers and adoptive parents from taking temporary leave to care for new children. Moreover, maternity leave policies do not recognize that employees other than pregnant women risk losing their jobs when they are temporarily unable to work because of a serious medical condition of their own or of other family members for whom they care.

The U.S. Needs Family Leave

If I asked you, "What do the United States and South Africa have in common?" your answer would probably be, "Not much, I hope." But would you know that we are the only two industrialized nations in the world without national family leave policies? All of our major competitors, including West Germany, Japan, Canada, as well as dozens of Third World nations, have recognized that there is a national interest in helping families balance work and family responsibilities.

The bottom line, quite frankly, is this: American parents ought to be able to have jobs and their families as well. And parents ought to be able to deal with rare family crises without losing those jobs. As a Nation, all of us have a stake in that, morally, socially, economically and politically.

What do American families do now when a crisis hits? The sad news is that many working people are on their own, caught in a choice between their families and their jobs.

Christopher J. Dodd, Statement made on the U.S. Senate floor, June 13, 1990.

Consequently, in 1987 I, along with William L. Clay (D-Mo.), introduced the Family and Medical Leave Act. After much negotiation and compromise, the final bill, backed by 151 cosponsors, required employers of 50 or more people to guarantee their employees up to 10 weeks of unpaid family leave to care for a newborn or newly adopted child, and up to 15 weeks of unpaid medical leave to recover from their own serious illness or to care for other family members during theirs. (This was a watered-down version of the original bill, which included smaller businesses and allowed for longer leave periods.)

Although the bill made great progress in the 100th Congress, it was not considered for passage in 1988. The Senate's version, S.2488, did come up in the last two weeks of Congress but was filibustered to death in the final days.

America Supports Family Leave

The Family and Medical Leave Act was again introduced in the 101st Congress. Support for such legislation continues to grow. A recent poll found that 79% of American voters support parental leave legislation. Nevertheless, business groups lobbied all out to defeat the Senate and House bills. We will face the same type of tough opposition but we remain determined to fight for a policy that we think helps families balance the competing demands of work and family. Federal legislation is necessary to ensure that leave benefits are extended to all people; we can no longer depend on a voluntary system that denies protections to many working parents.

"It is hard to find a single country in which parental leave has demonstrably and significantly strengthened family life."

The Government Should Not Mandate Family Leave

Bryce J. Christensen

Bryce J. Christensen is the editor of *The Family in America,* a monthly publication of The Rockford Institute, an organization in Rockford, Illinois, that works to maintain traditional gender roles. Christensen argues in the following viewpoint that family leave would destroy America's families by encouraging women to return to work shortly after the birth of their children and by increasing government's authority over families. Christensen believes that for the family to remain strong, mothers should stay at home and government involvement in the family should be minimal.

As you read, consider the following questions:

1. What conclusion does Christensen draw by comparing the United States to other countries?
2. According to the author, what specific negative effects would family leave have on the United States?
3. How should the government support families, according to the author?

Adapted from "Parental Leave: Domestic Opportunity or Foreign Failure?" by Bryce J. Christensen, *The Family in America* magazine, June 1991. Reprinted with permission.

Should the federal government require employers to give employees (especially women) time off for the birth of a child or for family emergencies? Advocates of a federally mandated parental leave have been pressing hard in recent years. They currently call their proposal family leave partly because it includes provisions for family responsibilities other than infant care, but mostly because of the political appeal of the word *family*. The demands of parenthood still define the key issue, so the debate is chiefly over parental leave. In 1990 activists persuaded Congress to pass a bill that would have required all firms with 50 or more employees to give three months' unpaid leave upon the birth of a child, but President Bush vetoed the measure. Now supporters of parental leave are back, more insistent than ever. One argument repeatedly made on behalf of parental leave—which usually means maternity leave—is not really an argument at all, but merely a call for America to fall in line with other industrial nations. In both the scholarly and popular press, activists point out again and again that "the United States stands alone among all industrialized nations in its lack of a statutory maternity leave policy." On rare occasions, the list of countries surveyed will include South Africa, lengthening the list of countries without maternity or parental leave to two, but usually the United States has no partner in disrepute. "The United States stands alone" is the usual refrain.

In this debate, standing alone is judged as inherently bad. But before succumbing to global groupthink, we ought to investigate the effects of parental leave abroad. Such an investigation is fair enough, since advocates of parental leave loudly insist on the relevance of foreign examples. At first blush, America's isolation on the question of mandated parental leave does appear suspect. But we need not look long or hard before serious doubts begin to arise about this policy.

Mandated Parental Leave

First, it should be noted that advocates of mandated parental leave almost invariably stress its supposed value as a support to childbearing and family life. Prominent pediatrician T. Berry Brazelton counts federally mandated parental leave as a critical first step in "strengthening the family system." Edward Zigler and his colleagues at Yale say they have "family well-being" in mind when they advocate federally mandated parental leave. Similarly, Sally Orr of the Association of Junior Leagues believes that the United States must adopt parental leave if we want to "have strong, healthy families." Family scholar and activist Urie Bronfenbrenner argues that the policy is essential to "family integrity." Congresswoman Patricia Schroeder claims the typical American couple needs parental leave to safeguard "their family's stability." John Sweeny of the AFL-CIO declares that "nothing short of the survival of the American family is at stake" in the debate over parental leave. A writer for *The Christian Century* feels federal parental-leave legislation would reflect "a willingness to take an honest look" at "the needs of families."

The European Birth Dearth

But an honest look abroad does not foster confidence in parental leave as a support to childbearing and family life. Indeed, it is hard to find a single country in which parental leave has demonstrably and significantly strengthened family life. American advocates of parental leave typically laud the virtues of policies found in Western Europe and Scandinavia, lands with long-established and generous provisions. It is more than a little strange that parental-leave advocates, who profess such strong concern for the family, rarely acknowledge that women in the countries they would have America imitate have stopped having babies—or at least have stopped having even enough babies to replace themselves. . . .

Chuck Asay by permission of the *Colorado Springs Gazette Telegraph.*

If advocates *know* that parental leave has not strengthened European family life, perhaps they advocate it out of despair. Perhaps they regard the retreat from childbearing and marriage evident in Western Europe and America as inevitable and irreversible, but they at least hope that parental leave will make life a bit easier for women who do have children while we all wait for the social extinction caused by our failure to reproduce. But it appears doubtful that most advocates of parental leave have

229

succumbed to such despair. Most speak and write in tones of ebullient confidence. Patricia Schroeder gives no hint of despair when she describes how parental leave will help Americans develop "a vibrant, dynamic model" of the family. With slightly more restraint, Eleanor Smeal of the National Organization for Women endorses parental leave as a sensible way of "adapting" to "our modern living experiences." If advocates of parental leave have been driven to their position by despair, they hide it well.

Rather, the conclusion appears inescapable that for most of those advocating parental leave, family life counts as merely a secondary or tertiary consideration, superseded by other cultural, political, or ideological objectives. Professed concern for the family melts away whenever these objectives are threatened. For instance, it is evident that the employment of women out of the home takes precedence over childbearing and rearing in the minds of many advocates of parental leave. Professor Zigler's definitive 1988 volume on *The Parental Leave Crisis* contains an essay arguing that "although the particular leaves in effect in France, Germany, and Sweden have proved beneficial to women, substantially longer leaves or leaves not based on attachment to the labor force might actually discourage women from working" and would therefore be undesirable. . . .

State Control of the Family

Many advocates of parental leave candidly admit that they regard unpaid parental leave as merely a first step in expanding the state's powers to redefine the relationship between work and family along European lines. Unpaid parental leave turns out to be only a stepping stone leading first to paid parental leave, then to expanded government child-care programs such as those found in Sweden, Denmark, or France. Aides to Congresswoman Schroeder have acknowledged that paid parental leave is their true objective. Berkeley psychologists Sheldon Zeduck and Kathleen Mosier call unpaid parental leave "only a first step toward resolving problems related to balancing roles in employing and family organizations." Parents need more help with day care, too, they assert. Dr. Brazelton urges the federal government to establish paid parental leave and to expand the system of government day care. The Women's Legal Defense Fund views unpaid parental leave as "a small first step" toward meeting "the needs and realities of American families today" and therefore considers it "sorely deficient by itself." The WLDF urges consideration of paid leaves as a next step. Writing in *The Nation*, law professor Nadine Taub endorses unpaid parental leave as "a vital step" but insists that it is "not enough." "The time has come," Taub writes, ". . . to move beyond a single-minded focus on the role of women as mothers of small children, to a broader discussion of the way society can meet all the caring needs traditionally assigned to women," including caring for the elderly as well as caring for children. "European countries provide helpful models" for Taub, who cites particularly Austria, Norway, France, and Sweden. . . .

Alternatives to Parental Leave

Federally mandated parental leave would also discourage individual American families from seeking new ways to reconcile work and home. Some professional women have postponed or suspended their careers to devote themselves to motherhood. A hopeful illustration of this pattern (often called "sequencing") may be seen among a group of women physicians interviewed in 1989 for *American Medical News*. Among these women who had deferred or delayed their medical careers for five years or more (20 years in one instance), "most are glad they spent time concentrating on their families." "I would advise my daughters," said one physician interviewed, ". . . to have children early and pursue a professional career later." Other young mothers in other fields might seriously consider this advice.

Opposition to Family Leave

Our longstanding opposition to federally mandated family and medical leave has always been and continues to be based on our strong belief that the Government should not have the power to mandate such a benefit even if employers and employees do not want or need it. . . .

Every Congress the Family and Medical Leave Act is introduced, it becomes less and less relevant because of the enormous strides employers have been making to accommodate work and family needs. . . .

A push for additional restrictions on our Nation's employers, such as those embodied in the Family and Medical Leave Act, ignores the reality outside the Capital Beltway. Although in our view there will never be a "right" time for mandated family and medical leave, this is probably the worst time in the legislation's history to pursue such a course of action.

Mary T. Tavenner, Statement before the Subcommittee on Labor-Management Relations of the U.S. House Education and Labor Committee, February 28, 1991.

Other American families have found that flexible hours or part-time employment make parental leave unnecessary. Still other American families are discovering the possibilities of at-home employment through telecommuting, piecework, and other arrangements. Over two million Americans—aside from farmers—had full-time, home-based jobs in 1985, with another

6 million reporting at least 8 hours of paid work at home during the previous week. About 600,000 married mothers with children under age 6 reported part- or full-time home-based work in 1985. The number of homeworkers has surely grown since then and will continue to grow if federal policymakers do not enact laws intended solely to benefit mothers who work out of the home. What Congress ought to be considering, in the view of policy analyst William R. Mattox, Jr., is a way to loosen restrictions on income-tax deductions permitted for home-based employment. Currently, the federal tax code permits a deduction for overhead expenses only for rooms used exclusively for income-producing activities. By dropping the exclusive-use test for families, Congress would take "the first step toward making home-based employment a more viable option."

Women and Work

Federal policies for home-based employment ought to be considered within a broader cultural reassessment of the developments that have brought so many women into paid employment. Poet Wendell Berry challenges Americans to consider why the workplace has replaced the home as the focal point for productive activity for both men and women. Berry thinks it is time "to ask why we should consider this general working away from home to be a desirable state of things, either for people or for marriage, for our society or for our country." In the strongest marriages, Berry observes, "the couple . . . makes around itself a household economy that involves the work of both wife and husband, that gives them a measure of economic independence and self-protection, a measure of self-employment, a measure of freedom, as well as a common ground and a common satisfaction."

Before pressing ahead with federally mandated parental leave, policymakers ought also to consider the financial sacrifices made by millions of households in which mothers devote themselves fully to homemaking and child rearing, thereby forgoing a second income. On average, that forgone second income means about $16,000 that the family chooses to do without. Though advocates of parental leave typically claim women work outside the home out of financial necessity, researchers at Pennsylvania State University found in a study published in 1990 that "the rising proportion of married mothers entering the labor force since 1960" is primarily due to "standard-of-living preferences" and not because a second income is needed for "basic necessities." Is it wise for the federal government to formulate national policies to accommodate "standard-of-living" preferences of some Americans, while slighting the family sacrifices of others? Even unpaid parental leave would create hidden subsidies, paid in part by one-income families who usually have lower household incomes. These are the hard issues that policymakers must not gloss over in a rush to imitate European models.

The United States may be the only industrialized Western country without mandated parental leave. American policymakers need feel no compulsion to make the consensus of failure complete. Americans still have the time and spirit to explore other more promising ways to combine work and family life. The United States need not regard itself as a rogue or pariah simply because our federal government does not mandate parental leave. Rather, on questions of family life and work, America may yet become a shining example and singular inspiration to other nations.

"Spending money for preventive health care, day care, and education and training programs not only saves lives but also saves money."

Funding Social Programs Would Benefit Families

Ruth Sidel

In the following viewpoint, Ruth Sidel argues that the government should fund a wide range of social policies including day care, job training, and health care to strengthen families. Sidel maintains that, without this support, many women and children live in poverty, and are without adequate health care. Funding social programs, according to Sidel, can alleviate these problems and can send the message that families are important. Sidel is a professor of sociology at Hunter College, City University of New York.

As you read, consider the following questions:

1. According to the author, why would funding social programs for everyone help those that need them the most?
2. What has been the result of governmental neglect of social programs for women and children, according to Sidel?
3. How will increased funding for social programs affect America's families, according to the author?

Adapted from "Putting Women and Children First: Priorities for the Future of America" by Ruth Sidel; paper presented at the conference of the National Foundation of Public Health Policy, Kansas City, Missouri, May 22, 1990. Reprinted with permission.

Between 11:40 p.m. on April 14, 1912 and 2:20 a.m. the following morning, the "unsinkable" *Titanic* would go down in the frigid waters of the Atlantic and more than 1500 lives would be lost.

On this magnificent ship, four city blocks long, were a French "sidewalk cafe," the finest band on the Atlantic, a Turkish bath with a mosaic floor, blue-green tiled walls and gilded beams, but a mere 20 lifeboats with room for only 1178 out of 2207 passengers and crew members on board.

Women and children were, indeed, the first to be saved that dreadful night. That is well known; less well-known is the fact that while the vast majority of First and Second Class women and children survived, the majority of women and children in steerage, as Third Class was then called, perished. In all, 8% of the women in First and Second Class drowned that night; 45% of the women in steerage died. The children's statistics are even more dramatic: only one child, 3%, in First and Second Class died; but 70% of the children in steerage died.

There were many reasons, of course, that First and Second Class passengers survived in such greater numbers. Access to the lifeboats was from the First and Second Class decks; the barriers to keep those in Third Class from going onto other decks were not removed during the disaster, and many could not find their way or, if they did, could not get through. Moreover, little effort was made to save the people in steerage; indeed some were forcibly kept down below by seamen standing guard.

Wealth and Poverty

The United States today surely glitters, gleams, and is considered by many to be unsinkable. The wealth of many Americans is truly incredible, and many others, less dramatically wealthy, are nonetheless doing very well. But despite our sidewalk cafes, our saunas, and our luxurious boutiques, we too do not have enough lifeboats for everyone. As on the *Titanic*, the United States is filled with locked gates, segregated decks and policies that assure that women and children will be first—not the first to be saved but the first to fall into poverty.

Of poor people in the United States today the vast majority are women—and their children. Two out of every three poor adults are women, and the economic status of families headed by women is declining. The impact of women's poverty on the economic status of children is even more shocking. One out of every five children under eighteen and nearly one out of every four preschool children lives in poverty. Among black children under the age of six, the poverty rate in 1987 was 48%; among black children living in female-headed families, 67% were poor.

Among Hispanic preschool children, 42% were poor; among Hispanic preschool children living in female-headed families the poverty rate was 70%.

What are the factors that are responsible for this "feminization of poverty?" In an era in which so many gains have been made by so many women, why do millions of women and their children live without adequate resources to provide food, clothing and shelter? A key factor in the pauperization of women is the continuing existence of a dual labor market that systematically discriminates against female workers. Women's magazines may suggest that most women work in glamorous, highly paid professions and carry a briefcase to work, but the data shows that the vast majority of women work in clerical and service and sales jobs and that working women earn only 68 cents on every dollar that men earn. . . .

© Joel Pett/*Lexington Herald Leader*. Reprinted with permission.

We have examined some of the problems of women and children in the United States who are living in poverty, and what is clear is that many of the events that precipitate Americans into poverty are beyond the control of any given person, and therefore cannot be handled by the individual alone. The United States must recognize, as have so many other industrialized societies, that the society must provide a humane environment in which people can live, work, thrive and raise their children.

The old supports of family and community must be replaced by new societal supports.

The United States must develop a comprehensive set of policies that will both strengthen family life and protect the well-being of women and children. I am not going to attempt here to map out the many reforms that are needed within American society generally; I am, rather, proposing a three-pronged family policy which, if implemented, would go far toward minimizing the number of women and children living in poverty, would begin to protect their health and well-being, and would facilitate family cohesion and mutual supports. There will be those who will say that we cannot afford such a program. To them I say we cannot afford to continue on our present course. We are an extraordinarily rich society; we simply must decide how we wish to spend our wealth, whether we wish to develop a national policy that will work toward eradicating the drastic extremes that are so injurious to a healthy democracy. There will also be those who will say that this program does not go nearly far enough—that *all* Americans must be protected against poverty. To them I say we have seen that women and children are particularly vulnerable to shifts in the economy, in family life, in social policy and therefore should be singled out, at this time, for special action. Perhaps a policy that puts women and children first will lead eventually to a more humane social policy for all Americans.

Needed Reforms

The agenda I am proposing includes three major areas of reform: the arena of work; universal entitlements specifically connected to the lives of families, particularly those with young children; and the welfare system. This is a broader agenda than is usually considered under the rubric, "family policy," but I believe it is extremely important to recognize that employment policy *is* family policy, welfare policy *is* family policy; and surely the amount of parental leave, prenatal care and day care a society provides constitutes family policy.

More specifically, we must mount a multifaceted effort to solve some of the problems of women in the workplace. We must, first of all, begin to pay women who work in traditionally female jobs a living wage. Ending the economic discrimination against "women's jobs," whether through some system of "comparable worth" or "pay equity," must be a central task of the 1990s. We must also build in dignity, a sense of autonomy and pathways to promotion in traditionally female occupations, for this is where the vast majority of women work and will continue to work in the foreseeable future. No matter what the trendy magazines and women's pages tell us, most women will never carry a briefcase to work. . . .

Beyond fundamental change in employment opportunity, Americans must rethink our special responsibility as a society to mothers and children. What is our societal responsibility toward the next generation and toward the women who nurture them? If we indeed believe that the next generation is our collective future, we must guarantee all mothers and children basic services necessary to their well-being. It is to society's benefit to protect the health of the pregnant woman and the new-born infant, the well-being of the small child, the care and education of the preschooler. But the investment must be in all mothers and children, not simply in one group. . . .

A Commitment to the Future

What we must work for today is a rethinking of our society's commitment to future generations, a commitment of certain fundamental supports that are due *every* mother and child. For it is only through universal entitlement that we will provide services of high quality. So long as services are provided for the poor alone, they will be inferior and constantly subject to cutback or elimination. Just as the passage of Medicaid institutionalized a two-class system of health care, and just as the emphasis on day care for the poor and nursery schools for the affluent has given us a two-class system of preschool care, so will any future programs for the poor alone produce unstable, stigmatized services vulnerable to every shift in the political winds. It is only through recognizing our common needs and our common rights that we can create a caring environment for all.

What are these fundamental supports that mothers and children need? The family policy I propose includes basic elements that are already available in most industrialized countries of the world. First, the United States must have a federally mandated parental leave policy. Virtually every industrialized country *except* the United States provides some statutory maternity leave or parental benefit. The U.S. must institute a national, universal, paid parental leave which should last for a minimum of six months. Either parent should be entitled to take any part or all of the leave provided that only one uses it at a given time. In this way the father would have the opportunity to participate in childrearing from the start and might develop more of a commitment to his children than many fathers have today.

Prenatal care must be available to all women. The health of the pregnant woman is too important—for her well-being, for the child's well-being and for the future of the nation—to be left simply to chance or to the vagaries of the marketplace. Every woman must be guaranteed first-rate, accessible health care, including family planning services, during pregnancy and in the postpartum period. This, of course, would be most effectively organized and promoted within a national health insurance system with universal entitlement and comprehensive coverage or within a national health service, but we cannot wait until the United States is ready to establish a health care system for all of its people; women and children must be given priority.

The infant and small child must also be guaranteed accessible, affordable care, both well-baby care and care in times of illness. It is a national disgrace that millions of American children have no regular source of health care, and that less than half of all poor preschool children are fully immunized against preventable diseases. Adequate health care must be a right, not a privilege, for the entire population, but particularly for children for whom regular health care is essential. . . .

Government Policies Are Needed

Right-wing glorification of the self-reliant, traditional family can be counterproductive in a modern world where only 11 percent of American families approximate the Norman Rockwell ideal of breadwinner husband, homemaker wife, and one or more dependent children. Most obviously it impedes the development of sensible family support policies. Half of all babies under one year old now have mothers in the labor force, and a quarter of all children are growing up in households with a mother but no father. What these nontraditional families need is free access to prenatal and maternity care, generous parenting leave, and a host of other rights and benefits—not another set of pressures. The misguided notion that government should not meddle in family affairs has made it extremely difficult for millions of American children to get a decent start in life.

Sylvia Ann Hewlett, *When the Bough Breaks*, 1991.

The United States must also establish a national system of day care and after-school care, not for the poor alone, but for all children in need. While the federal government should establish broad guidelines and contribute to funding, all other aspects of day-to-day administration, including licensing, hiring, inspection and quality control, must be left to the states, local governments and community groups. In a heterogeneous society such as the U.S., decentralization is crucial to the successful administration of a day care program. . . .

A Comprehensive Policy

Thus the heart of a new family policy for the United States would include paid parental leave, maternal and child health care, children's allowances, a national system of day care locally administered, an aggressive child support program, and a housing policy for those in greatest need. This program is no more than many other industrialized societies have instituted, and several components are in place in many developing countries. If we are truly "pro-family," we can do no less.

While many families' problems will be eased considerably by fundamental improvements in work opportunities and by the measures outlined above, a significant number of poor families will remain. Work is not the solution for all women, particularly for all women with preschool children. Some women will simply not have appropriate skills and/or education; others will wish to stay at home with their young children. And still others will need support to tide them over during periods of crisis. The third component of a unified, three-pronged family policy must be welfare reform. . . .

First, the application process and the determination of eligibility for Aid to Families with Dependent Children must be simplified. The length of the application, the myriad of forms, proofs of residency, copies of utility bills, birth certificates, letters from the landlord and other assorted pieces of paper would intimidate a PhD candidate. The assumption of guilt until the applicant is proven innocent is unacceptable. The length of time between the initial application and the first check is often unacceptable. The process must be simplified and the application evaluated with minimum hostility and maximum speed and courtesy. It is when people are in need and asking for help that they need the most support.

Second, the amount of grants must be raised dramatically. For one of the richest nations in the world to maintain millions of women and children far below the official poverty line is truly unconscionable. To force people to live in substandard housing, to skimp on food and, all too often, go hungry, to live at a standard significantly lower than others in the society, is to promote alienation, disease and hopelessness. This is what our welfare system is doing—humiliating recipients, making them feel like outsiders, demeaned and degraded in front of their children and neighbors. Why are we surprised when these children turn to drugs, alcohol or crime? We are telling them they do not matter; they are only acting out the message.

Government-Enforced Poverty

We must raise welfare payments at least to the poverty line. How else are families supposed to pay rent, eat, buy clothes, pay for a telephone and even buy a magazine or a newspaper once in a while? For some families this will mean that they will receive from the welfare system more than they would if they worked at the current minimum wage. Many in private industry will, of course, object to such a proposal since it would reduce the number of people who are forced to work, often at highly undesirable jobs, for such low wages. Others will object on the grounds that such a policy will undermine the work ethic. . . .

There is no question that helping people to be self-sufficient is cheaper for society in the long run. Spending money for preventive health care, day care, and education and training programs not only saves lives but also saves money. It is far cheaper to make sure people are well fed than to treat malnutrition; it is far cheaper to immunize children against infectious disease than to treat them once they are sick. The United States is acting in an incredibly shortsighted way when it cuts essential programs, permits the number of poor people to increase dramatically, and then treats them so shabbily that they opt out of society. We will, of course, pay in the long run—in escalating crime, in massive alienation, in wasted lives, and in dollars as well.

We must still raise the question of whether we can afford a family policy such as the one I have outlined. I believe we can. First, the billions of dollars we currently spend on subsidizing the poor, on care for the illnesses that result from poverty, on crime and on the other direct results of poverty, could be spent far more profitably on prevention and on appropriate programs that train people for real jobs. While the financial outlay may be significant at first, eventually many of those who now require help would be working, paying taxes, some of them providing the very services that are so necessary for the society at large.

Second, the U.S. at present has a lower tax rate than many other industrialized countries, and spends considerably less on social welfare than those societies. We have the resources; it is clearly a matter of determining our priorities.

Humane Policies Are Needed

And finally, the United States has a greater maldistribution of wealth and income than other industrialized countries. It is estimated that for the last 25 to 30 years, the richest fifth of the population has owned approximately three-quarters of the nation's wealth, and the bottom fifth approximately 0.2%. If we look at income, we see a similar pattern: By 1987 the wealthiest 40% of American families received 67.8% of total national family income, the highest percentage ever recorded, while the poorest 40% received 15.4%, the lowest percentage (along with that of 1986) ever recorded. One of the results of a family policy such as the one I have outlined would be some modest movement toward a more equitable distribution of the nation's economic resources. The real question, of course, is whether we can afford *not* to adopt a more humane social policy.

"The American family needs tax relief."

Tax Cuts Would Benefit Families

Robert Rector and Stuart M. Butler

Robert Rector is a policy analyst and Stuart M. Butler is the director of domestic and economic policy studies at The Heritage Foundation, a conservative think tank in Washington, D.C. In the following viewpoint, the authors contend that America's middle-class families have been harmed by increased taxes. To ease this crisis and help families, Rector and Butler propose tax cuts and tax incentives for middle-class families with children. These tax measures, argue the authors, would be far more effective than increasing funding for social programs.

As you read, consider the following questions:

1. How would tax cuts affect the family, according to the authors?
2. According to Rector and Butler, how would tax credits aid families?
3. How would increased funding for social programs affect families and America's economy, in the authors' opinion?

Adapted from "Reducing the Tax Burden on the Embattled American Family" by Robert Rector and Stuart M. Butler, the Heritage Foundation *Backgrounder*, August 12, 1991. Reprinted with permission.

Lawmakers from both parties in Washington have suddenly awakened to something well understood by Americans who struggle every month to stretch their paycheck to meet family needs: the American family is overtaxed. To cut this tax burden, bipartisan legislation has been introduced in Congress to raise the personal exemption for children in the federal tax code, which is the exemption to offset the cost of raising a child. Other proposed legislation would use a tax credit to reduce the tax bite on families with children. And most recently, the National Commission on Children, chaired by Senator Jay Rockefeller, the West Virginia Democrat, has recommended a $1,000 refundable annual tax credit for each child in a family.

Taxes Burden Families

These moves to relieve families with children of some of their tax burden is a welcome, if belated, recognition that action must be taken to reverse a trend in the tax system that has hurt American families. Thanks to huge increases in taxes during the past four decades, the average American family has seen a steadily larger slice of its income disappear, making it harder for many families to support their children. By the mid-1990s, federal tax revenue as a percentage of gross national product (GNP) will equal 20 percent, a rate reached only twice before in the post-World War II period: once in 1969 and once in 1981. The heaviest burden of the rise in taxation falls on families with children.

When state and local taxes are included, government now takes over one-third of the income of a two-parent family. Measured by average post-tax per capita income, families with children are now the lowest income group in the U.S.; their average post-tax income is below that of elderly households, single persons, and couples without children.

The federal tax code has become increasingly biased against families with children. The main reason for this is the steady decline in the value of the personal exemption applying to children, which is the tax allowance for the cost of raising children. During the past four decades the federal income tax burden on a family of four has increased by a staggering 150 percent. Single Americans and married couples with no children have escaped the bulk of this tax increase.

In 1948 a median income family of four paid virtually no income tax and only $60 in Social Security taxes (then set at 2 percent of its income). Today the equivalent family pays nearly 24 percent of its income to the federal government in taxes. The income loss in 1989 for the average family due to increases in federal taxes in the post-World War II period is approximately $8,200—or roughly the annual average mortgage paid on a family home.

This reduced tax benefit for children has reduced sharply the American family's ability to provide for its own needs. Worse still, families are caught in a vicious circle. The federal government responds to the financial worries of families by creating new programs to provide services to these families. Then to finance these new programs, Congress raises taxes, further diminishing the ability of families to provide for themselves and triggering calls for more government programs.

Working Wives: Uncle Sam—Not Family—Gains

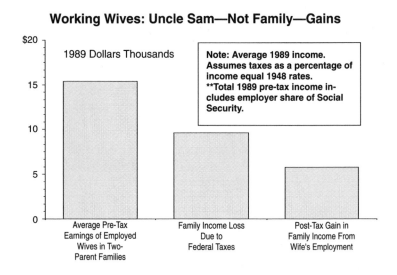

Note: Average 1989 income. Assumes taxes as a percentage of income equal 1948 rates.
**Total 1989 pre-tax income includes employer share of Social Security.

To break out of this vicious circle, the American family needs tax relief. Such tax relief can be accomplished in various ways, each with different implications for families and for federal finances.

Arguably the simplest method is to raise the personal exemption for children. This would involve no complicated change in the tax code and would mean, in effect, a larger tax deduction to offset the cost of raising each child. . . .

An alternative method would be to grant a tax credit for children. This differs from an increase in the exemption in two important ways. First, it grants each taxpaying family the same dollar amount of tax relief per child. By contrast, of course, an increase in the exemption would give more relief to families on higher tax brackets. Second, a credit can be used by families to offset their Social Security taxes as well as income tax. This would mean greater tax relief for low-income working families with children, most of whom pay heavy Social Security taxes that are deducted from their paychecks before any deductions or exemptions are applied. A tax credit also can be made "fully refundable," meaning that if the available credit exceeds a family's total tax liability the family receives the difference as a check from the Treasury. . . .

Tax relief for families can be funded by restraining the growth of federal, non-defense spending. With such a constraint on federal spending, reducing taxes on families would be deficit neutral. This means that each year the savings from slowing (not even cutting) the growth of new non-defense spending would offset the revenue losses from phasing in tax relief to families with children. . . .

Taxes on Children

American families face many problems, only few of which government can solve. When problems are caused by government policies, however, they can be solved by new policies. The most serious problem caused by government is the enormous financial burden imposed by a tax code now biased strongly against children.

Federal taxation of families with children has increased dramatically over the past four decades. In 1948, a family of four with the median family income level paid 2 percent of its income to the federal government in taxes. In 1989 the equivalent family paid nearly 24 percent of its income to the federal government. When state and local taxes are included, the tax burden would exceed one-third of family income.

A disproportionate share of the increase in federal income taxes over nearly 40 years falls on families with children. From 1954 to 1989, the average federal income tax rates for single persons and married couples with no children either remained the same or actually fell. But for a married couple with two children the average income tax rate more than doubled, and for a family with four children the average income tax rate rose from zero in 1954 to 2.6 percent in 1960 and to 6.3 percent in 1989. . . .

The personal exemption for children thus was intended to relieve part of the annual costs of raising a child from taxable income. In 1948, the personal exemption was $600, equal to roughly 20 percent of the median income of two-parent families, which was then $3,272. For a family of four, the $600 personal exemption shielded nearly 80 percent of family income from federal income tax. In addition, families could reduce their tax bill further by itemizing deductions or taking the standard deduction, and this protected most of the remaining 20 percent of income from income tax. The result: in the late 1940s and early 1950s the average family with children paid little or no income tax. . . .

The income loss due to increased taxation seriously strains family finances and profoundly affects family life in America. . . . Total pre-tax income for the median two-parent family in 1989 was $41,442. After taxes this family's income falls to $32,408. If federal taxes as a percentage of family income were restored to 1948 levels, the family's post-tax income would rise to $40,618. For the median income American family, the loss of income in 1989 because of the increase in federal taxes on families, due to the falling value of the personal exemption and the rise in payroll taxes since the early post-World War II period, was $8,210.

This income loss severely affects family finance. The median price of a single family home purchased in 1989 was $93,100; the average annual mortgage payment on this home (including principal and interest) was $7,920. Thus, the annual family income loss due to increased federal tax rates for the average family actually exceeds the annual cost of an average family home mortgage.

Taxes today also place a severe burden on working families with very modest incomes. Example: A truck driver working to support a wife and two children on $16,000 per year typically will pay $2,075 of this in federal taxes. A typical family with an income of $20,000 will pay $3,781 in taxes.

Family Time Famine

The loss of income due to rising taxes also helps explain why so many mothers have felt forced to join the work force to make ends meet—and yet seem to add little to the family budget by taking a job. For the average family in which both the husband and wife are employed, the wife's earnings equal about 32 percent of total family income.

Yet the average employed mother juggling her job and family demands would be dismayed to learn that only about one-third of her earnings are available to raise the family's standard of living—far less than the proportion of a similarly-placed mother's earnings in the late 1940s. The remaining two-thirds pay for the increase in federal taxes on family income during the post-World War II period. In fact, if federal tax rates as a percentage of family income were restored to 1948 levels, and if the average employed mother in a two-parent family were to leave the labor force entirely, the family would experience only a moderate dip in post-tax income today.

Average total pre-tax income in families where both spouses were employed was $50,267 in 1989. Of this, the husband's average earnings were $33,948 and the wife's average earnings were $16,319. After federal taxes, post-tax income for this family fell to $39,046. If federal tax rates as a percentage of family income were restored to 1948 levels, the family's post-tax income would be $32,591 if only the husband worked, or only $6,455 less than the family's current post-tax income today with both spouses working. Thus nearly two-thirds of the employed wife's average earnings go to pay for increased taxation; only one-third to support the family.

Reducing the Tax Burden

Once undermined, the family cannot be replaced by an array of government programs. The federal government could strengthen families and assist parents in their vital role of raising the next generation of Americans by reducing their tax burden—in every way possible.

Stuart M. Butler and Robert Rector, *Human Events*, August 31, 1991.

This does not suggest that all employed mothers would want to or should leave the labor force if taxes were lowered to early post-war levels. It does suggest strongly that mushrooming federal taxation has played a key role in the financial and personal strains that afflict many families and force many mothers reluctantly into the work force. It also, in turn, helps to explain why parents today typically spend 40 percent less time with their children than did parents in 1965. While parents in 1965 spent 30 hours per week in direct contact with their children, such time spent with children had dropped to only 17 hours by 1985.

Parents Under Pressure

Surveys indicate that the pressure on parents to work harder and longer to keep the family financially afloat is beginning to erode the quality of family life. A 1989 survey by the *New York Times*, for example, finds that 72 percent of employed fathers and 83 percent of employed mothers feel torn between the demands of their jobs and their desire as parents to spend more time with their families. Over half of the fathers and mothers surveyed in a similar *Los Angeles Times* poll state that they feel guilty about spending too little time with their children. A 1988 *USA Today* survey finds that 73 percent of two-parent families would choose to have one parent remain at home full time to care for their children if "money were not an issue." And a 1989 Cornell University study finds that two-thirds of mothers employed full-time would prefer to work fewer hours in order to devote more time to family life.

The conclusion drawn from these data is clear: the federal government could strengthen families and assist parents in their vital role of raising the next generation of Americans by reducing the tax burden on these families.

Families of course would benefit from a range of tax cuts, such as a reduction in general income tax rates or, importantly, from cuts in the capital gains tax or business taxes which create new and better jobs for all workers. These tax reductions would help all Americans and should be enacted.

Tax cuts targeted specifically to families also are needed, to undo the damage of the past four decades in which families have shouldered a disproportionately heavy tax burden due to the increasing bias in the tax code. Tax cuts for families would help restore the key principles of the U.S. income tax and reduce the need for many expensive welfare and other assistance programs designed to "help" financially strapped families. . . .

Restraining the Domestic Spending Spree

While there is growing agreement that families are overtaxed, there is no consensus about how to provide tax relief without increasing the federal deficit. Some proponents of tax relief for families with children argue that it should be funded by levying higher taxes on other Americans or by hiking business taxes. This would not help families, for it would slow economic growth and cut job opportunities. Revenues to pay for the reductions in taxes on families instead should come from restraining the growth in new government spending.

A large part of the initial tax increases on families after 1948 were to fund the Cold War's defense costs. Defense spending rose from 3.7 percent of gross national product in 1948 to nearly 10 percent in 1960 and fell to 5.4 percent in 1990.

U.S. defense spending continues to plummet. Under the proposed Bush budgets, defense spending falls to 3.8 percent of GNP in 1996, the lowest level since the late 1940s. In constant 1990 dollars, defense spending will fall from $299 billion in fiscal 1990 to $233 in fiscal 1996. Savings in fiscal 1996 alone will equal $66 billion. None of this "peace dividend" is being returned to the taxpayer. Instead, for every $1.00 cut in constant dollar defense below 1990 levels, there is $2.00 in new, non-defense spending.

Soaring Federal Spending

Tax relief for families could be financed simply by controlling domestic spending growth. Under the budget agreement reached by Bush and Congress, domestic spending in nominal terms soared 12 percent in fiscal 1991, will increase 8.2 percent in fiscal 1992, and will increase an average of 7.3 percent annually from 1993 to 1996. This is up from the annual nominal rate of 4.75 percent in the Reagan years. At the rate of domestic spending growth established in the 1990 budget agreement, the federal government will spend a cumulative $667 billion above the Reagan growth rate through 1995. This massive increase amounts to $4.00 in projected new domestic spending for every new dollar in taxes raised by 1990's budget agreement. . . .

The family is the foundation of American society. The often-disparaged middle class family is the principal institution by which the work ethic, self discipline, intellectual motivation, and moral character are passed on to the next generation. The family is the original Department of Health and Human Services. Once undermined it cannot be replaced by any array of government programs.

The American family is, however, in deep financial trouble. With federal and state taxes taking nearly one-third of the average family's income, parents are having a difficult time raising and educating their children. While most Americans grumble about rising federal taxes, these taxes have risen faster on families with children than on any other households.

Investing in the Future

Since America's children are America's future, the federal government should invest in the future by strengthening families. It can do this in large measure by curtailing the excessive taxation which has been slowly undermining the family. Families with children of course would be helped to a degree by a general reduction in tax rates on all Americans. But this would not alleviate significantly the disproportionate hike in taxes on such families due to the tax code's increasing bias against families since the late-1940s.

Yet such tax relief for families should not be achieved by allowing the deficit to widen further or by placing ever higher tax burdens on other members of society. Nor should it come by putting the economy in a tailspin through new taxes on business and investment. The proper way to finance tax relief to families with children is to restrain the increase in new government spending. What families need from government is not new spending and new social programs. These programs not only have done little or nothing to preserve families—in many cases the programs actually have triggered the breakup of families. What families really need is for government to allow them to keep a greater share of their own hard-earned money.

Recognizing Statements That Are Provable

We are constantly confronted with statements and generalizations about social and moral problems. In order to think clearly about these problems, it is useful if one can make a basic distinction between statements for which evidence can be found and other statements which cannot be verified or proved because evidence is not available, or the issue is so controversial that it cannot be definitely proved.

Readers should be aware that magazines, newspapers, and other sources often contain statements of a controversial nature. The following activity is designed to allow experimentation with statements that are provable and those that are not.

The following statements are taken from the viewpoints in this chapter. Consider each statement carefully. *Mark P for any statement you believe is provable. Mark U for any statement you feel is unprovable because of the lack of evidence. Mark C for any statement you think is too controversial to be proved to everyone's satisfaction.*

If you are doing this activity as a member of a class or group, compare your answers with those of other class or group members. Be able to defend your answers. You may discover that others will come to different conclusions than you do. Listening to the reasons others present for their answers may give you valuable insights into recognizing statements that are provable.

P = *provable*
U = *unprovable*
C = *too controversial*

1. The governments of most Western nations require employers to offer maternity leave to their employees.

2. The majority of the poor people in the United States are women and children.

3. The government's lack of support for poor families is a deliberate policy to oppress blacks and Hispanics.

4. Discrimination against women in the labor force prevents them from obtaining high-paying jobs.

5. The traditional support networks of family and community are no longer relevant to families and must be replaced by new support systems.

6. Providing comprehensive prenatal care to poor women can help prevent babies from being born addicted to drugs, with fetal alcohol syndrome, or other health and social problems.

7. Reducing income tax rates for the middle class can remove some of the economic burden from parents.

8. Most middle-class parents would prefer a tax credit from the government over an increase in the tax exemption.

9. Decreasing non-defense spending would provide enough government revenue to finance the tax relief policy that families deserve.

10. The slow pace of wage increases coupled with the rapid increase in taxes has impoverished many American families.

11. Tax cuts for families with children would help strengthen America's families and reduce the social problems that tax increases caused.

12. State and federal taxes take nearly one-third of the average family's income.

13. Family leave benefits can relieve working parents' anxieties about their jobs and their children by allowing new families to have time together.

14. Many critics argue that families should be self-sufficient and should not receive help from the government.

15. The family leave benefit will not strain the finances of most businesses and therefore is not a valid reason for opposing the policy.

Periodical Bibliography

The following articles have been selected to supplement the diverse views presented in this chapter.

Doug Bandow   "Family Leave Hurts Women the Most," *The New York Times*, October 6, 1991.

Monika Bauerlein   "Why Doesn't the U.S. Have a Family Policy?" *Utne Reader*, September/October 1991.

Aaron Bernstein   "Family Leave May Not Be That Big a Hardship for Business," *Business Week*, June 3, 1991.

Allan Carlson   "Helping Children: Income Tax Reform," *The Public Interest*, Winter 1989.

Congressional Digest   "Family Leave and Medical Act," April 1991.

Susan B. Garland   "The Family-Leave Bill Could Stick This Time," *Business Week*, October 28, 1991.

Kim A. Lawton   "Family Leave Stirs Profamily Feud," *Christianity Today*, May 27, 1991.

Mary Lord   "Modest Gains for Family Civil Rights," *U.S. News & World Report*, November 18, 1991.

Connaught C. Marshner   "What Social Conservatives Really Want," *National Review*, September 2, 1988.

Daniel Patrick Moynihan   "Families Falling Apart," *Society*, July/August 1990.

William Raspberry   "Pro-Family Policies: A Matter of Commonsense," *Liberal Opinion*, October 22, 1990. Available from PO Box 468, Vinton, IA 52349.

John D. Rockefeller   "Bipartisan Agenda for America's Children," *The World & I*, December 1991.

Robert J. Samuelson   "Political Child Abuse," *Newsweek*, February 3, 1992.

Roberto Suro   "The New American Family: Reality Is Wearing the Pants," *The New York Times*, December 29, 1991.

Time   "The Changing Family," special issue, Fall 1990.

Working Mother   "Will American Women Ever Get Maternity Leave?" November 1991.

Organizations to Contact

The editors have compiled the following list of organizations that are concerned with the issues debated in this book. All have publications or information available for interested readers. For best results, allow as much time as possible for the organizations to respond. The descriptions below are derived from materials provided by the organizations. This list was compiled upon the date of publication. Names, addresses, and phone numbers of organizations are subject to change.

Children's Defense Fund (CDF)
122 C St. NW
Washington, DC 20001
(202) 628-8787

The CDF works to promote the interests of children, especially the needs of poor, minority, and handicapped children. It supports government funding of education and health-care policies that benefit children. In addition to its monthly newsletter, *CDF Reports*, the fund publishes many books, articles, and pamphlets promoting children's interests.

Concerned Women for America (CWA)
370 L'Enfant Promenade SW
Suite 800
Washington, DC 20024
(202) 488-7000

CWA works to support the traditional nuclear family by lobbying Congress to pass laws that will strengthen families. It is opposed to government-funded day care and abortion. It publishes a newsletter eleven times a year along with position papers critiquing government policy.

Eagle Forum
PO Box 618
Alton, IL 62002
(618) 462-5415

The Eagle Forum advocates traditional family values. It opposes any political forces that it believes are anti-family, anti-religious, or anti-morality. Its members believe that mothers should stay at home to raise their children. It publishes the monthly *Phyllis Schlafly Report* as well as various brochures.

Focus on the Family
420 N. Cascade Ave.
Colorado Springs, CO 80903
(719) 531-3400

Focus on the Family is a Christian, conservative organization dedicated to preserving and strengthening the traditional family. It maintains that the family should be defined, legally and socially, as a married man and woman with children. It believes that the breakdown of the traditional family is linked to increases in poverty, teen pregnancy, and drug abuse. The organization publishes books including *The Family: Preserving America's Future* and *Whatever Happened to the Human Race?* as well as a monthly magazine, the *Citizen*.

Gay and Lesbian Parents Coalition International (GLPCI)
PO Box 50360
Washington, DC 20091
(202) 583-8029

GLPCI is a worldwide advocacy and support group that represents more than four million gay and lesbian parents. GLPCI believes that the American family has changed drastically. Among these changes are an increasing number of families headed by gay and lesbian parents. GLPCI helps develop support organizations for gay and lesbian families, supports research on these families, and works to educate society about gay and lesbian families. It publishes the quarterly newsletter, *GLPCI Network*.

The Heritage Foundation
214 Massachusetts Ave. NE
Washington, DC 20002
(202) 546-4400

The Heritage Foundation is a public-policy research institute that supports limited government and the free-market system. The foundation opposes government-funded day care and believes the private sector, not government, should ease social problems such as teen pregnancy, drug abuse, and childhood poverty. It also advocates providing tax benefits to families in place of various social programs. The foundation publishes the quarterly journal *Policy Review* in addition to hundreds of monographs, books, and papers on public-policy issues.

Institute for American Values (IAV)
1841 Broadway, Suite 211
New York, NY 10023
(212) 246-3942

The institute studies family life and the family as a social institution. It researches and analyzes public-policy decisions related to family issues such as child care, family and the workplace, teen pregnancy, and family values in America. Through its work, the institute hopes to strengthen family life in America. IAV publishes the quarterly newsletter *Family Affairs* and the book *Rebuilding the Nest: A New Commitment to the American Family*. It also publishes position papers, including "Life in the Express Lane: America's Time-Starved Families with Children," "The Family Values of Americans," and "Perspectives on the New Familism."

Intinet Resource Center
PO Box 150474-H
San Rafael, CA 94915-0474
(415) 507-1739

Intinet serves as a clearinghouse for information on nonmonogamous relationships and a network for people interested in alternative family life-styles. The center also promotes nonmonogamous relationships as an alternative to the traditional family. The center publishes the quarterly newsletter *Floodtide* and a *Resource Guide for the Responsible Non-Monogamist*.

The Libertarian Party
1528 Pennsylvania Ave. SE
Washington, DC 20003
(202) 543-1988

The Libertarian Party is the third largest political party in the United States. It supports individual rights and opposes government interference. It maintains that government programs and social services have undermined the American family. It publishes position statements and disseminates articles.

Men's Rights Association
17854-CH Lyons St.
Forest Lake, MN 55025-8854
(612) 464-7887

The association works to promote stronger marriage and family relations through public education. It conducts informal research and compiles statistics on topics such as men's rights and divorce. It also provides attorney referrals to men. The association publishes the monthly *The Liberator* and a newsletter, as well as the books *Divorce: What Everyone Should Know to Beat the System, A Manifesto of Men's Liberation*, and *Rape of the Male*.

Men's Rights, Inc. (MR)
PO Box 163180
Sacramento, CA 95816
(916) 484-7333

Men's Rights believes that divorce and custody laws oppress men and keep them away from their families. MR opposes feminism and believes that men's opinions and feelings about abortion should be considered. MR publishes the newsletter *New Release* along with position papers and articles.

Mothers at Home (MAH)
8310A Old Courthouse Rd.
Vienna, VA 22182
(703) 827-5903

Mothers at Home is an advocacy group for mothers who have chosen to stay home with their children. MAH supports workplace policies such as flexible job schedules, part-time work, and favorable job reentry policies which make it easier for women to stay home. It opposes raising taxes to support federally funded day care. It disseminates position papers and pamphlets, and publishes the monthly magazine *Welcome Home* and the book *Discovering Motherhood*.

National Council on Family Relations (NCFR)
3989 Central Ave. NE, Suite 550
Minneapolis, MN 55421
(612) 781-9331

The council is a nonprofit organization made up of social workers, clergy, counselors, psychologists, and others who research family issues such as education, social work, psychology, sociology, home economics, anthropology, and health care. NCFR publishes the quarterly journals *Journal of Marriage and Family Relations* and *Family Relations*.

National Council for Research on Women (NCRW)
Sara Delano Roosevelt Memorial House
47-49 East 65th St.
New York, NY 10021
(212) 570-5001

The council is composed of seventy centers and organizations that support and conduct feminist research, policy analyses, and educational programs. The NCRW promotes an increased corporate awareness of family needs and of alternatives for parents in the workplace as the traditional family declines in prevalence. It supports corporate benefits that aid families, including child-care options, family emergency leave, job sharing, and flextime. It publishes a newsletter, *Women's Research Network News*, and a variety of reports and position papers.

Organization for the Enforcement of Child Support, Inc. (OECS)
119 Nicodemus Rd.
Reisterstown, MD 21136
(301) 833-2458

OECS helps children and families by publicizing the difficulties of enforcing child-support laws. Through publicity, OECS attempts to persuade the public to support enforcing these laws. The organization also publicizes the costs of child-support delinquency to taxpayers. OECS has a wide variety of publications, including the newsletter *Pied Piper* and the pamphlets "Your Rights and Responsibilities to Your Children After Divorce," "Kids Need to Know About Child Support," and "Locating Absent Parents and Serving Process."

The Rockford Institute
934 N. Main St.
Rockford, IL 61103-7061
(815) 964-5819

The institute works to return America to Judeo-Christian values and supports traditional roles for men and women. It maintains that mothers who work or place their children in day care harm their children. The institute publishes the newsletter *Main Street Memorandum* and the monthly periodical *The Family in America.*

Select Committee on Children, Youth, and Families
U.S. House of Representatives
385 House Office Building Annex 2
Washington, DC 20515-6401
(202) 226-7692

The committee was created in 1983 to conduct an ongoing assessment of the condition of American children and families and to make recommendations to Congress and the public about how to improve public and private sector policies. It publishes reports and transcripts of hearings it holds on family issues.

Single Mothers by Choice (SMC)
PO Box 1642, Gracie Square Station
New York, NY 10028
(212) 988-0993

SMC is a support and information group for women who have chosen to become single mothers. It believes that single motherhood is a viable option for women who believe they have the emotional and financial resources to support a family alone. SMC publishes a quarterly newsletter.

Single Parent Resource Center (SPRC)
1165 Broadway
New York, NY 10001
(212) 213-0047

The SPRC is a clearinghouse for information about and for single parents. It maintains that as a growing number of children are raised in single-parent families, more aid will be needed to help single parents make good decisions for themselves and their children. The SPRC publishes pamphlets on single-parent issues.

Bibliography of Books

Gary L. Bauer — *Ideology, Politics, and the American Family.* Washington, DC: The Heritage Foundation, 1989.

William R. Beer — *American Stepfamilies.* New Brunswick, NJ: Transaction Publishers, 1992.

T. Berry Brazelton — *Families, Crisis, and Caring.* Reading, MA: Addison-Wesley, 1989.

T. Berry Brazelton — *Working and Caring.* Reading, MA: Addison-Wesley, 1985.

Andree Aelion Brooks — *Children of Fast-Track Parents.* New York: Viking Penguin, 1989.

Allan Carlson — *Family Questions.* New Brunswick, NJ: Transaction Publishers, 1989.

Andrew J. Cherlin, ed. — *The Changing American Family and Public Policy.* Washington, DC: Urban Institute Press, 1988.

Bryce J. Christensen — *Utopia Against the Family: The Problems of the American Family.* San Francisco: Ignatius Press, 1990.

Helen Corr and Lynn Jamieson, eds. — *Politics of Everyday Life: Continuity and Change in Work and the Family.* London: Macmillan, 1990.

David T. Ellwood — *Poor Support: Poverty in the American Family.* New York: Basic Books, 1988.

Martha Albertson Fineman — *The Illusion of Equality: The Rhetoric and Reality of Divorce Reform.* Chicago: University of Chicago Press, 1991.

Frank F. Furstenberg Jr. and Andrew J. Cherlin — *Divided Families: What Happens to Children When Parents Part.* Cambridge, MA: Harvard University Press, 1989.

Maggie Gallagher — *Enemies of Eros.* Chicago: Bonus Books, 1989.

George Gilder — *Men and Marriage.* Gretna, LA: Pelican Publishing Co., 1986.

Frances K. Goldscheider and Linda J. Waite — *New Families, No Families?* Berkeley: University of California Press, 1991.

Cheryl D. Hayes, John L. Palmer, and Martha J. Zaslow, eds. — *Who Cares for America's Children?: Child Care Policy for the 1990s.* Washington, DC: National Academy Press, 1990.

James M. Henslin, ed. — *Marriage and Family in a Changing Society.* New York: The Free Press, 1989.

Arlie Hochschild with Anne Machung — *The Second Shift: Working Parents and the Revolution at Home.* New York: Viking Penguin, 1989.

Brenda Hunter — *Home by Choice.* Portland, OR: Multnomah Press, 1991.

Jean E. Hunter and Paul T. Mason — *The American Family: Historical Perspectives.* Pittsburgh: Duquesne University Press, 1991.

K. Sue Jewell — *Survival of the Black Family: The Institutional Impact of U.S. Social Policy.* New York: Praeger, 1988.

Colleen Leahy Johnson — *Ex Familia: Grandparents, Parents, and Children Adjust to Divorce.* New Brunswick, NJ: Rutgers University Press, 1988.

Edward L. Kain	*The Myth of Family Decline.* Lexington, MA: Lexington Books, 1990.
Paula Kamen	*Feminist Fatale.* New York: Donald I. Fine, Inc., 1991.
Lester A. Kirkendall and Arthur E. Gravett, eds.	*Marriage and the Family in the Year 2020.* Buffalo, NY: Prometheus Books, 1991.
Sar A. Levitan, Richard S. Belous, and Frank Gallo	*What's Happening to the American Family?* Baltimore: Johns Hopkins University Press, 1988.
Frank Levy	*The Economic Future of American Families.* Washington, DC: Urban Institute Press, 1991.
Richard Louv	*Childhood's Future.* Boston: Houghton Mifflin Co., 1990.
Elaine Tyler May	*Homeward Bound: American Families in the Cold War Era.* New York: Basic Books, 1988.
Steve Mintz and Susan Kellogg	*Domestic Revolution: A Social History of American Family Life.* New York: Free Press, 1988.
Leslie A. Morgan	*After Marriage Ends: Economic Consequences for Midlife Women.* Newbury Park, CA: Sage Press, 1991.
Ann Phoenix, Anne Woollett, and Eva Lloyd	*Motherhood: Meanings, Practices, and Ideologies.* Newbury Park, CA: Sage Press, 1991.
Glenda Riley	*Divorce: An American Tradition.* New York: Oxford University Press, 1991.
Harrell R. Rodgers	*Poor Women, Poor Families.* Armonk, NY: M.E. Sharpe, 1990.
Juliet Schor	*The Overworked American.* New York: Basic Books, 1992.
Pat Schroeder with Andrea Camp and Robyn Lipner	*Champion of the Great American Family.* New York: Random House, 1989.
Jocelynne A. Scutt, ed.	*The Baby Machine: Reproductive Technology and the Commercialization of Motherhood.* London: Green Print, 1990.
Ruth Sidel	*Women and Children Last: The Plight of Poor Women in Affluent America.* New York: Penguin Books, 1986.
Arlene Skolnick	*Embattled Paradise: The American Family in an Age of Uncertainty.* New York: Basic Books, 1991.
Dayle Smith	*Kin Care and the American Corporation: Solving the Work/Family Dilemma.* Homewood, IL: Business One Irwin, 1991.
Judith Stacey	*Brave New Families: Stories of Domestic Upheaval in Late Twentieth-Century America.* New York: Basic Books, 1990.
Sandra S. Volgy, ed.	*Women and Divorce, Men and Divorce.* Binghamton, NY: The Haworth Press, 1991.
Judith S. Wallerstein	*Second Chances: Men, Women, and Children a Decade After Divorce.* New York: Ticknor & Fields, 1990.
Shirley L. Zimmerman	*Family Policies and Family Well-Being.* Newbury Park, CA: Sage Press, 1992.

Index

Abrahamson, Alan, 145
adoption
  homosexuals and, 57, 64, 68, 69
  surrogacy and, 75-76
adult children of divorce (ACOD),
  116-120
Ahrons, Constance R., 92
AIDS
  effect on relationships, 34
  homosexuals and, 60, 65
  legal issues and, 56
Aid to Families with Dependent
  Children (AFDC), 106, 240
alimony, 123-124, 133-134
Allen, David, 49
American Academy of Pediatrics,
  171, 176
American Bar Association, 131
American Enterprise Institute, 206
American Home Economics
  Association, 48
American Society of Law and
  Medicine, 85
Angell, Marcia, 76
Annas, George, 72
Aries, Philippe, 31
artificial insemination by donor
  (AID), 72, 75, 81-82
AT&T, 155

Baby M, 86
Beck, Joan, 160, 161
Bellah, Robert, 27, 31
Belsky, Jay, 170, 171
Benedict, Ruth, 76
Besharov, Douglas, 174
birth control, 80
Blakeslee, Sandra, 68, 108
Blankenhorn, David, 204
Blum, Barbara, 157
Brazelton, T. Berry, 219, 228, 230
Bronfenbrenner, Urie, 69, 117, 188,
  228
Brothers, Joyce, 143, 145
Buchanan, Patrick, 208
Burtless, Gary, 187, 191
Bush, George
  child-care credit and, 160
  parental leave bill and, 228
  U.S. budget and, 248
businesses
  meet needs of families, 152-158,
    169, 173-174, 222-223

con, 159-166
Butler, Stuart M., 242, 247

Cahill, Mary Ann, 149
capitalism
  effects on family, 214-217
Capron, Alexander M., 75
Cardozo, Arlene Rossen, 209
Carlson, Allan, 205
Catholic church, 72
Charen, Mona, 148
child abuse, 212, 218
childbirth
  homosexuals and, 58
  rate decline, 18-19, 229
child care, 26
  benefits children, 173
  can harm children, 170-172
  centers run by employers
    are beneficial, 154-158, 174, 222
    con, 161
  characteristics of high quality, 173,
    174
  government programs for, 188-189,
    239
  statistics on, 169, 173, 212
  studies on, 170-171
  two-career parents' need for,
    167-174
    alternatives to, 148, 177-178, 189
Child Care Action Campaign, 173,
  222
children
  crime and, 168
  custody of, in divorce, 96-97, 105
  drug use and, 168, 171, 213
  effects of divorce on
    age factors and, 113-114
    are harmful, 68, 104-105, 108-114,
      123-128, 206
      con, 38, 115-120
    boys, 112
    economic, 106-107
    emotional, 110-114, 206,
      212
    girls, 111
  effects of reproductive technology
    on, 82-83
  health care for, 239
  heterosexual parents and, 64, 66
  homosexual parents and, 57, 58,
    60, 77, 214
  latchkey, 168, 171, 174, 204, 212

need for mother's care, 149-150,
172, 180-181
poverty and, 204, 212, 216,
235-236
divorce causes, 123-128, 130, 215
pressures on, 168
quality of life is declining for,
21-22, 24
rearing of
responsibility for, 30
traditional family and, 18, 57
tax exemptions for, 189, 243, 244
test scores and, 168, 212
time spent with parents
is declining, 158, 184-190,
204-207, 210, 247
is enough, 191-197
child support
fathers defaulting on, 101, 106, 125
inadequacy of, 134-135
Christensen, Bryce J., 47, 113, 172,
180, 227
Clay, William L., 225
Coalition for Labor Union Women,
213
cohabitation
is increasing, 26-27
Colt, George Howe, 188
communes, 34, 42
Coontz, Stephanie, 211, 213, 216
Craswell, Ellen, 106

day care. *See* child care
Decter, Midge, 49
DeMarco, Donald, 79
Denmark, 56
divorce
alimony and, 123-124, 133-134
as abnormal, 100-107
as normal, 38, 92-99
children and
benefits for, 116-118
custody of, 96-97
effects on, 38, 68, 104-106
harms, 104-105, 108-114
con, 115-119
support of, 101, 106, 123-124, 134
economic effects of
on men, 131
on women, 101, 106-107, 121-126,
129-135, 212
education about, 107
effect on traditional family, 18, 20
emotional problems from, 103, 107,
109-114
history of, 101-102
interferes with parenting skills,
105-106, 111, 119

myths about, 36, 101, 103, 104, 107
no-fault
economic effects of, 101, 121-122,
133
problems with, 101, 106
reasons for, 95, 96, 102-103, 121,
130
older women and, 124-125
rates of, 38, 73, 94, 101
are constant, 34
are decreasing, 29
are increasing, 20, 26, 102, 106
reasons for, 98, 101
reforms needed, 106-107
stigma of, 94, 96, 97
Dodd, Christopher J., 225
Donovan, J., 35
Dornbusch, Sanford M., 28
Dun & Bradstreet, 174
Duncan, Gregory, 127, 132

Eco, Umberto, 53
education
about divorce, 107
free-choice system, 210
elderly
care for, 154-156, 217, 231
embryo transfer, 81
Erbe, Bonnie, 37
Eskey, Kenneth, 151
Evans, Rae Forker, 144-145
Ewing, Stephen E., 165

Faludi, Susan, 126-128, 129
Families and Work Institute, 156, 189
family
as restrictive, 216-217
changes in
benefits from, 21
problems from , 21-22, 35
characteristics of, 41, 43-44, 74
definition of, 41, 64, 73, 78
is expanding, 40-46, 74, 77-78
legal, 46
should be limited, 47-54
social roles and
changing of, 29-30, 48-50, 94-95
effects of, 197, 206-207
traditional, 18, 217
dependence upon, 27-28
determined by
custom, 76-77
law, 75-76
effect of urbanization on, 93, 96
history of, 30-31, 35-36, 93-94
in the 1950s, 18, 23, 27-28
in the 19th century, 214
in Europe, 24

legal rulings on, 56
needs funding for social programs,
  234-241
  con, 244, 249
nuclear. *See* family, traditional
privacy and, 217-218
reasons for, 18, 28, 42, 46
single-parent
  increase in, 20, 125-126, 172, 220,
    223-224
  problems of children in, 68-69,
    113, 206
support policies for, 153-158,
  167-174
support systems, 27-28, 36, 42,
  93-94, 153
taxes and
  averages, 243-244, 245, 246
  cuts would benefit, 242-249
  exemptions for children, 189,
    243, 244
  increases in, 243-244, 245, 246,
    249
  relief for, 208, 232
traditional
  alternatives to, 37, 41-42
  benefits of, 64-65
  characteristics of, 18, 20, 41
  government should support,
    203-210
    con, 211-218
  is declining, 17-24, 37, 64
  is not perfect, 23, 28, 35-36, 38,
    94
  is obsolete, 33-39
  problems with, 214, 215
  traditions of, 44
  transition of, 25-32
  violence in, 36, 37, 218
  working mothers benefit, 141-146
    con, 147-151
Family and Medical Leave Act, 220,
  221, 225-226, 231
  biases against, 222
Family and Work Institute, 222
family law, 75-76
Family Service America, 45
Fassel, Diane, 35, 115
fathers
  changes in parenting and, 22, 143
  defaulting on child support, 101,
    106, 134-135
  parental leave and, 161, 238
  separation from children, 105-106,
    113, 206
  time spent with children, 186-188,
    205-207, 210
Fein, Bruce, 66

Feldman, Linda, 196
fertility
  decline in, 18-19
Fields, Suzanne, 205
Fletcher, Jan, 159
Fletcher, John, 84
flextime
  benefits working parents, 154-158,
    208, 222, 231
    con, 160-161
Footlick, Jerrold K., 49
Frantz, Marge, 172
Free Congress Foundation, 210
Freud, Anna, 150
Friedan, Betty, 130

Galston, William, 188, 204
Gay and Lesbian Parents Coalition,
  83
Gimenez, Martha, 134
government programs
  cannot replace the family, 24, 53,
    189, 204-205, 244, 249
  for child care, 188-189, 239
  should mandate family leave,
    219-226, 238
    con, 227-233
  should support traditional families,
    203-210
    con, 211-218
government spending
  should be reduced, 245, 248-249
Green, Richard, 83
Greer, Germaine, 48

Hartinger, Brent, 55
Hayakawa, S.I., 52
Hayton, Bradley P., 63, 69
Henslin, James M., 96
Hewlett, Sylvia Ann, 152, 223, 239
Hobart, Charles, 32
Hochschild, Arlie, 135
Hoffman, Saul, 127, 132
home-based work
  can benefit families, 151, 162-166,
    189, 208-209, 231-232
homosexuals
  AIDS and, 60, 65
  as parents, 214
    adoption and, 57, 64, 68, 69
    do not harm children, 57, 58, 60
    harm children, 65-70
  as partners
    are changing the family, 20,
      55-62, 77
    are undermining the family,
      63-70, 83
    childbirth and, 58

promiscuity and, 61, 66, 67
statistics on, 56-57, 65-66, 67
studies on, 58
use of artificial insemination, 77, 83, 84
Hunnicutt, Benjamin, 192, 194
Hymowitz, Carol, 194

IBM
family-support policies of, 155, 156, 169, 174
incest, 37, 61, 218
cultural taboos about, 76-77
individualism, 21, 27-28
infants
addiction at birth, 212, 220
mortality rate, 212, 220
stages after birth, 221-222
Institute for American Values, 204
in vitro fertilization (IVF), 72, 74, 76, 81
Irons, Peter, 48

Jeter, Kris, 43
Jeter, Mildred, 58, 59
Johnson & Johnson
family-support policies of, 154, 169

Kamarck, Elaine, 189, 204
Kamerman, Sheila B., 164
Kingston, Paul William, 185, 186, 206
Kirkpatrick, Jeane, 209
Knight, Robert, 52
Kowalski, Sharon, 60

Labich, Kenneth, 167
Lauritzen, Paul, 74
Lawlor, Julia, 163
lesbians
as mothers, 42, 57, 65, 83
marriage laws and, 56
statistics on, 65
Lindsey, Karen, 50
Loving, Richard, 58, 59

Macklin, Ruth, 71
Marciano, Teresa, 40
marriage
family definition and, 41, 43, 50
homosexual
church and, 58, 61, 62
laws on, 56, 60
limited rights of, 46, 56-58
should be legal, 58-61
would harm the family, 63-70
con, 55-62
interracial, 58
in the 1950s, 18, 23, 142

kinds of, 43
legal benefits of, 56
longer life spans and, 35, 36
myths about, 36, 104
reasons for, 95
statistics on, 27
Martin, Sue, 83
Mason, Linda, 174
Mason, Mary Ann, 130
Mattox, William R., Jr., 183, 203, 232
Mead, Margaret, 36
Medved, Diane, 105
men
economic effects of divorce on, 131
sexuality and, 64
Millett, Kate, 48
Moody, Fred, 100
mothers
postpartum depression and, 222
working
benefit the family, 141-146
breast-feeding and, 148-149
children of, 143, 170-172, 207
are harmed by, 186, 204-207, 210
effect on traditional family, 18, 19-20
harms the family, 147-151
kinds of employment, 177-180
necessity of, 148, 172
statistics on, 153, 157, 176-178, 193
want time at home, 181-182, 207, 247
Mothers at Home, 175
Moynihan, Daniel Patrick, 208

National Center for Lesbian Rights, 57
National Commission for Children, 220, 222
National Commission on Children, 205, 243
National Employer Supported Childcare Project, 153
National Organization of Women, 131, 230
National Survey of Families and Households, 28
National Women's Economic Alliance, 146
Nock, Steven, 185, 186, 206

O'Connor, Sandra Day, 150, 209
Office of Child Support Enforcement, 135
Okin, Susan Moller, 127, 143
Orr, Sally, 228

Orthner, Dennis K., 25

Papazoglou, Orania, 22
parental leave
  businesses should offer, 153-156,
    162, 173
  fathers and, 161
  government should mandate,
    219-226, 238
    con, 227-233
  worldwide policies on, 221,
    223-225, 228, 238
    do not support the family,
      229-231, 233
parents
  heterosexual, 64, 66
  homosexual, 57-58, 60, 65-70, 77,
    214
  single
    increase in, 20, 126, 172, 220,
      223-224
    problems of children of, 68-69,
      113, 206
  skills affected by divorce, 105-106,
    111, 119
  surrogate, 72, 74-76, 84-86
  two-career
    businesses meet needs of,
      152-158, 169
      con, 159-166
    have too little family time, 168,
      184-190, 204-207, 247
      con, 191-197
    leisure time and, 186-187,
      192-194, 195-197
    necessity of, 172, 232
    need more child care, 167-174
      con, 175-182, 188, 204
    reasons for, 184-185, 246
    stresses of, 153, 156, 161, 171,
      180, 220
Parker, Robin, 141
People for the American Way, 50
Pogrebin, Letty Cottin, 49-50
Popenoe, David, 17, 27
pornography, 213
poverty
  children and, 204, 212, 216,
    235-236
  divorce causes, 121-128, 130,
    215
  feminization of
    causes of
      discrimination, 130, 134, 215,
        235-236
      divorce, 121-128, 212
Pregnancy Discrimination Act, 224,
  225

Progressive Policy Institute, 189, 204
Prudential Insurance Company, 174

Rector, Robert, 242, 247
Repository for Germinal Choice, 82
reproductive technology
  is changing the family, 71-78
  is undermining the family, 79-86
  problems of, 80-82
Robinson, John, 186, 194, 196, 204,
  206
Rockefeller, Jay, 243
Rodgers, Roy H., 92
Roosevelt, Franklin Delano, 222

Samuelson, Robert J., 186, 187, 191
Scanzoni, John, 32, 43
Schlafly, Phyllis, 130
Schroeder, Patricia, 219, 228, 230
Seligmann, Jean, 57
sexual revolution
  effect on traditional family, 18, 19
Sidel, Ruth, 234
single-parent families
  increase in, 20, 125-126, 172, 220,
    223-224
  problems of children in, 68-69,
    113, 206
Skolnick, Arlene, 31
Skrzycki, Cindy, 161
Smeal, Eleanor, 230
social programs
  increases in would benefit families,
    234-241
    con, 244, 249
society
  changes in, 34
  mobility of
    effect on relationships, 34, 36-37
Socrates, 51-52
suicide
  teenage, 60, 113, 168, 213
support groups, 36-37
Suro, Robert, 31
surrogate parenting, 72, 74-76, 84-86
Sussman, Marvin B., 40

Tavenner, Mary T., 231
taxes
  cuts in would benefit families,
    242-249
  exemptions for children, 189, 243,
    244
  relief for families, 208, 232
  Social Security and, 244
  spent on social welfare, 241
Taylor, Paul, 169
teenagers

homosexuality and, 60, 62
pregnancy and, 212
suicide and, 60, 113, 168, 213
television
  interferes with family time, 187,
    193-194, 197
Thompson, Karen, 60
Time, 60
Trump, Donald, 195

Uniform Parentage Act, 75
unions, 215-216
United States
  Census Bureau
    divorce statistics, 134
  Department of Labor
    working mother statistics, 177-179
  economic inequalities in, 235-238,
    240, 241
  family welfare and, 24
  must fund social programs for
    families, 234-241
  national health-care program,
    238-239

Veevers, Jean E., 94
Verbrugge, Lois, 142

Wallerstein, Judith S., 36, 68, 104,
  105, 108
Walsh, Joan, 50
Weitzman, Lenore J., 120, 130-135
welfare
  family decline and, 24
  programs for women and children,
    240-241
Whitehead, Mary Beth, 86
Wiley, Juli Loesch, 147
Wimberger, Herbert, 103, 104
women
  choosing to stay at home, 23-24,

144, 148-151, 178-179, 181
  deferring a career, 150-151, 189,
    209
  economic effects of divorce on, 101,
    106-107, 212
  are harmful, 121-128, 212, 215
  family roles of, 217
  health care for, 238-239
  pay discrepancies in the workplace,
    124, 125, 135, 236, 237
  poverty and
    causes for
      discrimination, 130, 134, 215,
        235-236
      divorce, 125-127, 212
  reasons for marriage, 95
  sexuality and, 64
  status has improved, 21
  Superwoman myth and, 145
  working outside the home, 19-21,
    23, 26, 95, 124-125, 172
    benefit the family, 141-146
    harm the family, 147-151
    health and, 142-145, 173
    work stereotypes and, 213
Women's Legal Defense Fund, 230
work
  flextime, 154, 155, 160-161, 164
  home-based, 151, 162-166, 189,
    208-209, 231-232
  part-time, 155, 156, 231
  time spent at, 184, 186, 192-194,
    195-197

Zeduck, Sheldon, 230
Zerbe, Diane, 103, 104, 105
Zigler, Edward
  on child care, 158, 168, 173
  on family time, 192
  on parental leave, 228, 230
Zinsmeister, Karl, 184, 206-207, 208